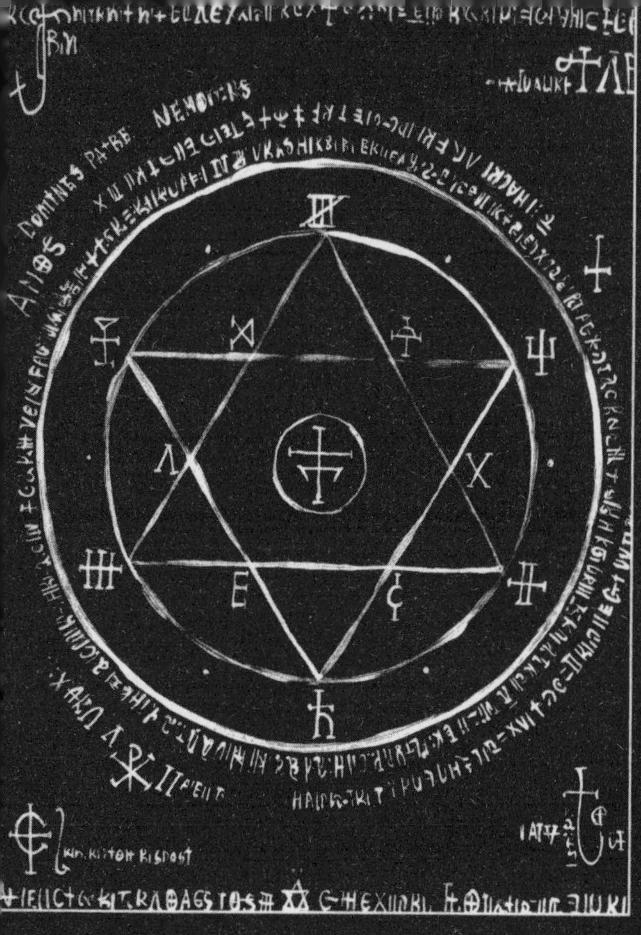

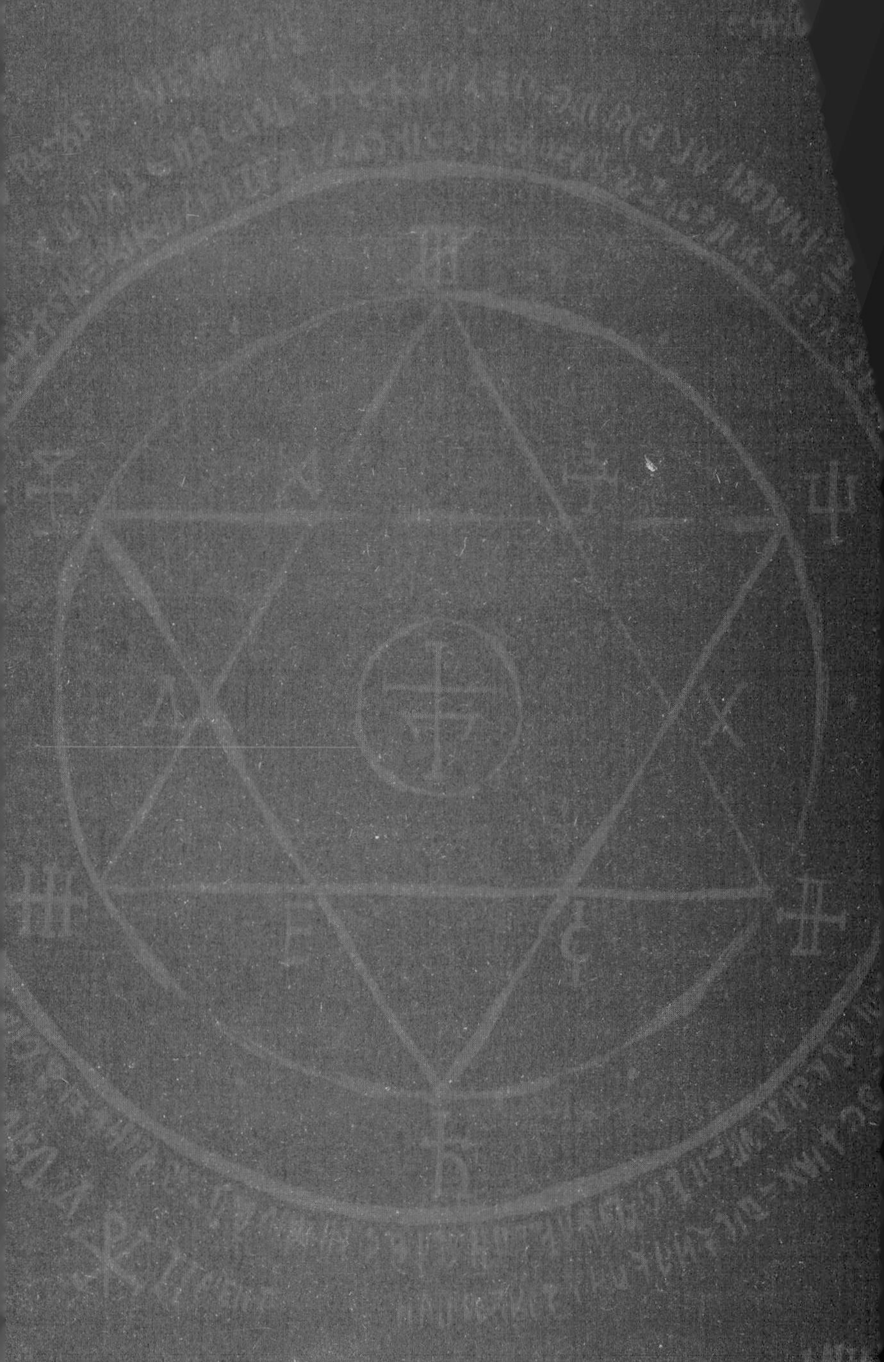

PRIEST

VOLUME 3

BY
MIN-WOO HYUNG

TOKYOPOP®

LOS ANGELES • TOKYO • LONDON

Translator - Lauren Na
English Adaptation - Jake Forbes
Layout- Melissa Hackett
Cover Artist - Raymond Swanland
Graphic Designer - Anna Kernbaum

Editor - Jake Forbes
Digital Imaging Manager - Chris Buford
Pre-Press Manager - Antonio DePietro
Production Managers - Jennifer Miller, Mutsumi Miyazaki
Art Director - Matt Alford
Managing Editor - Jill Freshney
VP of Production - Ron Klamert
President & C.O.O. - John Parker
Publisher & C.E.O. - Stuart Levy

E-mail: info@TOKYOPOP.com
Come visit us online at www.TOKYOPOP.com

A  MANGA

TOKYOPOP Inc.
5900 Wilshire Blvd. Suite 2000
Los Angeles, CA 90036

Priest Vol. 3: Requiem for the Damned

ISBN: 1-59182-010-3

First TOKYOPOP Printing: November 2002

10 9 8 7 6 5

Printed in the USA

THE STORY SO FAR...

ie, leader of the infamous Rebel Angels, was being carried by train
an escort of federal marshals to her trial (and most likely, execution),
n her gang decided to spring her. Much to the surprise of robbers and
nen alike, the train carried a secret cargo—reanimated corpses with
irst for blood. Everyone on the train was slaughtered, except for
e, who was saved by a mysterious priest, Ivan Isaacs.

wards, Lizzie followed her dark savior to the frontier town of St.
'as, where she witnessed an even more brutal battle between Ivan
he demon Jarbilong, a servant of the fallen angel Temozarela. Again,
overcame his enemies with silver bullets, a wicked knife, and an
nan strength, fueled by his own rage and the power of the Devil
who resides within his soul. Again, Lizzie was the only survivor, but
e battle she too became infected by the plague of Temozarela.
e blacking out, she was picked up by a local sheriff who had been
tigating the accident on the train. But the one who holds all the
ers, Ivan Isaacs, disappeared into the desert.

PRIEST

프리스트

3

REQUIEM FOR THE DAMNED

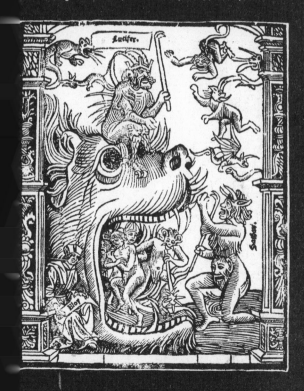

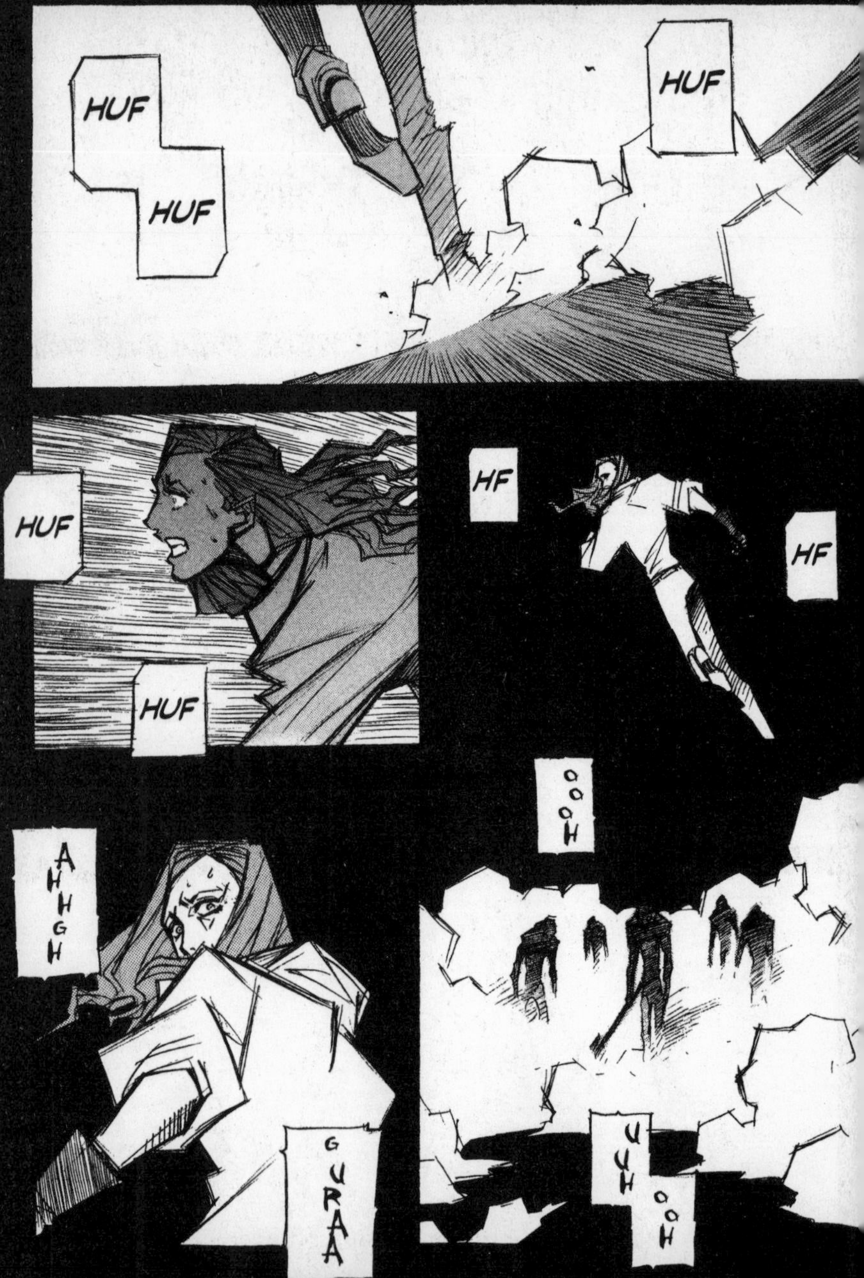
HUF
HUF
HUF
HUF
HUF
HF
HF
AHHGH
GURAA
OOOH
UUH OOH

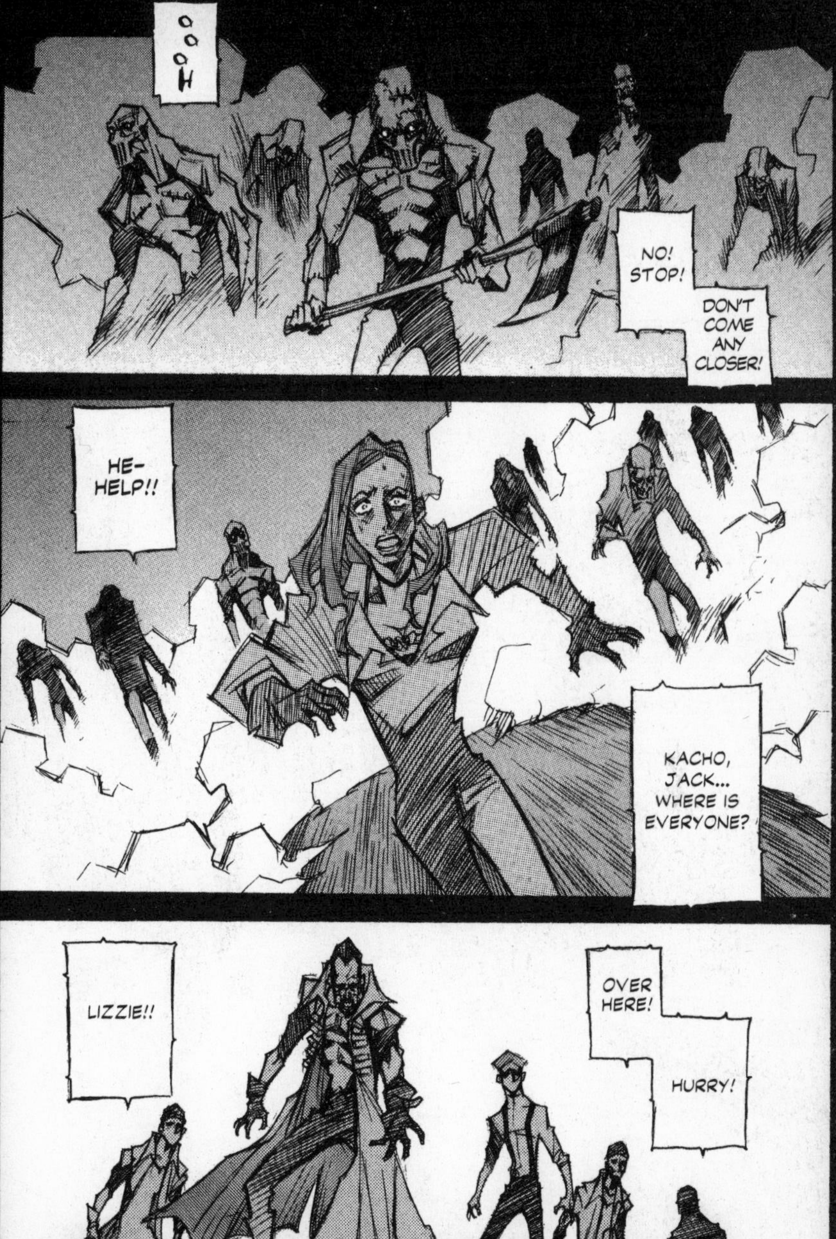
OOOH
NO! STOP!
DON'T COME ANY CLOSER!
HE-HELP!!
KACHO, JACK... WHERE IS EVERYONE?
LIZZIE!!
OVER HERE!
HURRY!

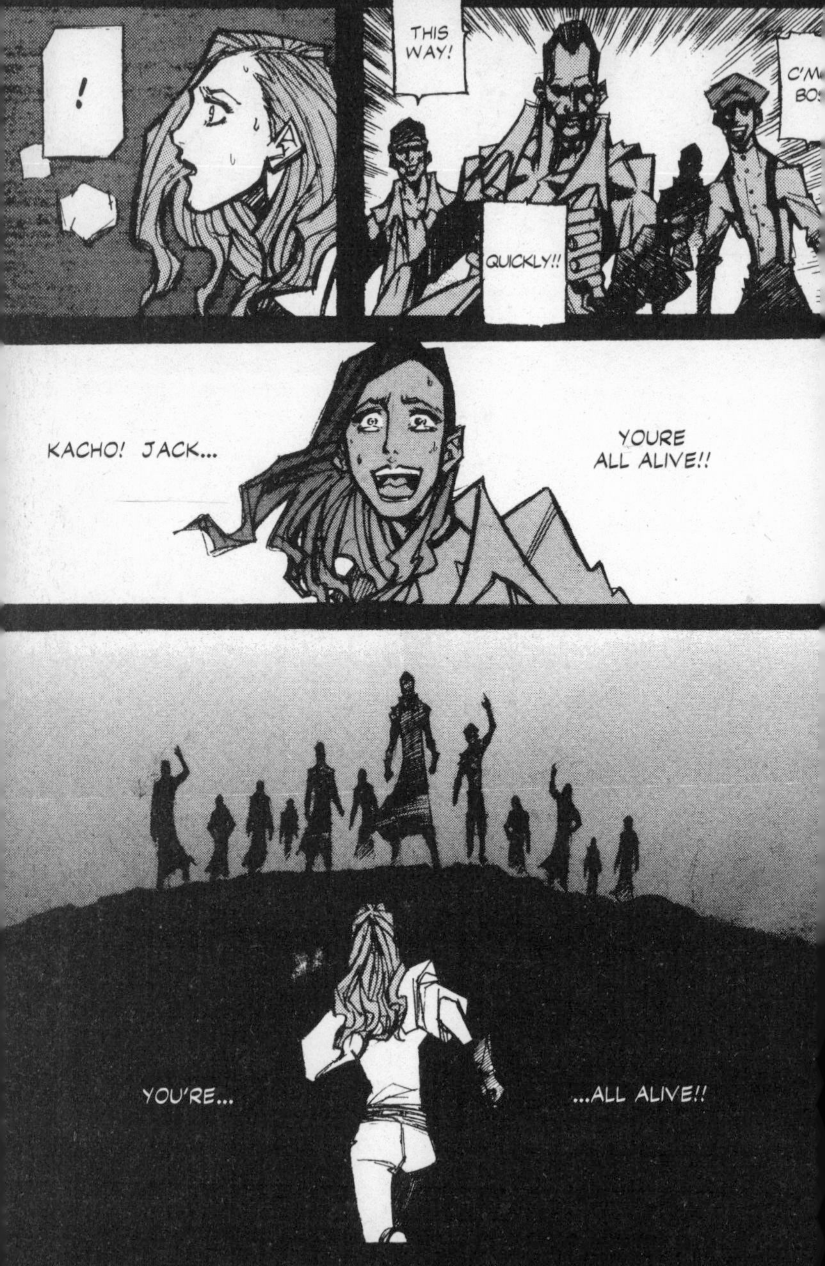
!
THIS WAY!
QUICKLY!!
KACHO! JACK...
YOURE ALL ALIVE!!
YOU'RE...
...ALL ALIVE!!

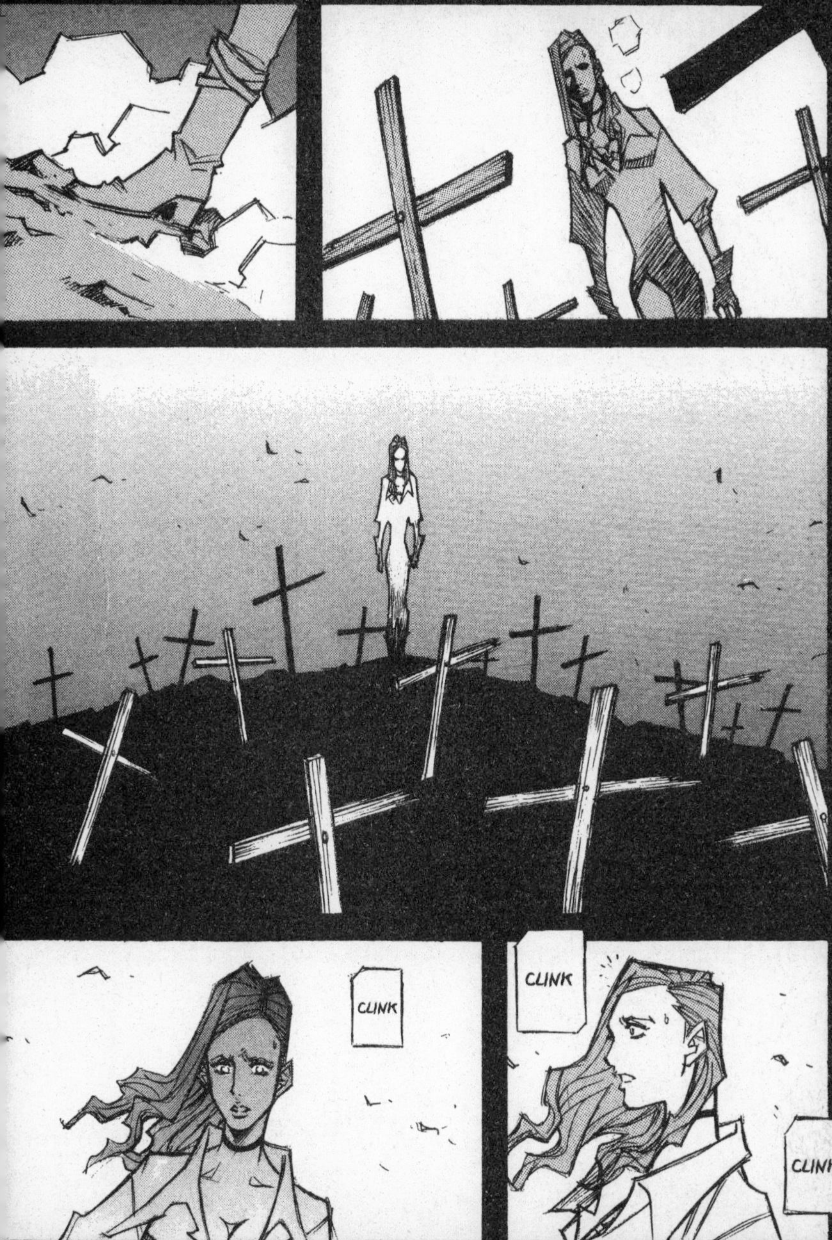
CLINK
CLINK
CLINK

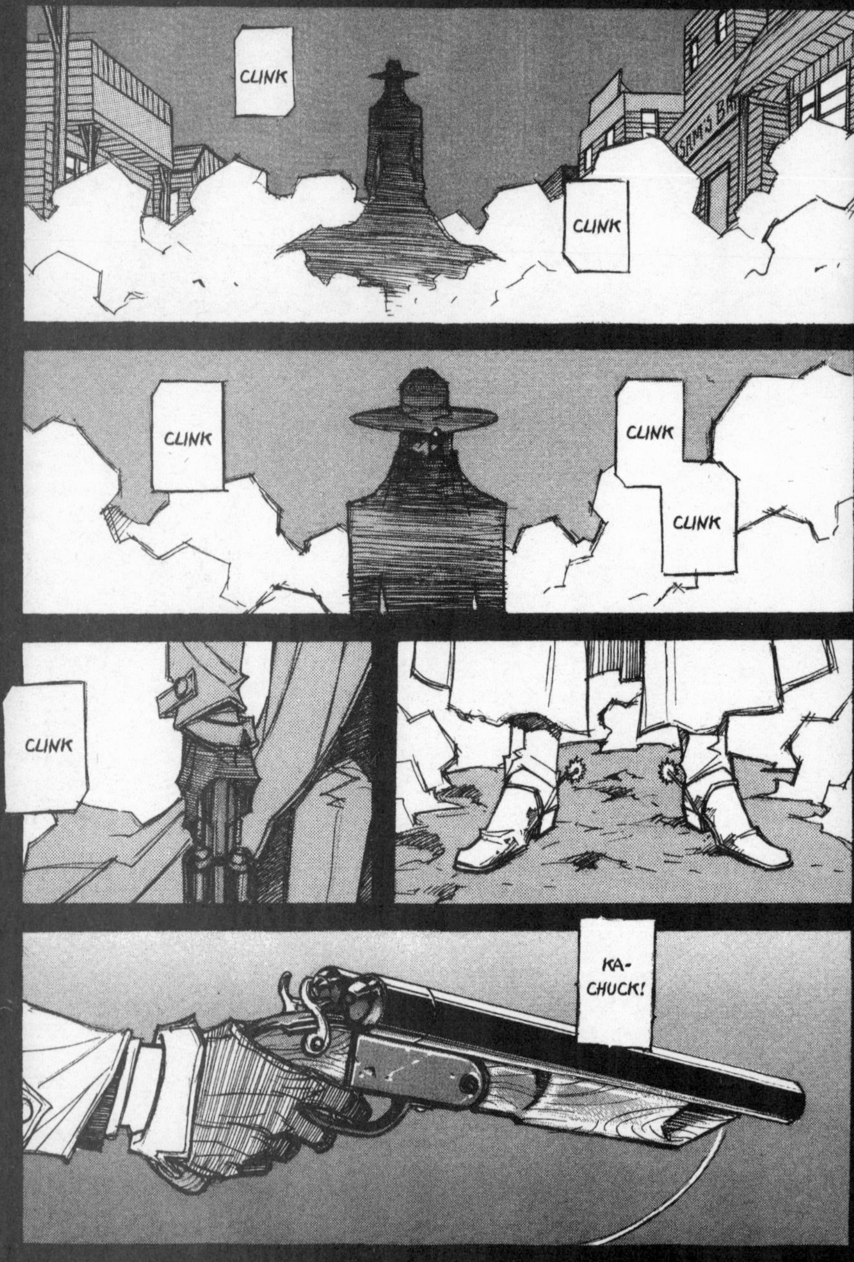
CLINK
CLINK
CLINK
CLINK
CLINK
CLINK
KA-
CHUCK!

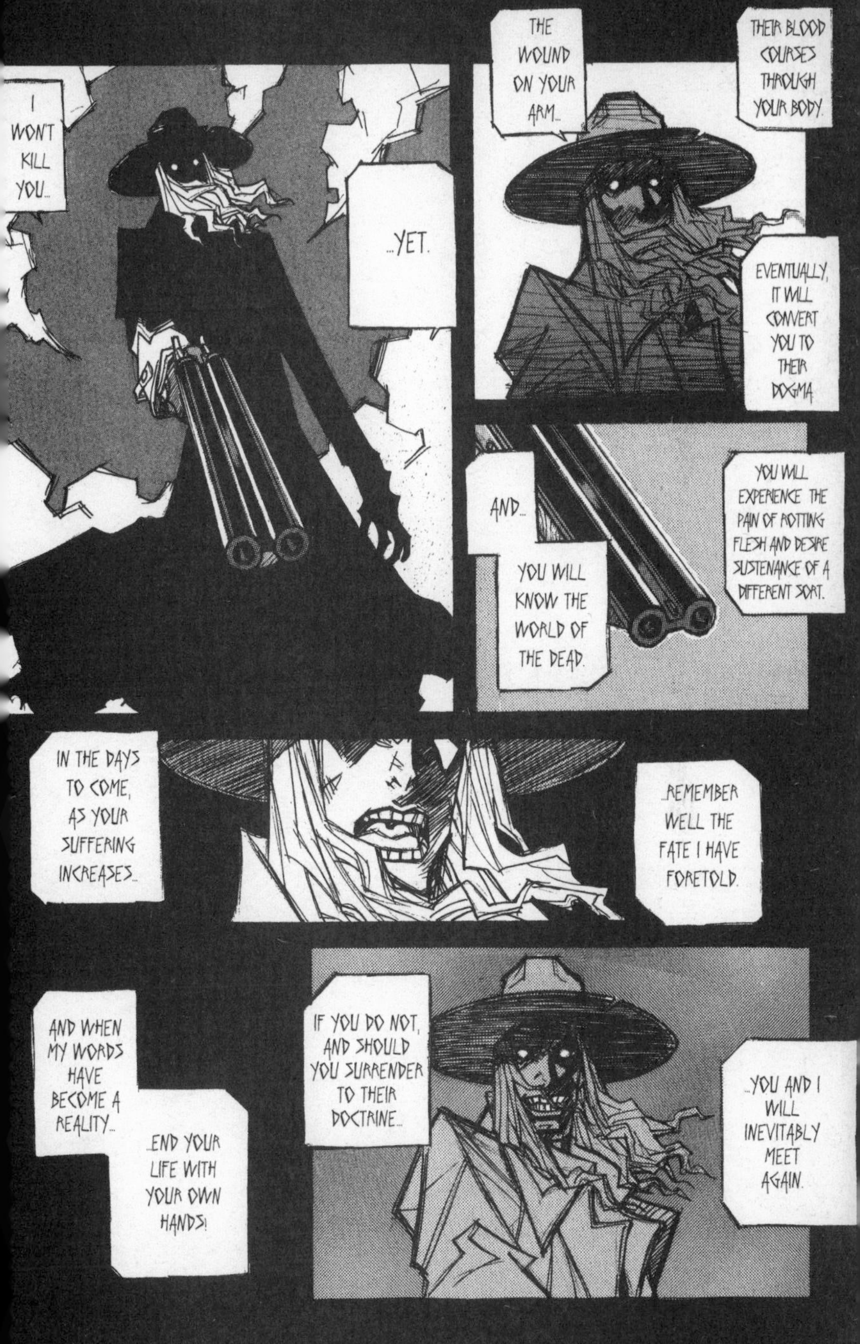
I WON'T KILL YOU...
...YET.
THE WOUND ON YOUR ARM...
THEIR BLOOD COURSES THROUGH YOUR BODY.
EVENTUALLY, IT WILL CONVERT YOU TO THEIR DOGMA
AND...
YOU WILL KNOW THE WORLD OF THE DEAD.
YOU WILL EXPERIENCE THE PAIN OF ROTTING FLESH AND DESIRE SUSTENANCE OF A DIFFERENT SORT.
IN THE DAYS TO COME, AS YOUR SUFFERING INCREASES...
...REMEMBER WELL THE FATE I HAVE FORETOLD.
AND WHEN MY WORDS HAVE BECOME A REALITY...
...END YOUR LIFE WITH YOUR OWN HANDS!
IF YOU DO NOT, AND SHOULD YOU SURRENDER TO THEIR DOCTRINE...
...YOU AND I WILL INEVITABLY MEET AGAIN.

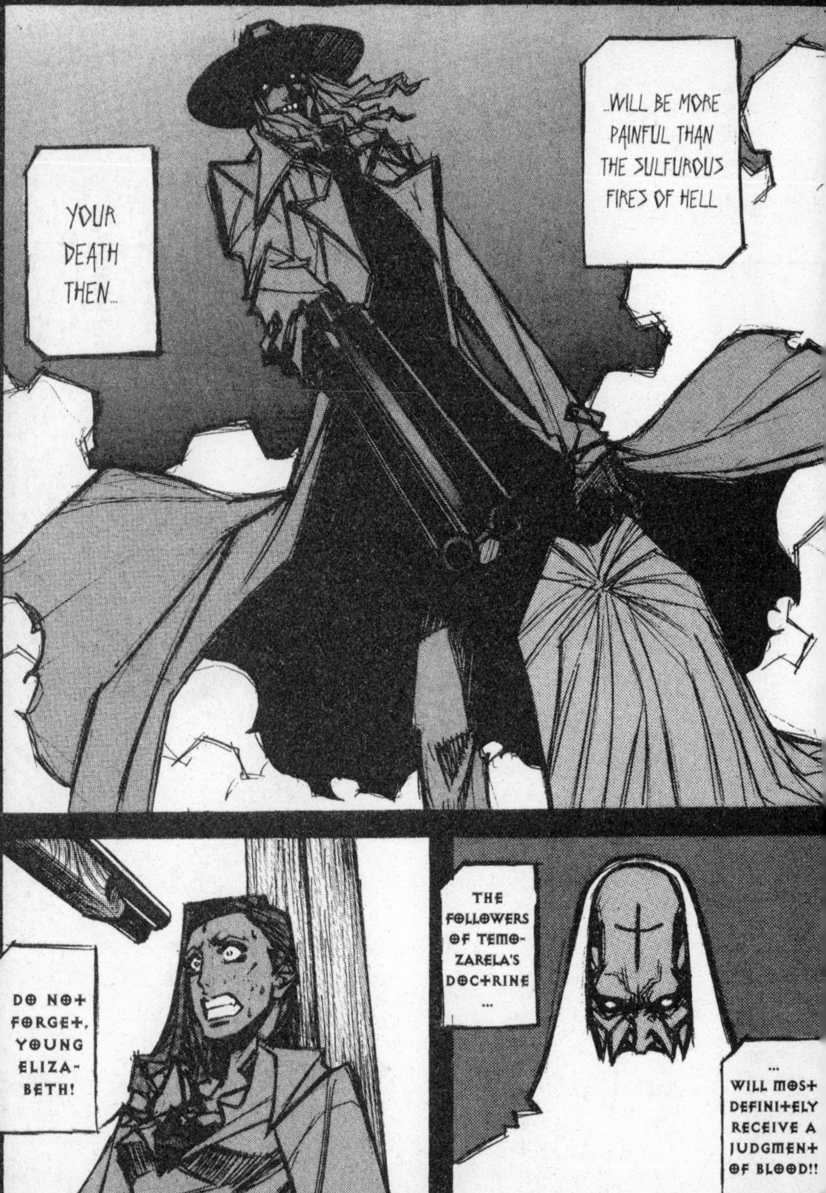
YOUR DEATH THEN...
...WILL BE MORE PAINFUL THAN THE SULFUROUS FIRES OF HELL
DO NOT FORGET, YOUNG ELIZA-BETH!
THE FOLLOWERS OF TEMO-ZARELA'S DOCTRINE ...
... WILL MOST DEFINITELY RECEIVE A JUDGMENT OF BLOOD!!

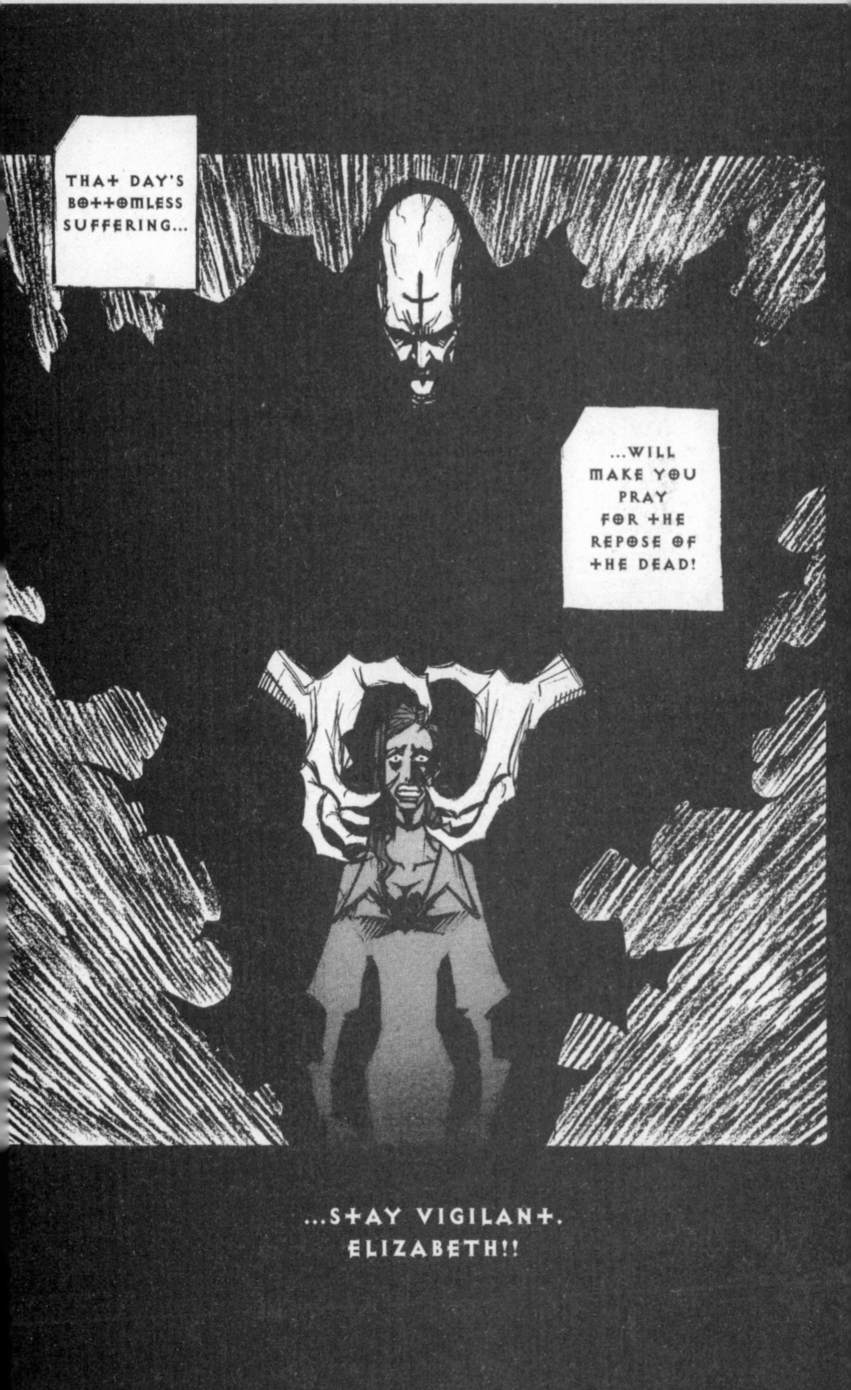
THAT DAY'S BOTTOMLESS SUFFERING...
...WILL MAKE YOU PRAY FOR THE REPOSE OF THE DEAD!
...STAY VIGILANT. ELIZABETH!!

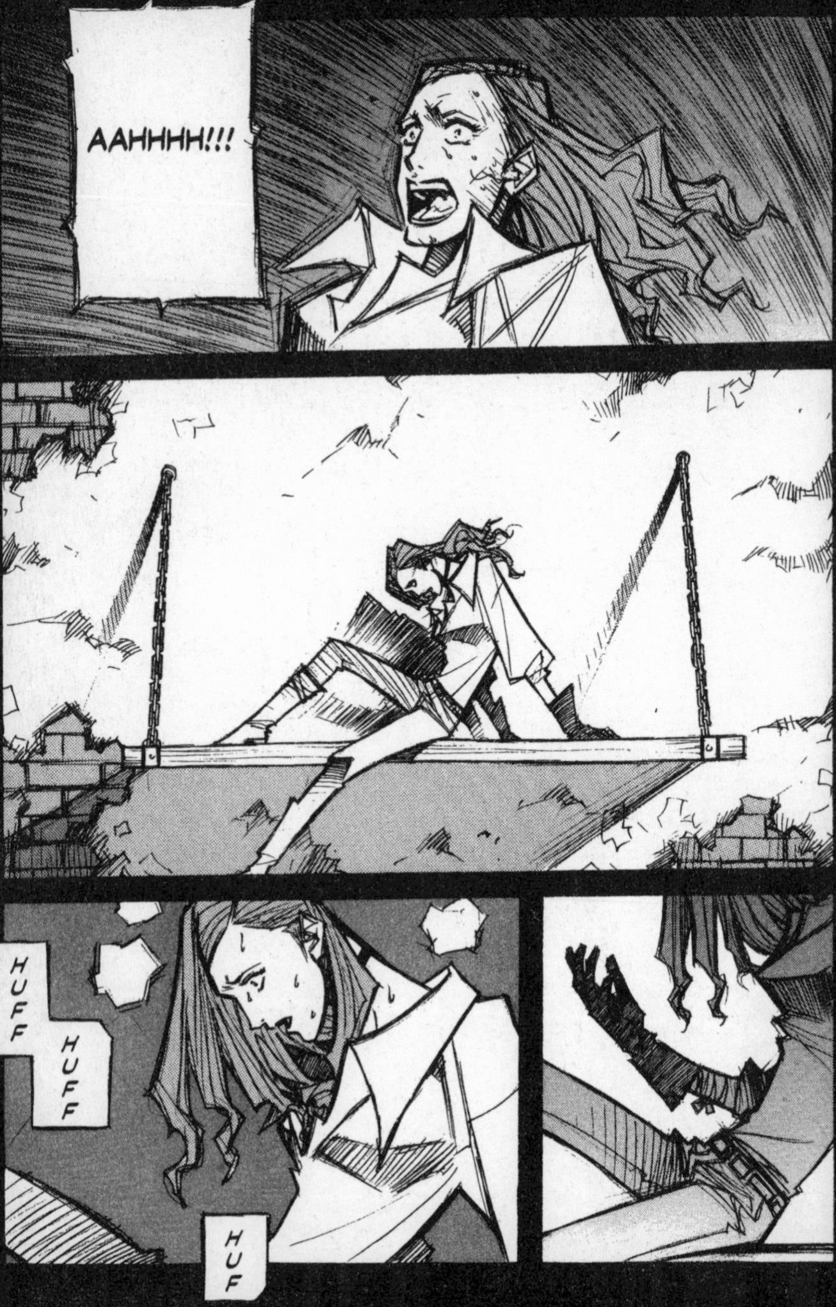
AAHHHH!!!
HUFF
HUFF
HUFF
HUF

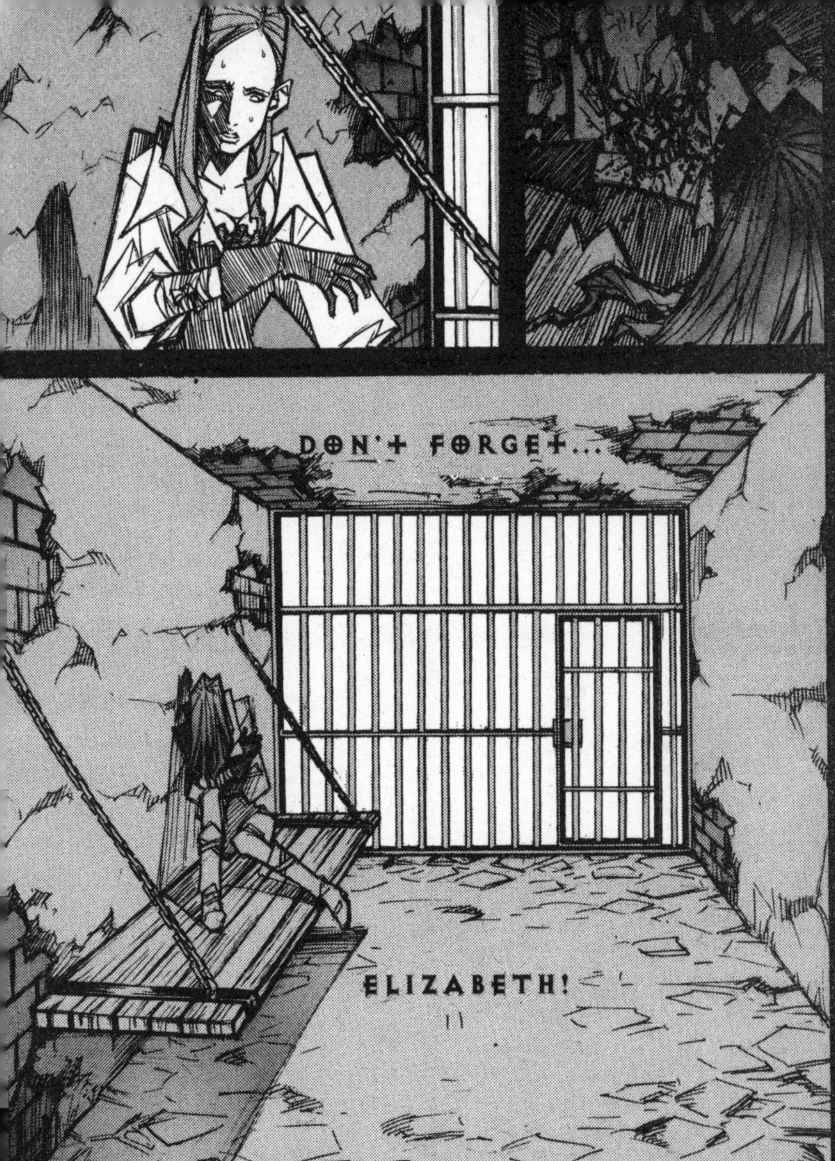
DON'T FORGET...
ELIZABETH!

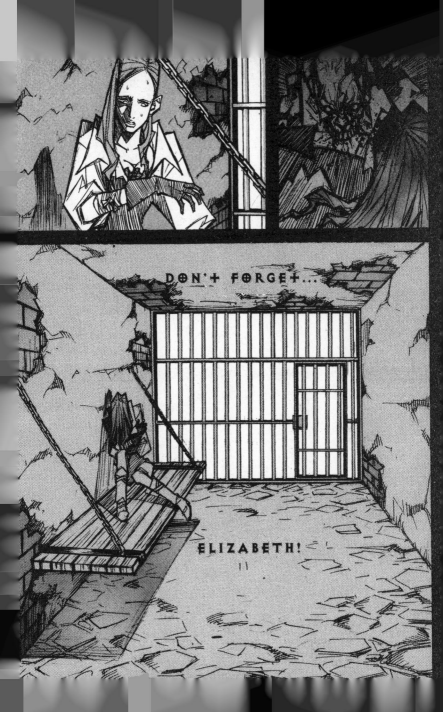

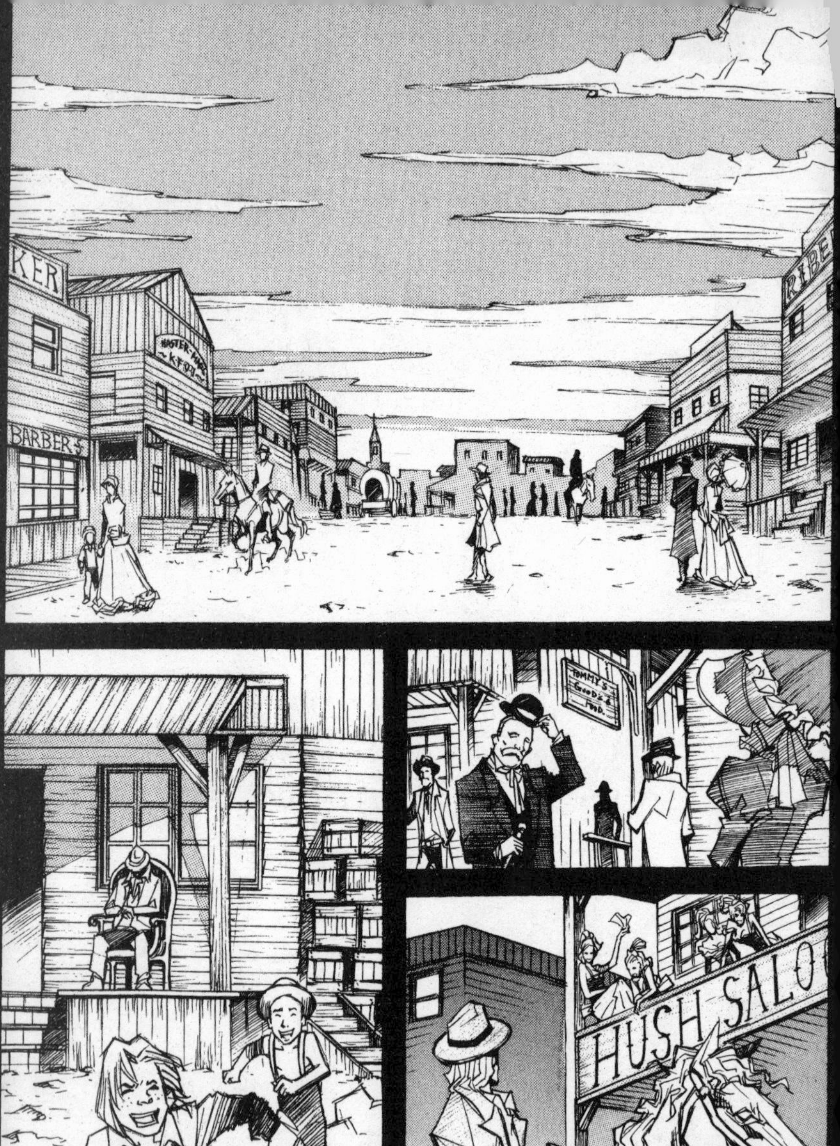
KER
BARBER'S
RIBE
TOMMY'S
HUSH SALO

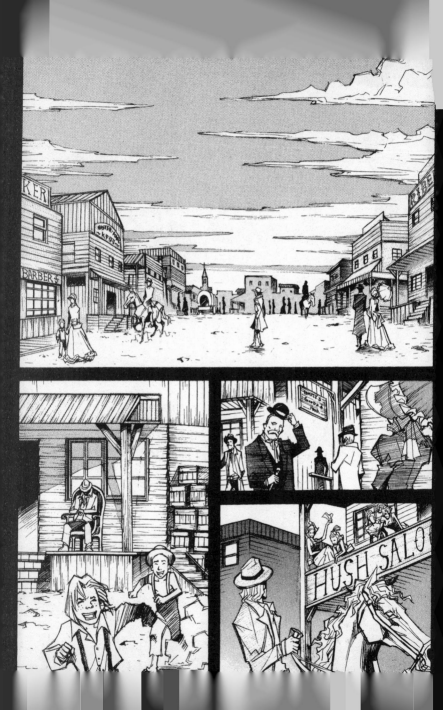

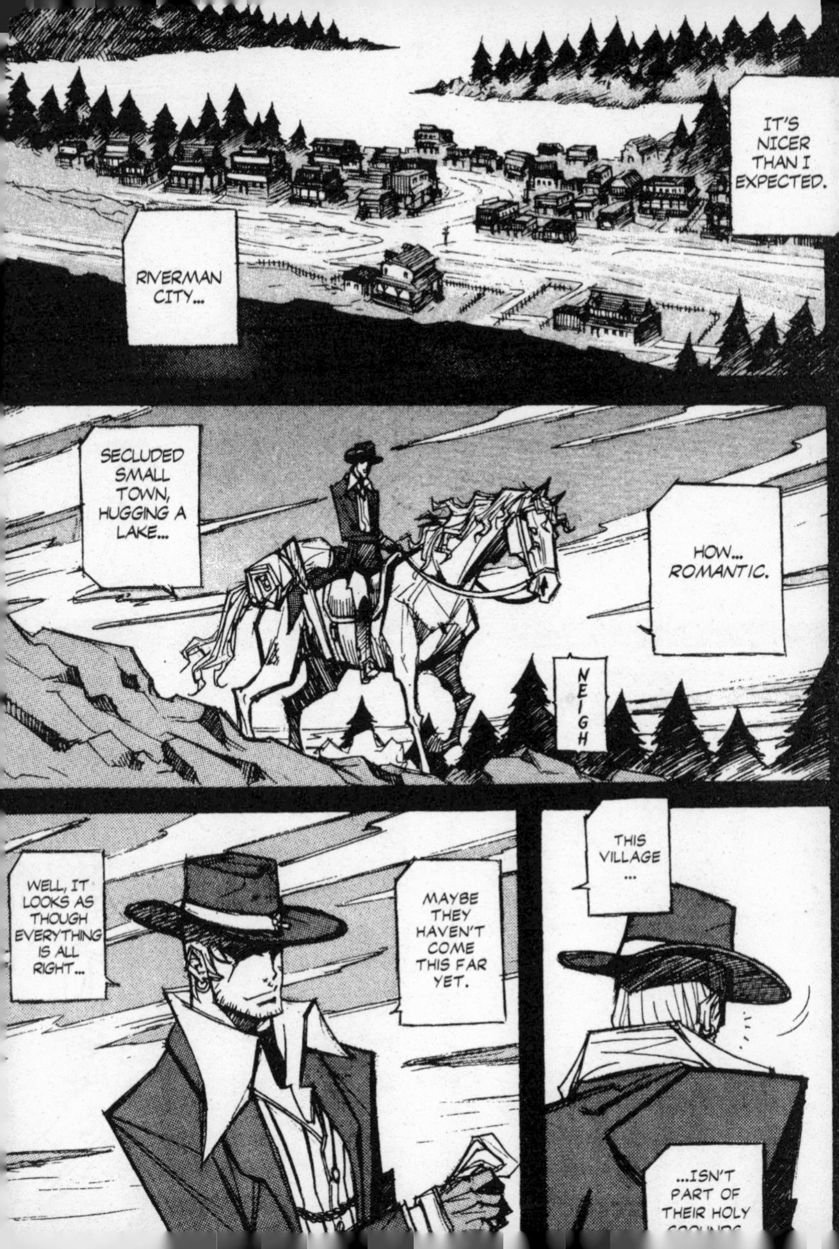
RIVERMAN CITY...
IT'S NICER THAN I EXPECTED.
SECLUDED SMALL TOWN, HUGGING A LAKE...
HOW... *ROMANTIC.*
NEIGH
WELL, IT LOOKS AS THOUGH EVERYTHING IS ALL RIGHT...
MAYBE THEY HAVEN'T COME THIS FAR YET.
THIS VILLAGE ...
...ISN'T PART OF THEIR HOLY

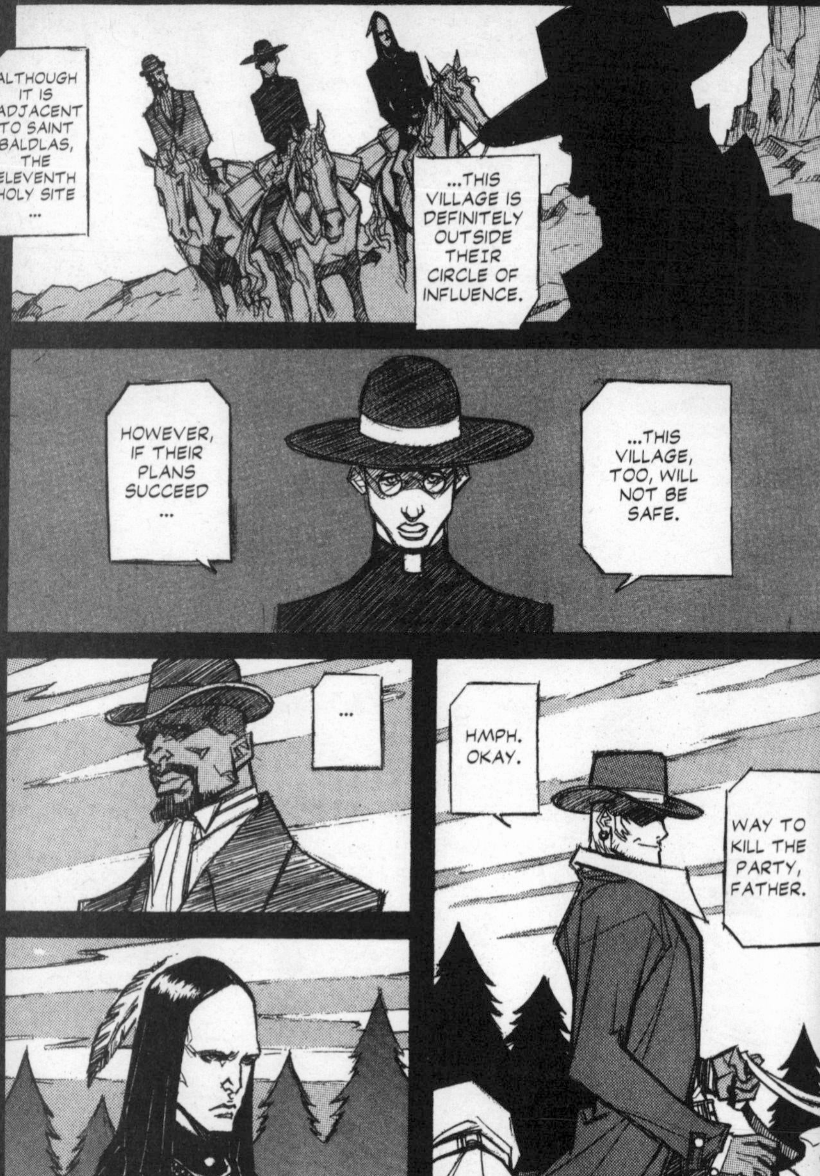
ALTHOUGH IT IS ADJACENT TO SAINT BALDLAS, THE ELEVENTH HOLY SITE ...
...THIS VILLAGE IS DEFINITELY OUTSIDE THEIR CIRCLE OF INFLUENCE.
HOWEVER, IF THEIR PLANS SUCCEED ...
...THIS VILLAGE, TOO, WILL NOT BE SAFE.
...
HMPH. OKAY.
WAY TO KILL THE PARTY, FATHER.

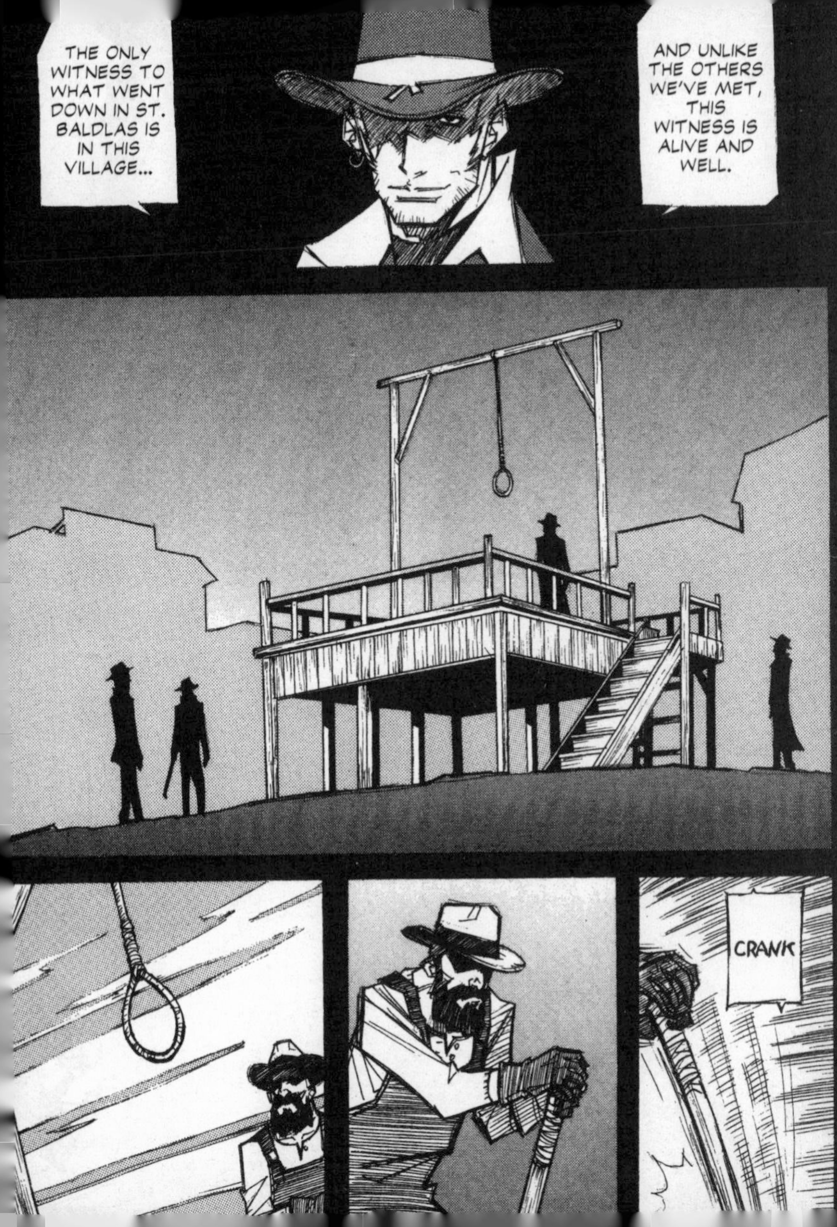
THE ONLY WITNESS TO WHAT WENT DOWN IN ST. BALDLAS IS IN THIS VILLAGE...
AND UNLIKE THE OTHERS WE'VE MET, THIS WITNESS IS ALIVE AND WELL.
CRANK

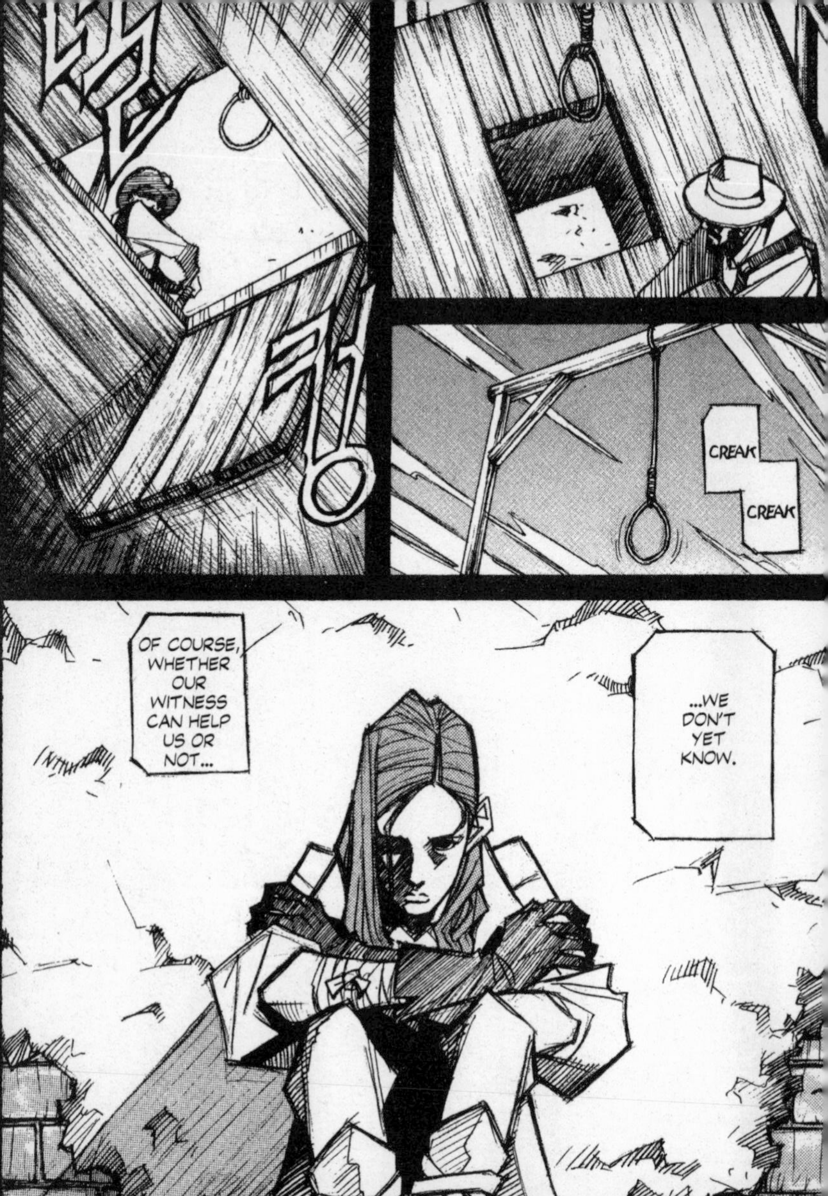
CREAK
CREAK
OF COURSE, WHETHER OUR WITNESS CAN HELP US OR NOT...
...WE DON'T YET KNOW.

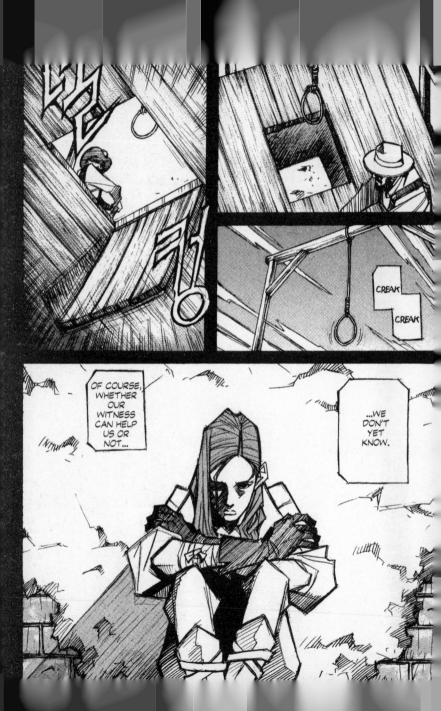

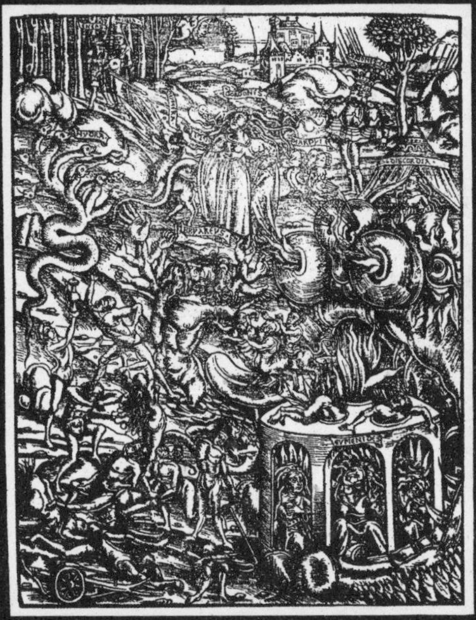
HYDRA
DISCORDIA

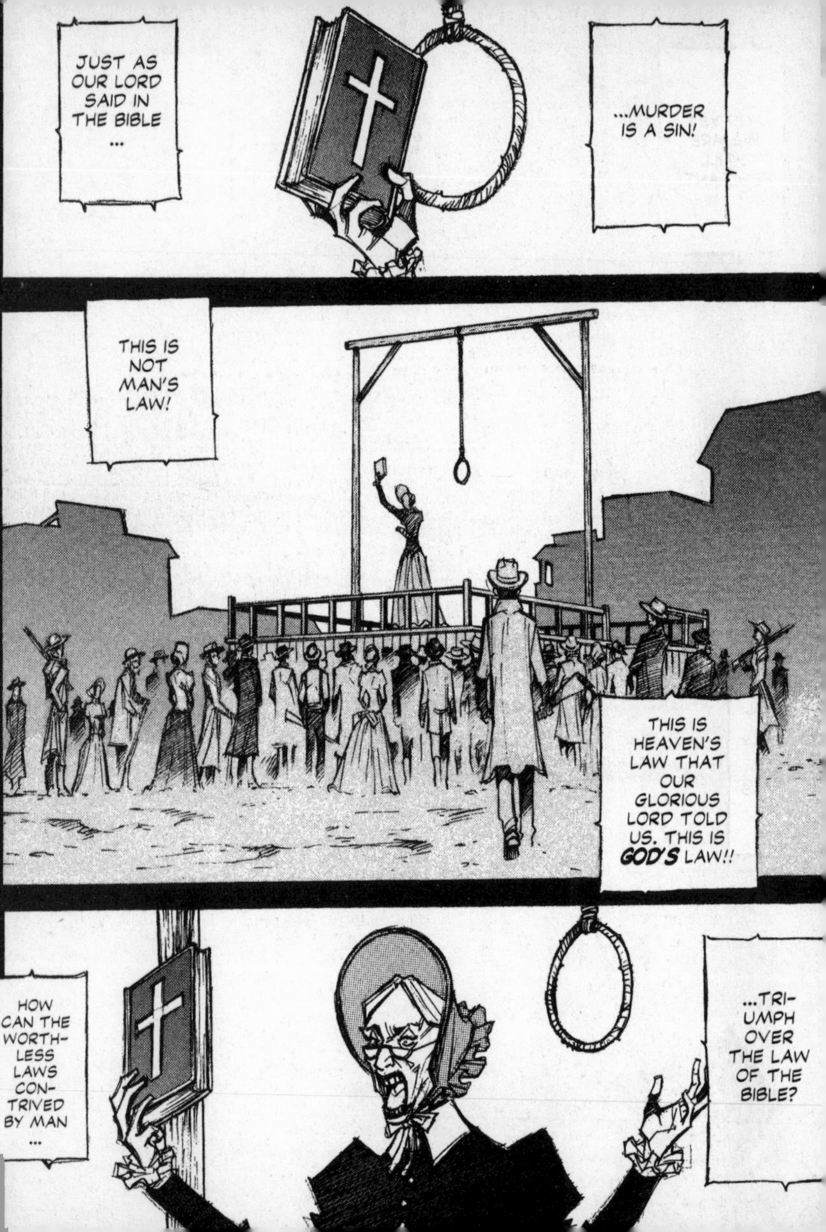

JUST AS OUR LORD SAID IN THE BIBLE ...
...MURDER IS A SIN!
THIS IS NOT MAN'S LAW!
THIS IS HEAVEN'S LAW THAT OUR GLORIOUS LORD TOLD US. THIS IS **GOD'S** LAW!!
HOW CAN THE WORTH-LESS LAWS CON-TRIVED BY MAN ...
...TRI-UMPH OVER THE LAW OF THE BIBLE?

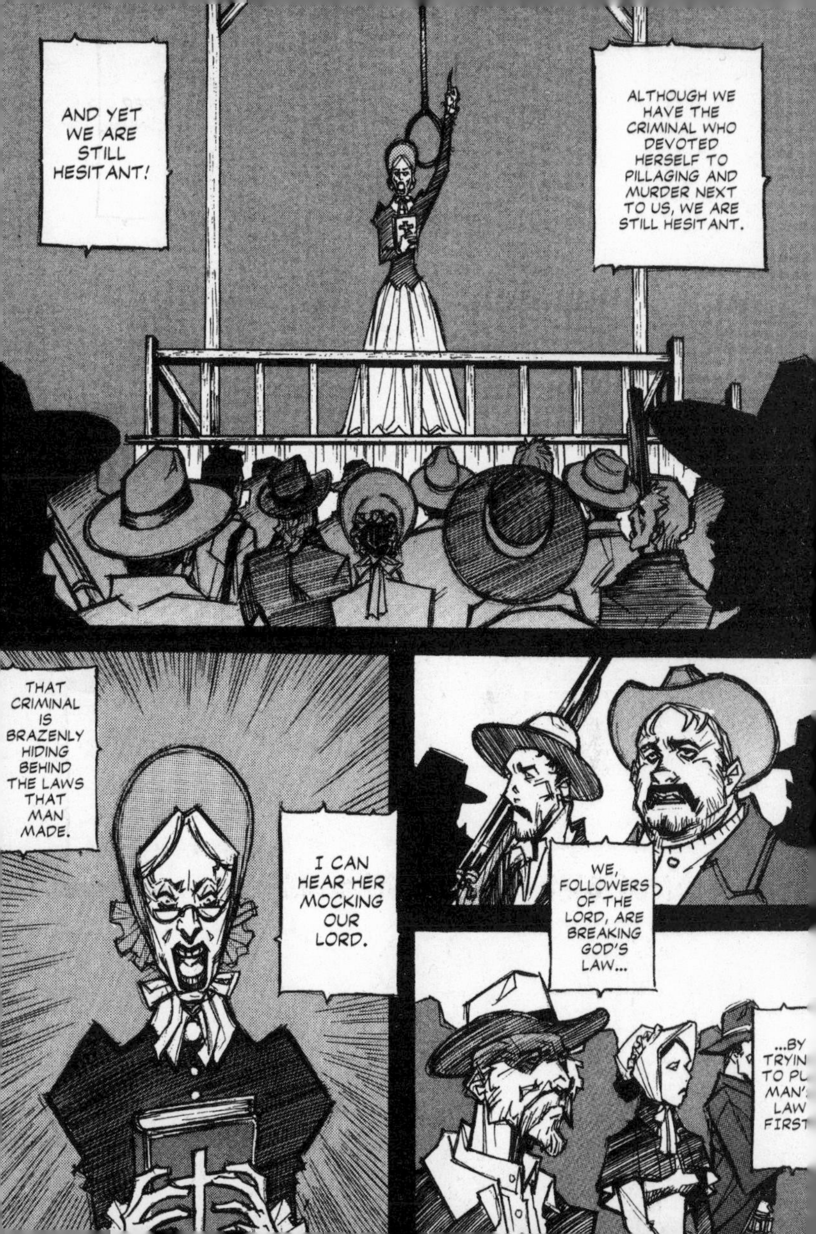
AND YET WE ARE STILL HESITANT!
ALTHOUGH WE HAVE THE CRIMINAL WHO DEVOTED HERSELF TO PILLAGING AND MURDER NEXT TO US, WE ARE STILL HESITANT.
THAT CRIMINAL IS BRAZENLY HIDING BEHIND THE LAWS THAT MAN MADE.
I CAN HEAR HER MOCKING OUR LORD.
WE, FOLLOWERS OF THE LORD, ARE BREAKING GOD'S LAW...
...BY TRYIN TO PU MAN' LAW FIRST

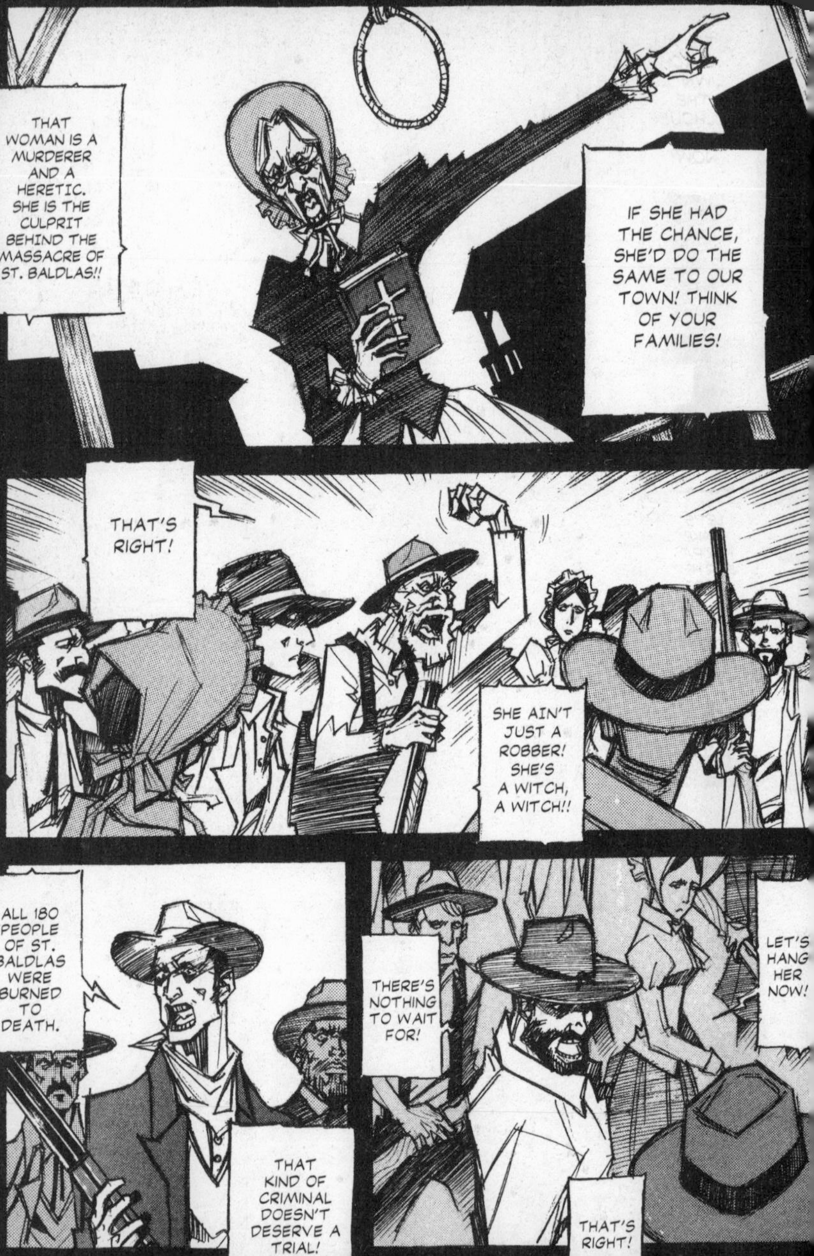

THAT WOMAN IS A MURDERER AND A HERETIC. SHE IS THE CULPRIT BEHIND THE MASSACRE OF ST. BALDLAS!!
IF SHE HAD THE CHANCE, SHE'D DO THE SAME TO OUR TOWN! THINK OF YOUR FAMILIES!
THAT'S RIGHT!
SHE AIN'T JUST A ROBBER! SHE'S A WITCH, A WITCH!!
ALL 180 PEOPLE OF ST. BALDLAS WERE BURNED TO DEATH.
THAT KIND OF CRIMINAL DOESN'T DESERVE A TRIAL!
THERE'S NOTHING TO WAIT FOR!
LET'S HANG HER NOW!
THAT'S RIGHT!

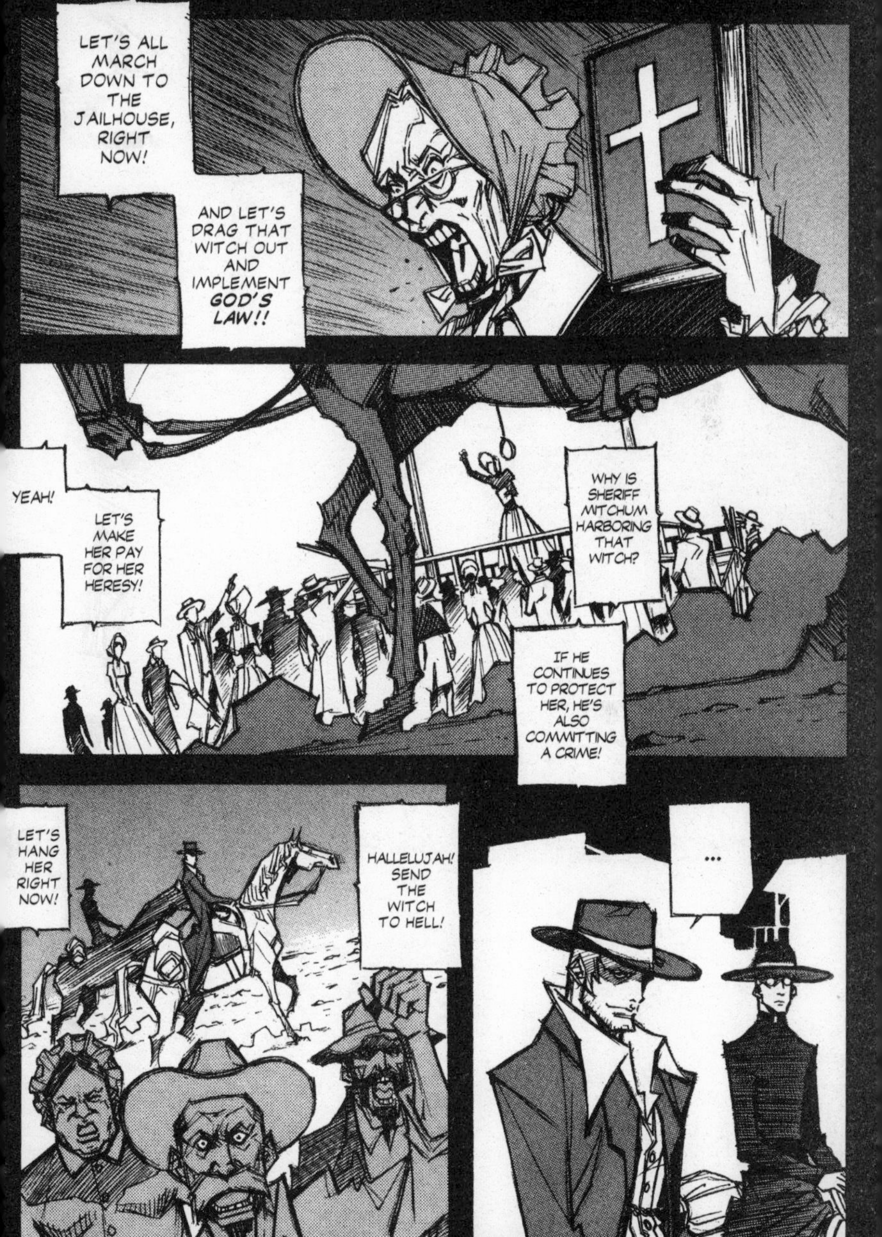
LET'S ALL MARCH DOWN TO THE JAILHOUSE, RIGHT NOW!
AND LET'S DRAG THAT WITCH OUT AND IMPLEMENT GOD'S LAW!!
YEAH!
LET'S MAKE HER PAY FOR HER HERESY!
WHY IS SHERIFF MITCHUM HARBORING THAT WITCH?
IF HE CONTINUES TO PROTECT HER, HE'S ALSO COMMITTING A CRIME!
LET'S HANG HER RIGHT NOW!
HALLELUJAH! SEND THE WITCH TO HELL!
...

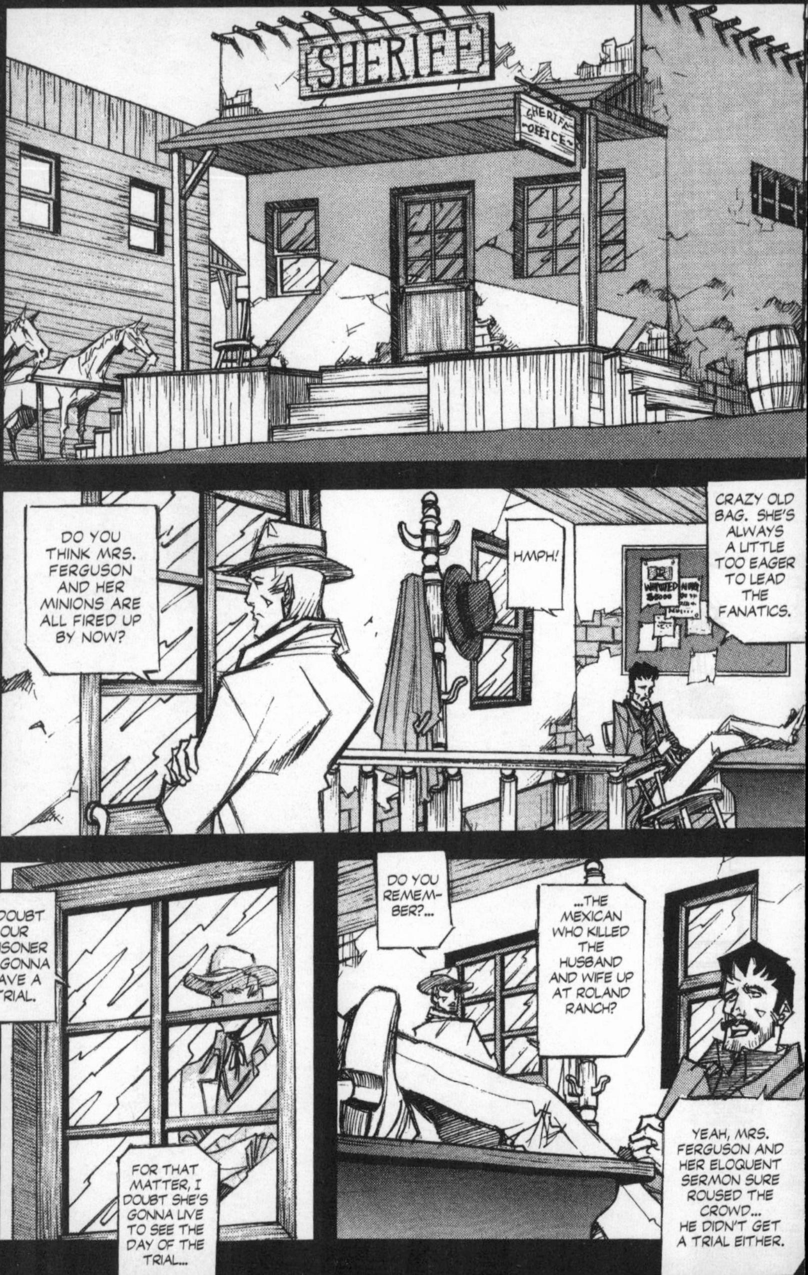
SHERIFF
SHERIFF OFFICE
DO YOU THINK MRS. FERGUSON AND HER MINIONS ARE ALL FIRED UP BY NOW?
HMPH!
CRAZY OLD BAG. SHE'S ALWAYS A LITTLE TOO EAGER TO LEAD THE FANATICS.
I DOUBT OUR PRISONER IS GONNA HAVE A TRIAL.
FOR THAT MATTER, I DOUBT SHE'S GONNA LIVE TO SEE THE DAY OF THE TRIAL...
DO YOU REMEMBER?...
...THE MEXICAN WHO KILLED THE HUSBAND AND WIFE UP AT ROLAND RANCH?
YEAH, MRS. FERGUSON AND HER ELOQUENT SERMON SURE ROUSED THE CROWD... HE DIDN'T GET A TRIAL EITHER.

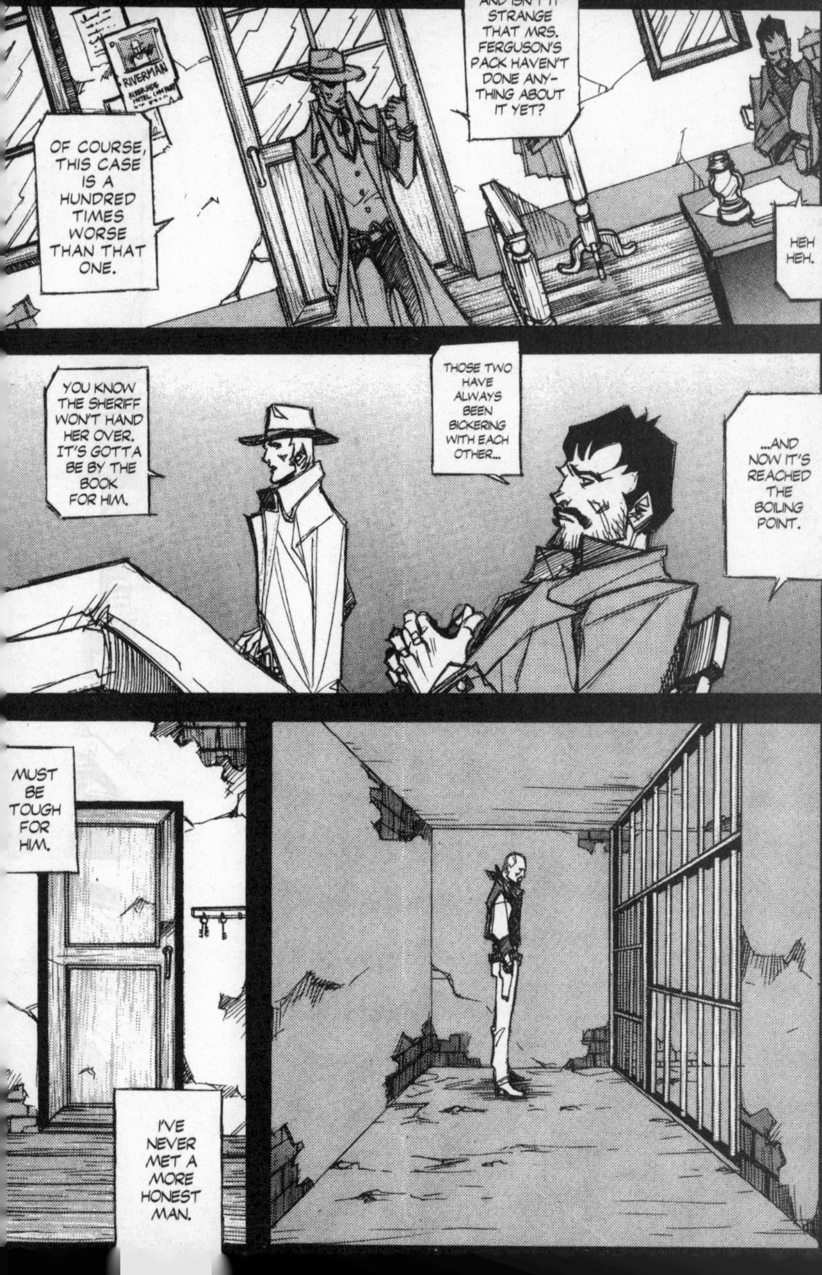
RIVERMAN
OF COURSE, THIS CASE IS A HUNDRED TIMES WORSE THAN THAT ONE.
AND ISN'T IT STRANGE THAT MRS. FERGUSON'S PACK HAVEN'T DONE ANYTHING ABOUT IT YET?
HEH HEH.
YOU KNOW THE SHERIFF WON'T HAND HER OVER. IT'S GOTTA BE BY THE BOOK FOR HIM.
THOSE TWO HAVE ALWAYS BEEN BICKERING WITH EACH OTHER...
...AND NOW IT'S REACHED THE BOILING POINT.
MUST BE TOUGH FOR HIM.
I'VE NEVER MET A MORE HONEST MAN.

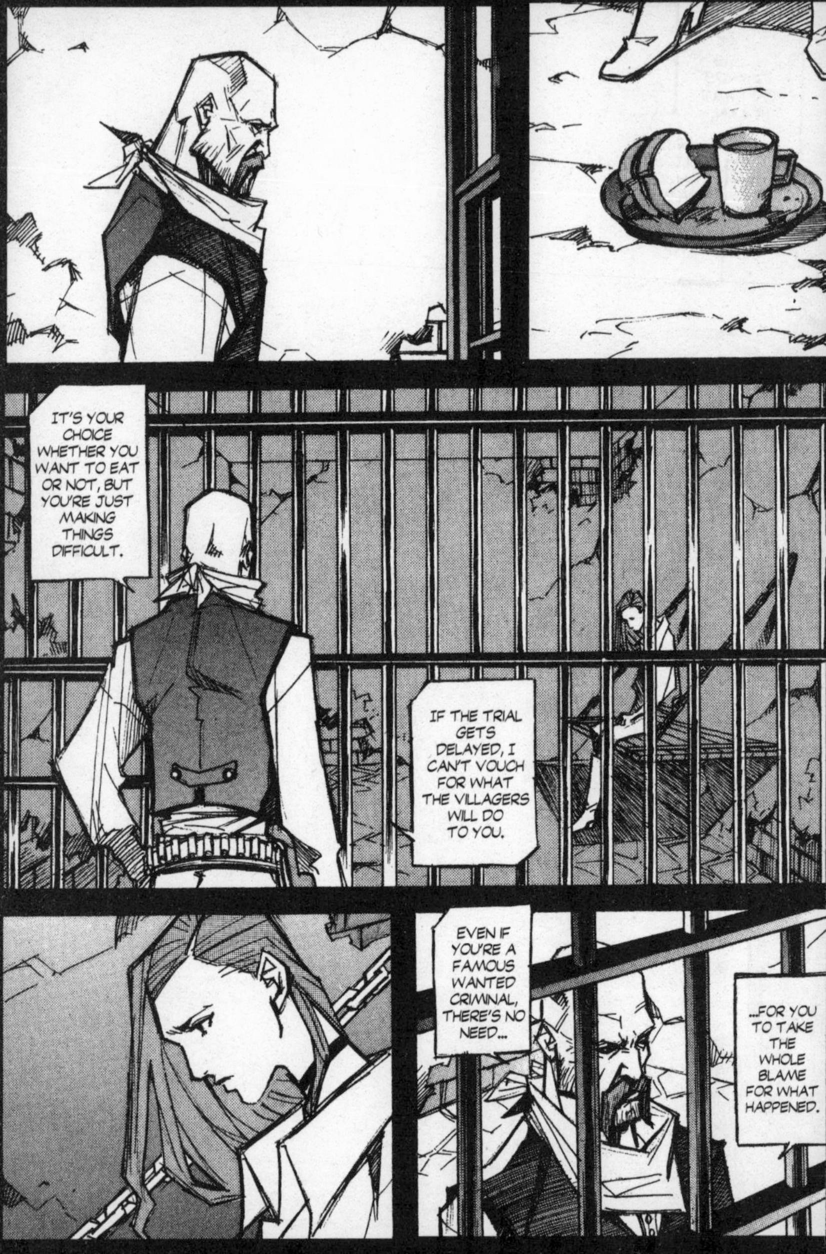
IT'S YOUR CHOICE WHETHER YOU WANT TO EAT OR NOT, BUT YOU'RE JUST MAKING THINGS DIFFICULT.
IF THE TRIAL GETS DELAYED, I CAN'T VOUCH FOR WHAT THE VILLAGERS WILL DO TO YOU.
EVEN IF YOU'RE A FAMOUS WANTED CRIMINAL, THERE'S NO NEED...
...FOR YOU TO TAKE THE WHOLE BLAME FOR WHAT HAPPENED.

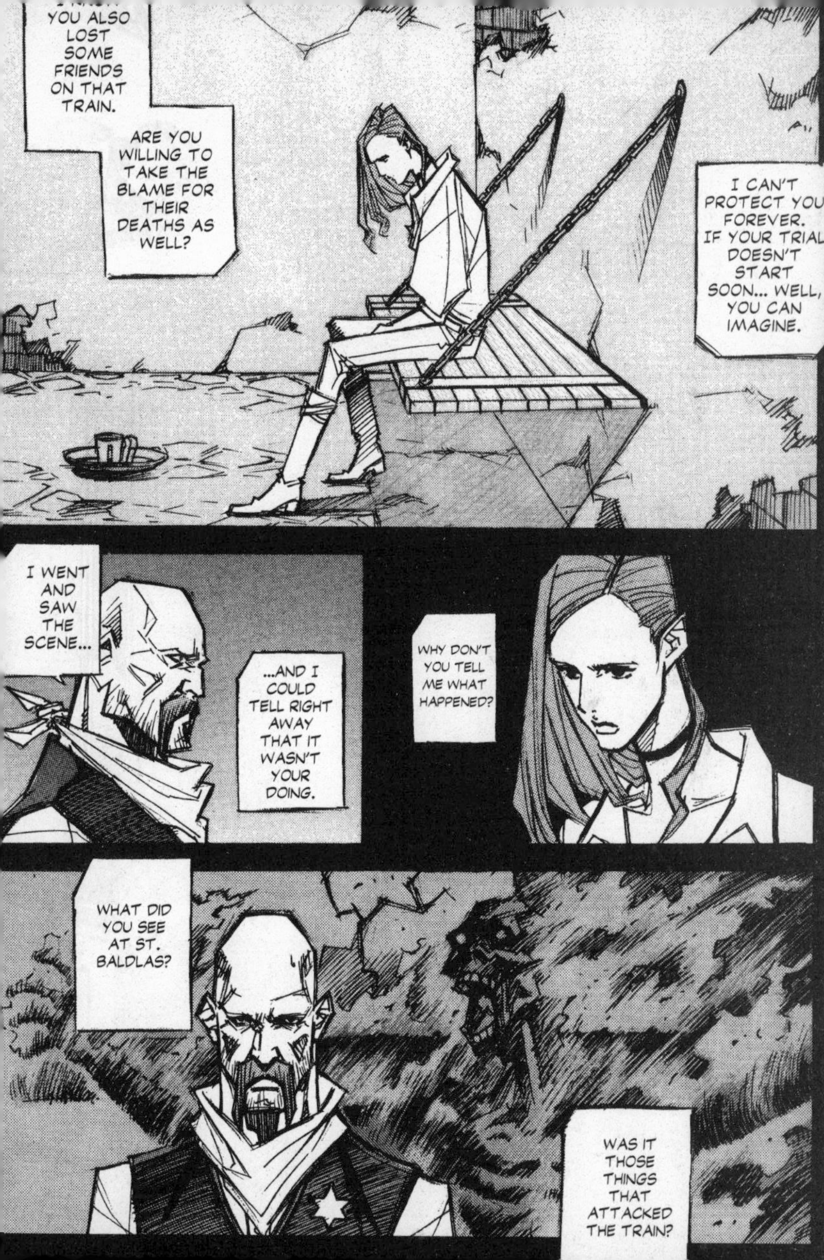
YOU ALSO LOST SOME FRIENDS ON THAT TRAIN.
ARE YOU WILLING TO TAKE THE BLAME FOR THEIR DEATHS AS WELL?
I CAN'T PROTECT YOU FOREVER. IF YOUR TRIAL DOESN'T START SOON... WELL, YOU CAN IMAGINE.
I WENT AND SAW THE SCENE...
...AND I COULD TELL RIGHT AWAY THAT IT WASN'T YOUR DOING.
WHY DON'T YOU TELL ME WHAT HAPPENED?
WHAT DID YOU SEE AT ST. BALDLAS?
WAS IT THOSE THINGS THAT ATTACKED THE TRAIN?

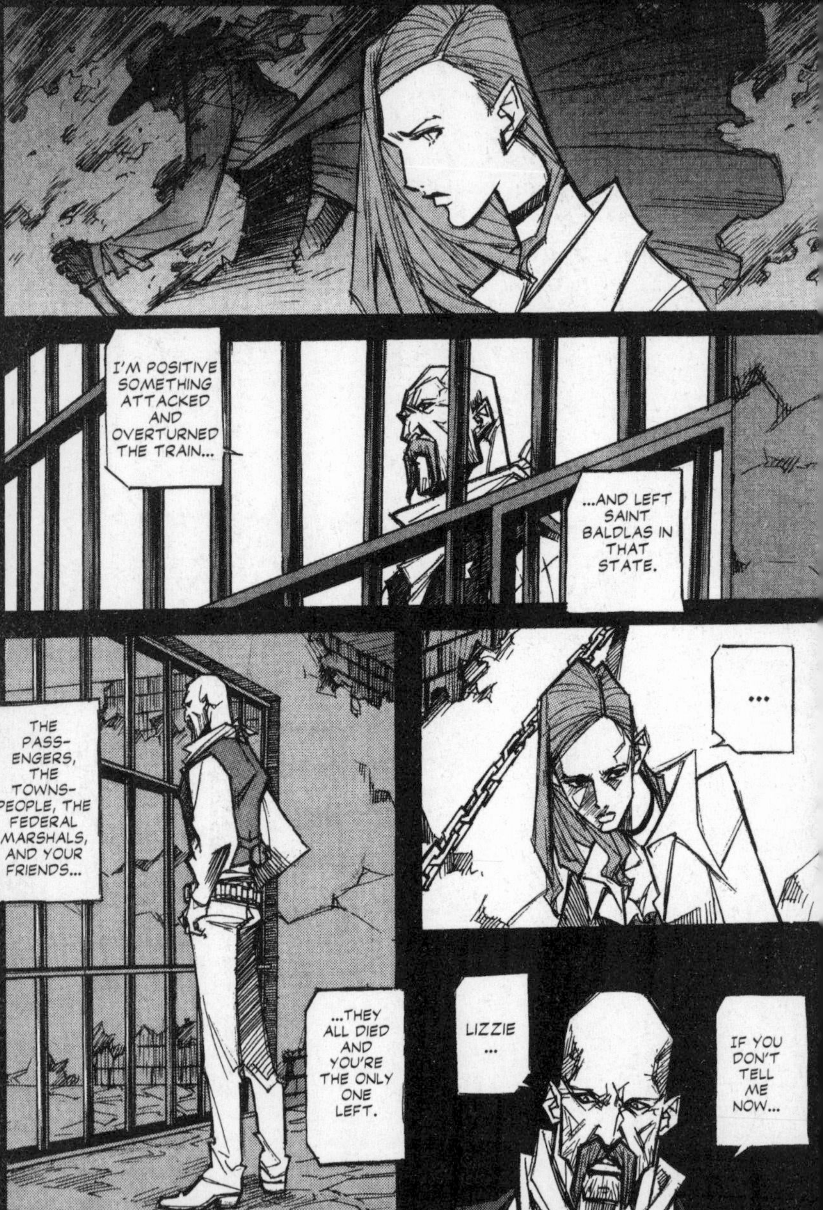
I'M POSITIVE SOMETHING ATTACKED AND OVERTURNED THE TRAIN...
...AND LEFT SAINT BALDLAS IN THAT STATE.
THE PASSENGERS, THE TOWNSPEOPLE, THE FEDERAL MARSHALS, AND YOUR FRIENDS...
...THEY ALL DIED AND YOU'RE THE ONLY ONE LEFT.
...
LIZZIE...
IF YOU DON'T TELL ME NOW...

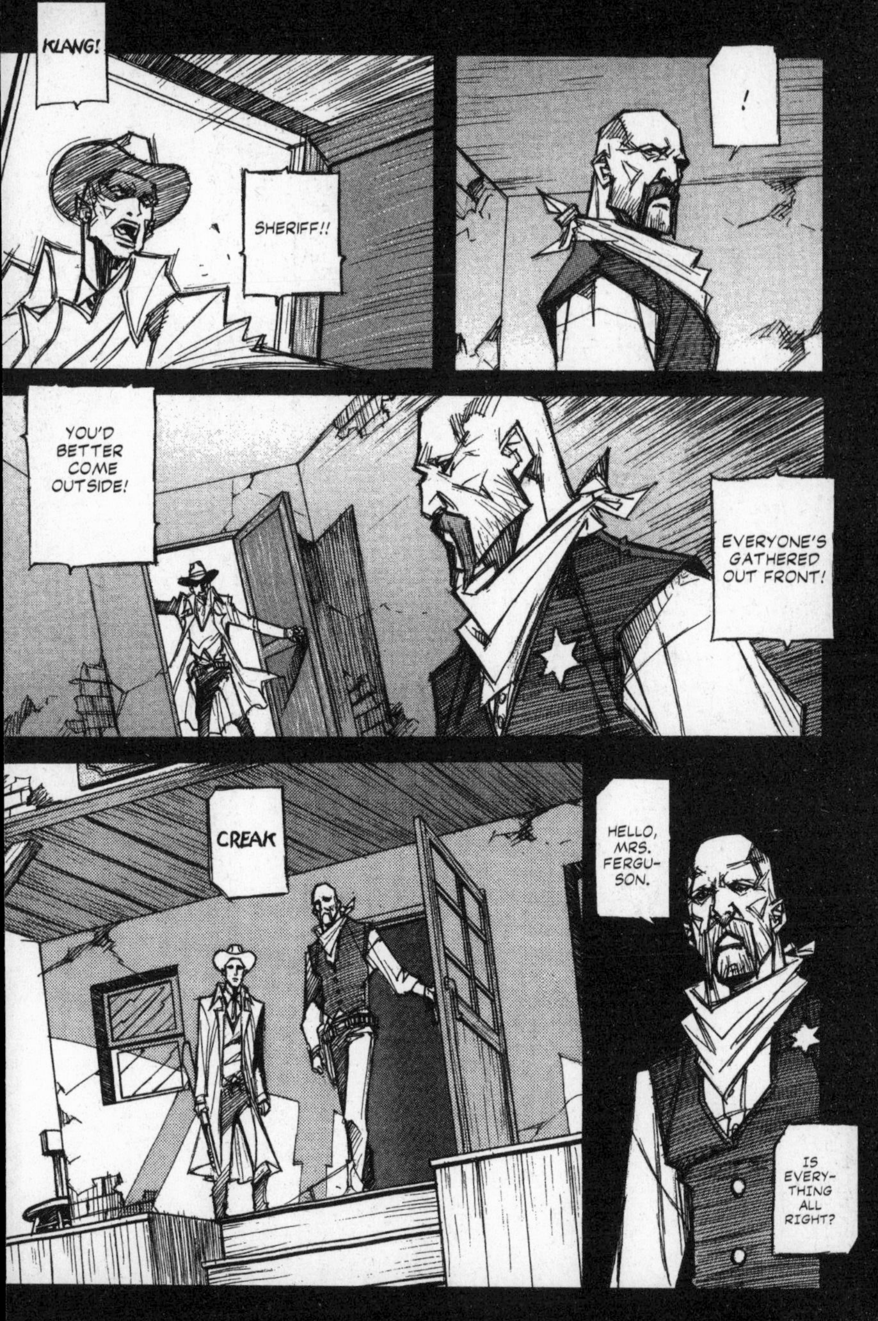
KLANG!
SHERIFF!!
!
YOU'D BETTER COME OUTSIDE!
EVERYONE'S GATHERED OUT FRONT!
CREAK
HELLO, MRS. FERGU-SON.
IS EVERY-THING ALL RIGHT?

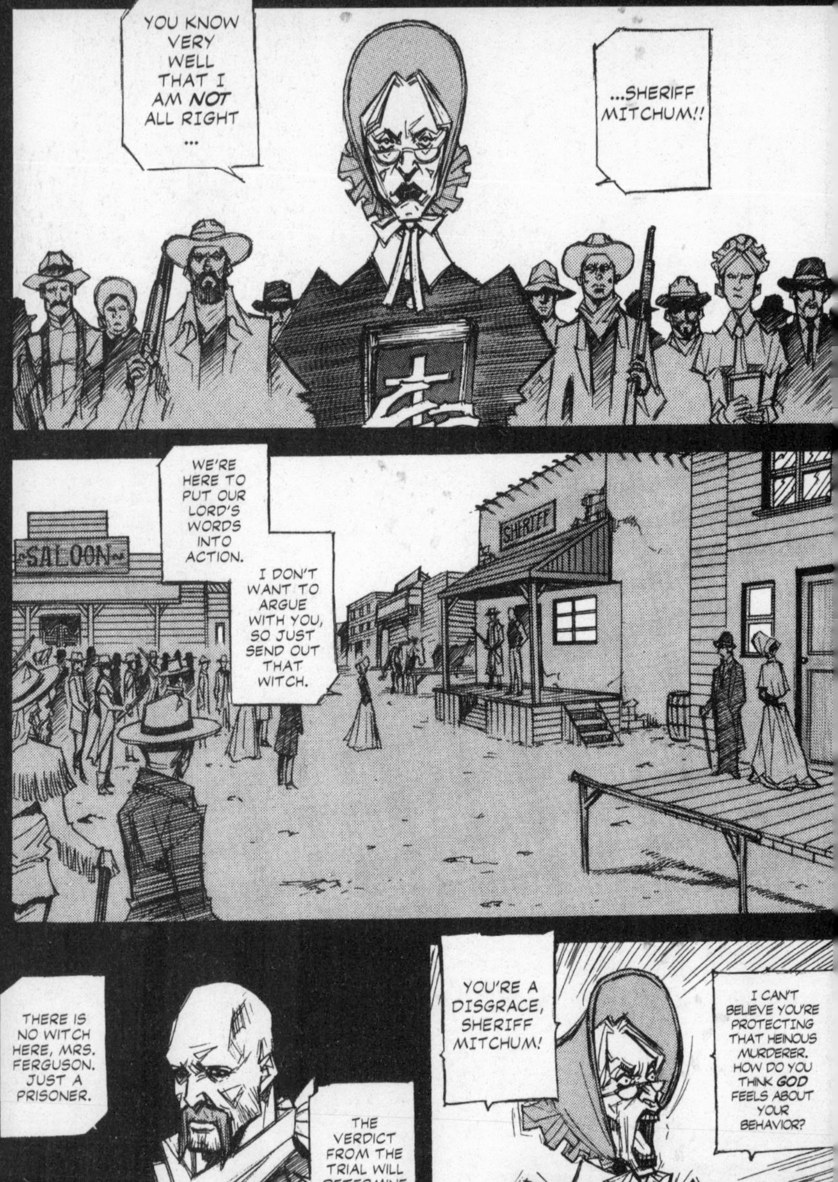
YOU KNOW VERY WELL THAT I AM **NOT** ALL RIGHT ...
...SHERIFF MITCHUM!!
WE'RE HERE TO PUT OUR **LORD'S** WORDS INTO ACTION.
I DON'T WANT TO ARGUE WITH YOU, SO JUST SEND OUT THAT WITCH.
SALOON
SHERIFF
THERE IS NO WITCH HERE, MRS. FERGUSON. JUST A PRISONER.
THE VERDICT FROM THE TRIAL WILL DETERMINE THE PUNISHMENT.
YOU'RE A DISGRACE, SHERIFF MITCHUM!
I CAN'T BELIEVE YOU'RE PROTECTING THAT HEINOUS MURDERER. HOW DO YOU THINK **GOD** FEELS ABOUT YOUR BEHAVIOR?

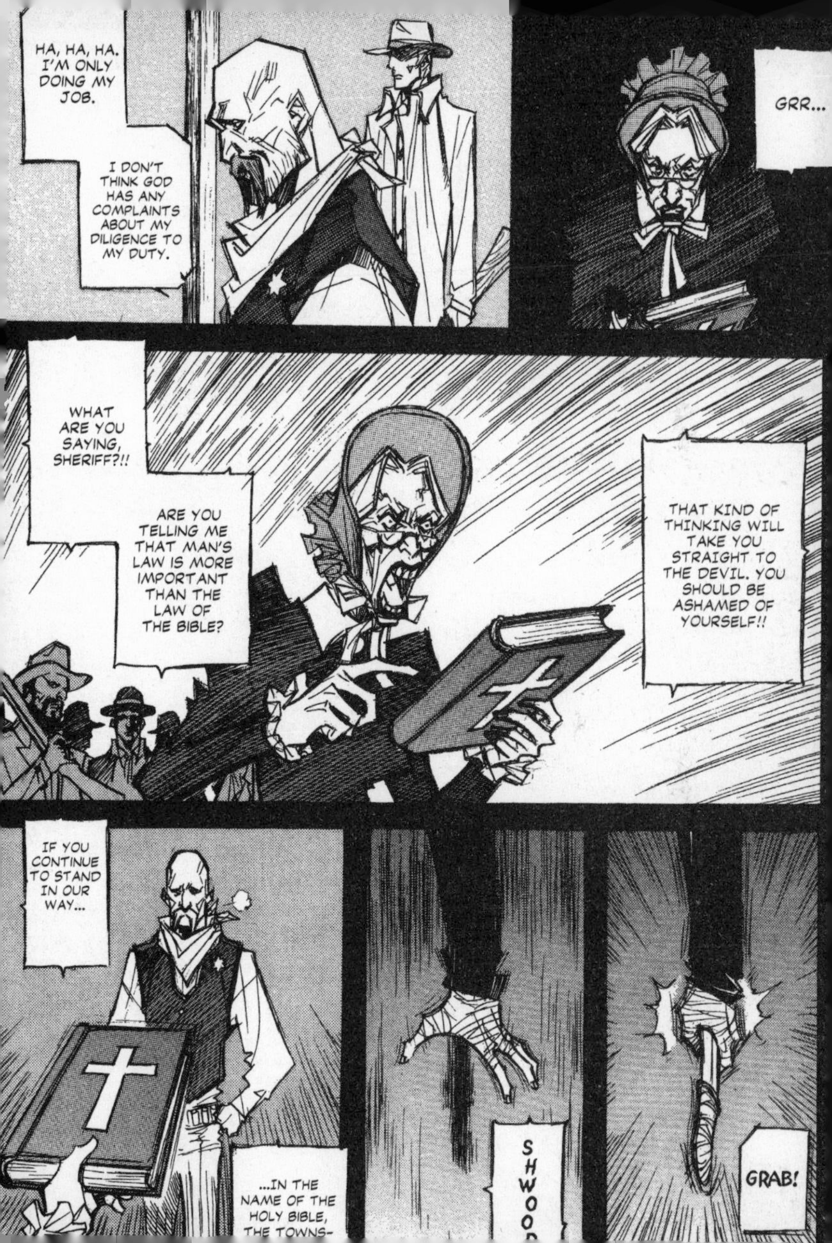
HA, HA, HA. I'M ONLY DOING MY JOB.
I DON'T THINK GOD HAS ANY COMPLAINTS ABOUT MY DILIGENCE TO MY DUTY.
GRR...
WHAT ARE YOU SAYING, SHERIFF?!!
ARE YOU TELLING ME THAT MAN'S LAW IS MORE IMPORTANT THAN THE LAW OF THE BIBLE?
THAT KIND OF THINKING WILL TAKE YOU STRAIGHT TO THE DEVIL. YOU SHOULD BE ASHAMED OF YOURSELF!!
IF YOU CONTINUE TO STAND IN OUR WAY...
...IN THE NAME OF THE HOLY BIBLE, THE TOWNS-
SHWOO
GRAB!

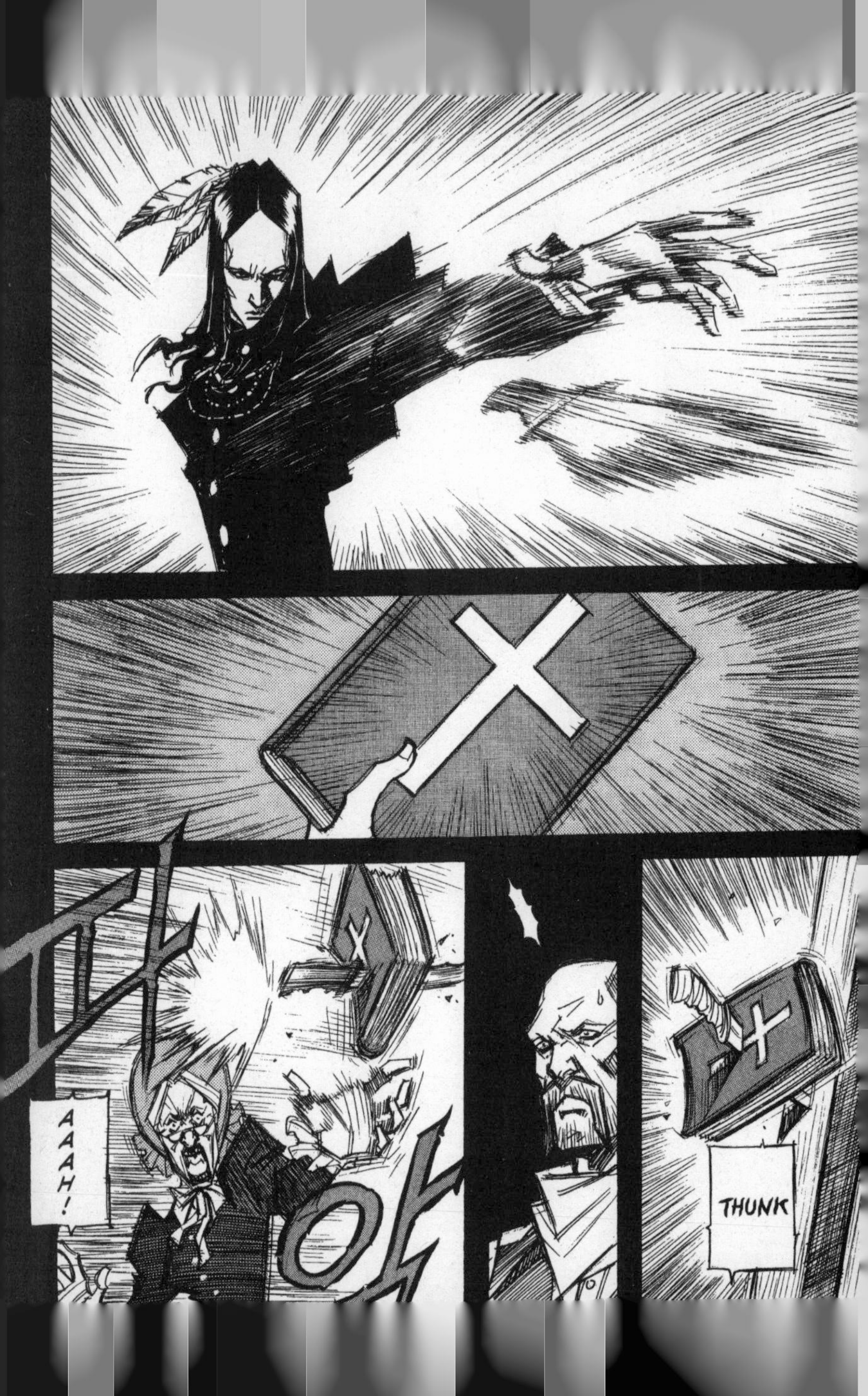
AAAH!
THUNK

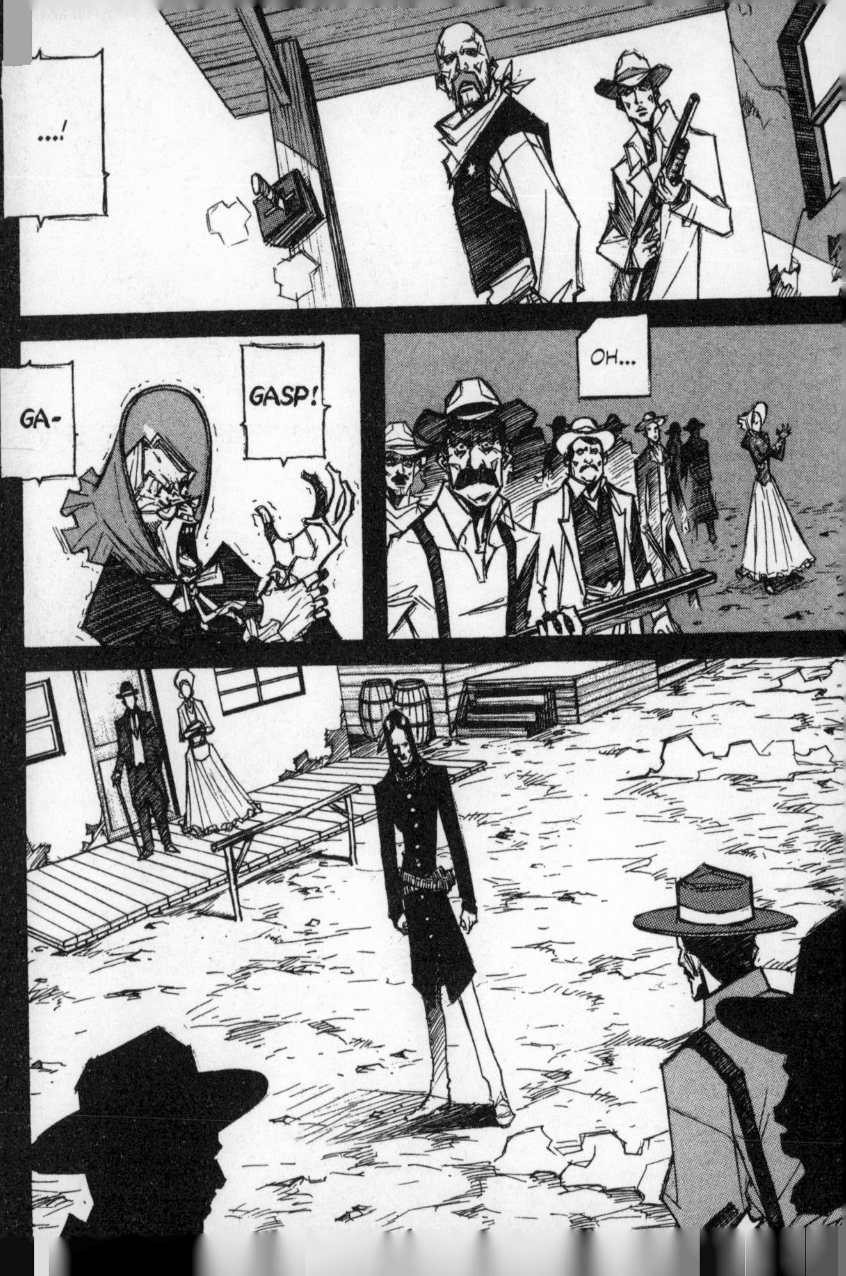
....!
GA-
GASP!
OH...

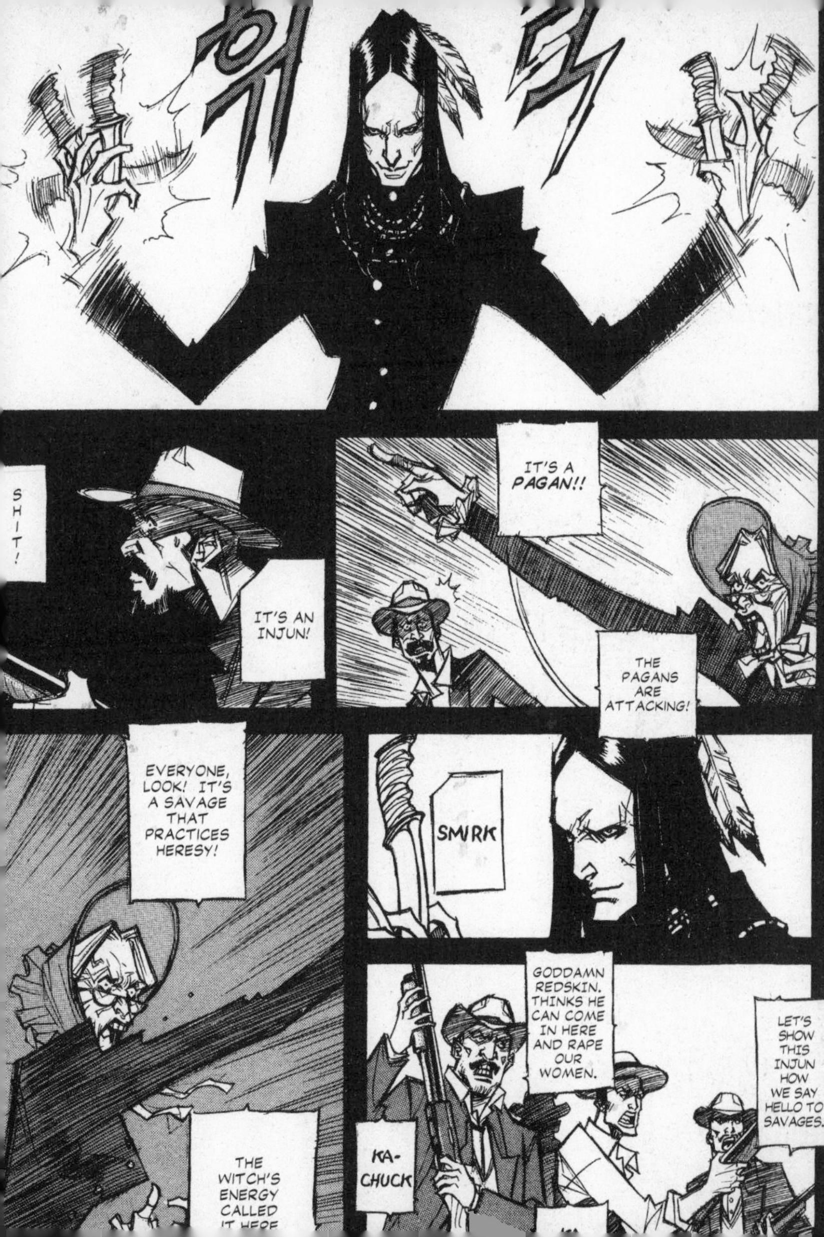
SHIT!
IT'S AN INJUN!
IT'S A *PAGAN*!!
THE PAGANS ARE ATTACKING!
EVERYONE, LOOK! IT'S A SAVAGE THAT PRACTICES HERESY!
THE WITCH'S ENERGY CALLED
SMIRK
GODDAMN REDSKIN. THINKS HE CAN COME IN HERE AND RAPE OUR WOMEN.
LET'S SHOW THIS INJUN HOW WE SAY HELLO TO SAVAGES.
KA-CHUCK

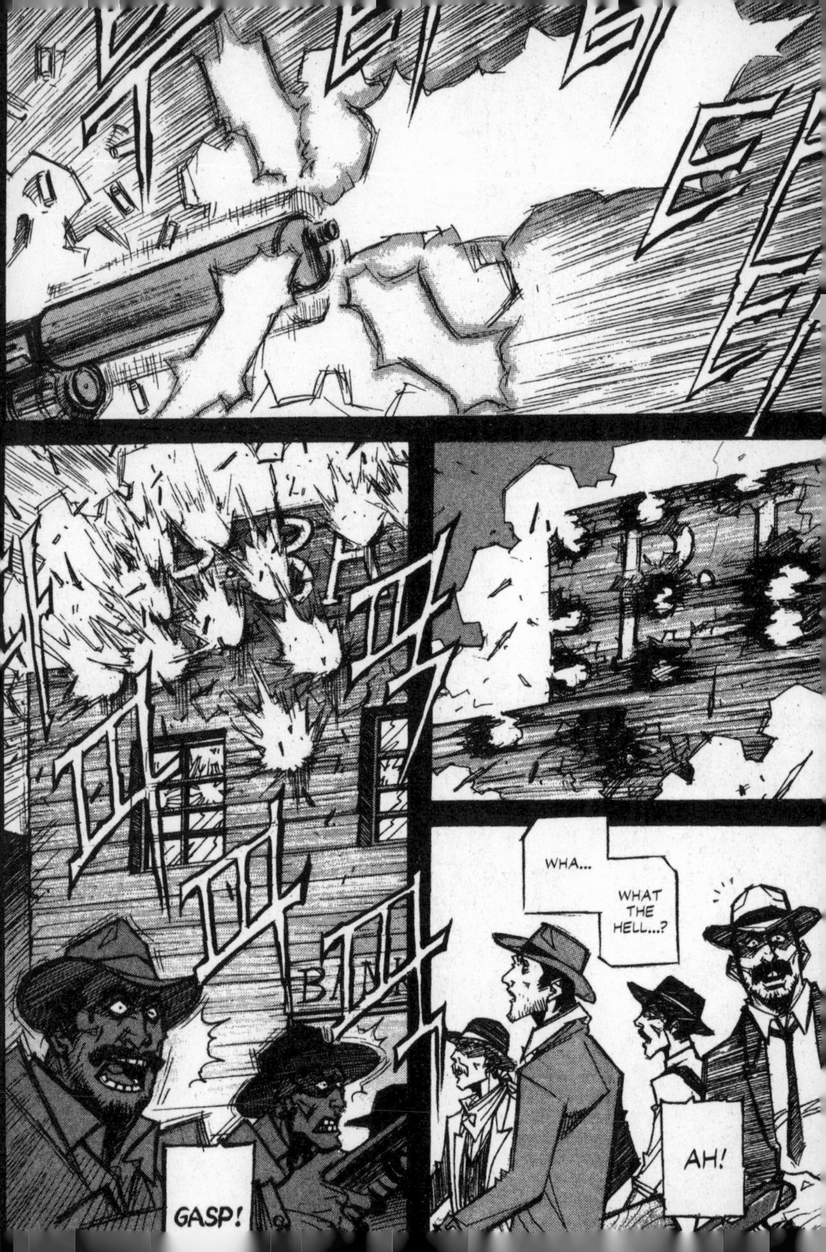
GASP!
WHA...
WHAT THE HELL...?
AH!

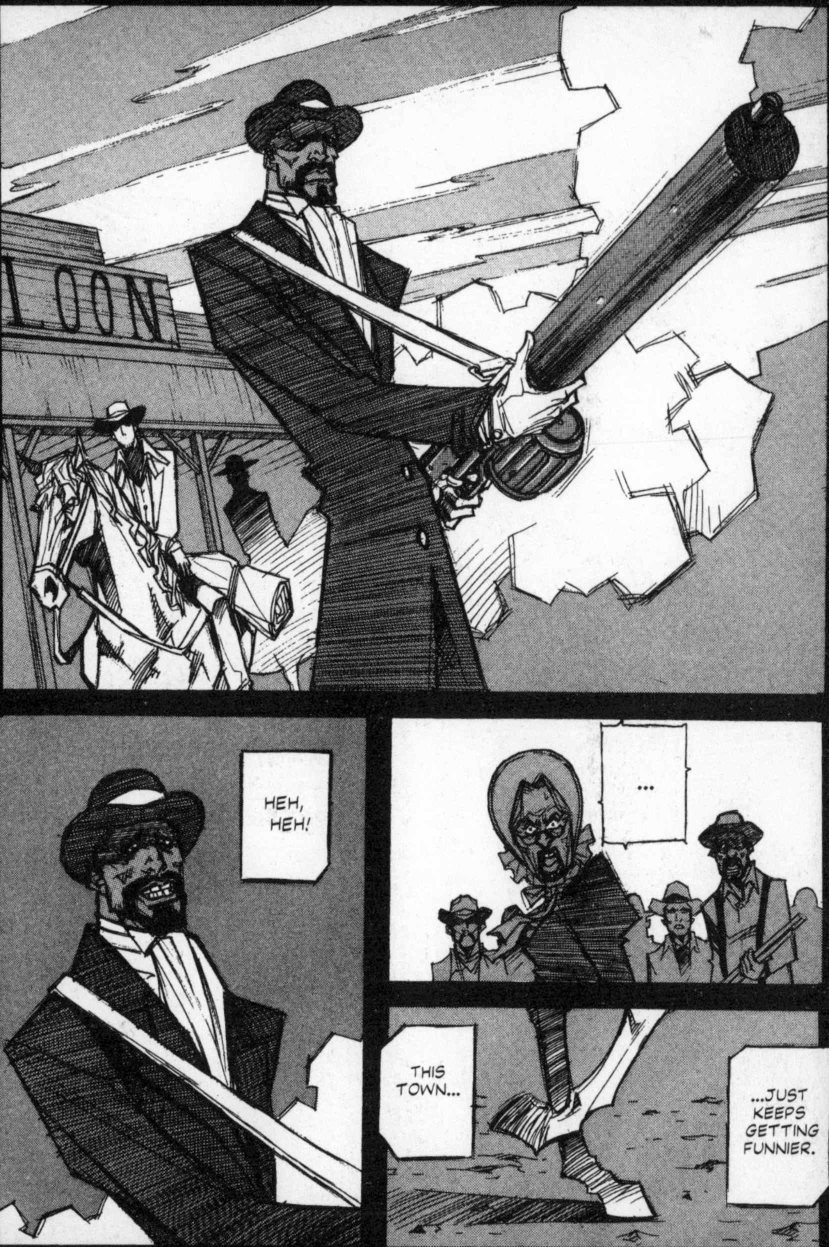

LOON
HEH, HEH!
...
THIS TOWN...
...JUST KEEPS GETTING FUNNIER.

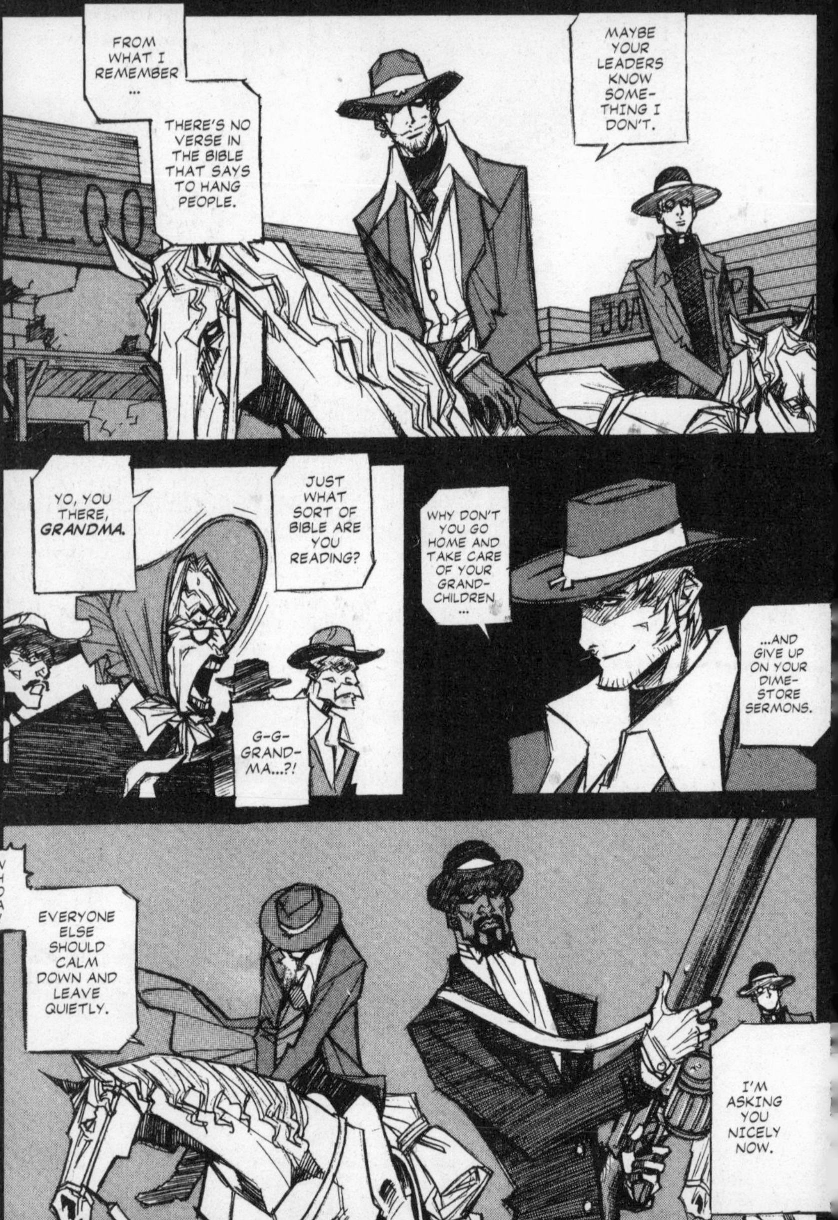
FROM WHAT I REMEMBER ...
THERE'S NO VERSE IN THE BIBLE THAT SAYS TO HANG PEOPLE.
MAYBE YOUR LEADERS KNOW SOME-THING I DON'T.
YO, YOU THERE, ***GRANDMA.***
JUST WHAT SORT OF BIBLE ARE YOU READING?
G-G-GRAND-MA...?!
WHY DON'T YOU GO HOME AND TAKE CARE OF YOUR GRAND-CHILDREN ...
...AND GIVE UP ON YOUR DIME-STORE SERMONS.
WHOA!
EVERYONE ELSE SHOULD CALM DOWN AND LEAVE QUIETLY.
I'M ASKING YOU NICELY NOW.

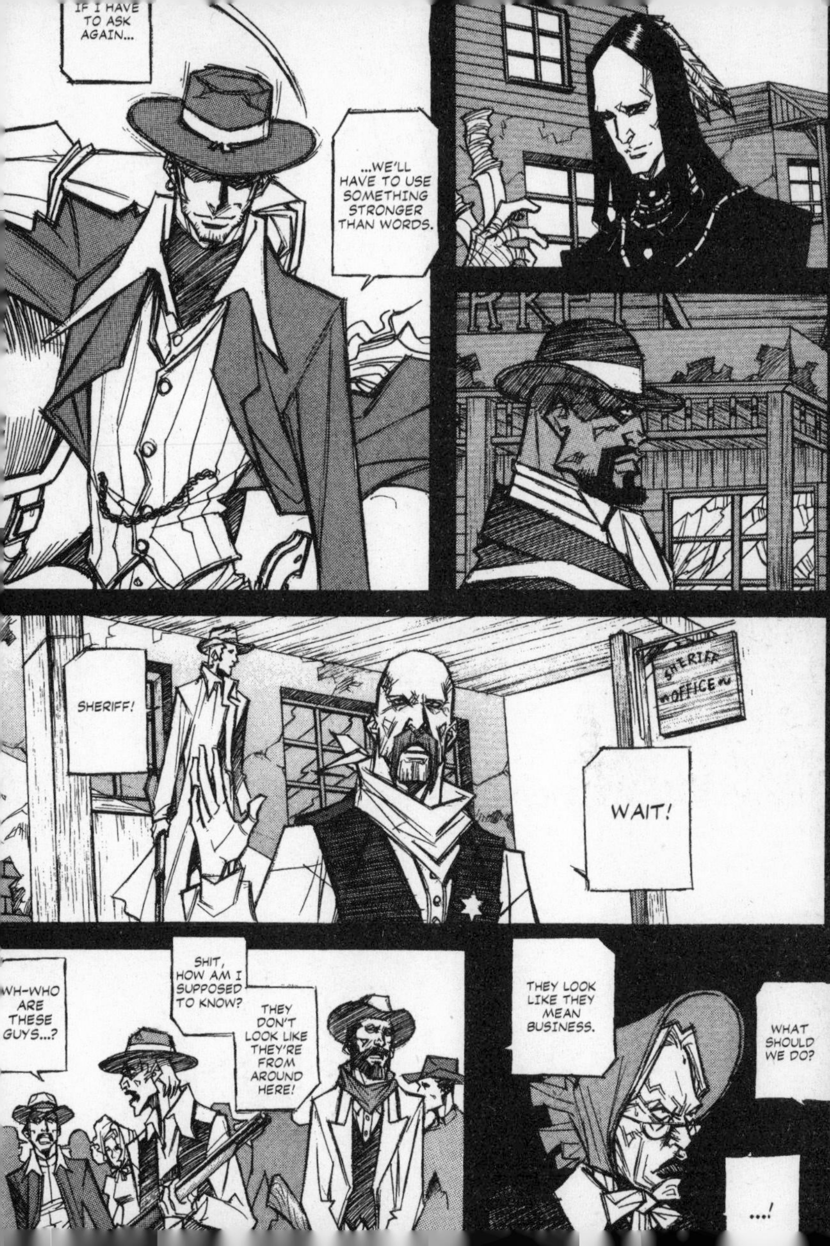
IF I HAVE TO ASK AGAIN...
...WE'LL HAVE TO USE SOMETHING STRONGER THAN WORDS.
SHERIFF!
SHERIFF OFFICE
WAIT!
WH-WHO ARE THESE GUYS...?
SHIT, HOW AM I SUPPOSED TO KNOW?
THEY DON'T LOOK LIKE THEY'RE FROM AROUND HERE!
THEY LOOK LIKE THEY MEAN BUSINESS.
WHAT SHOULD WE DO?
...!

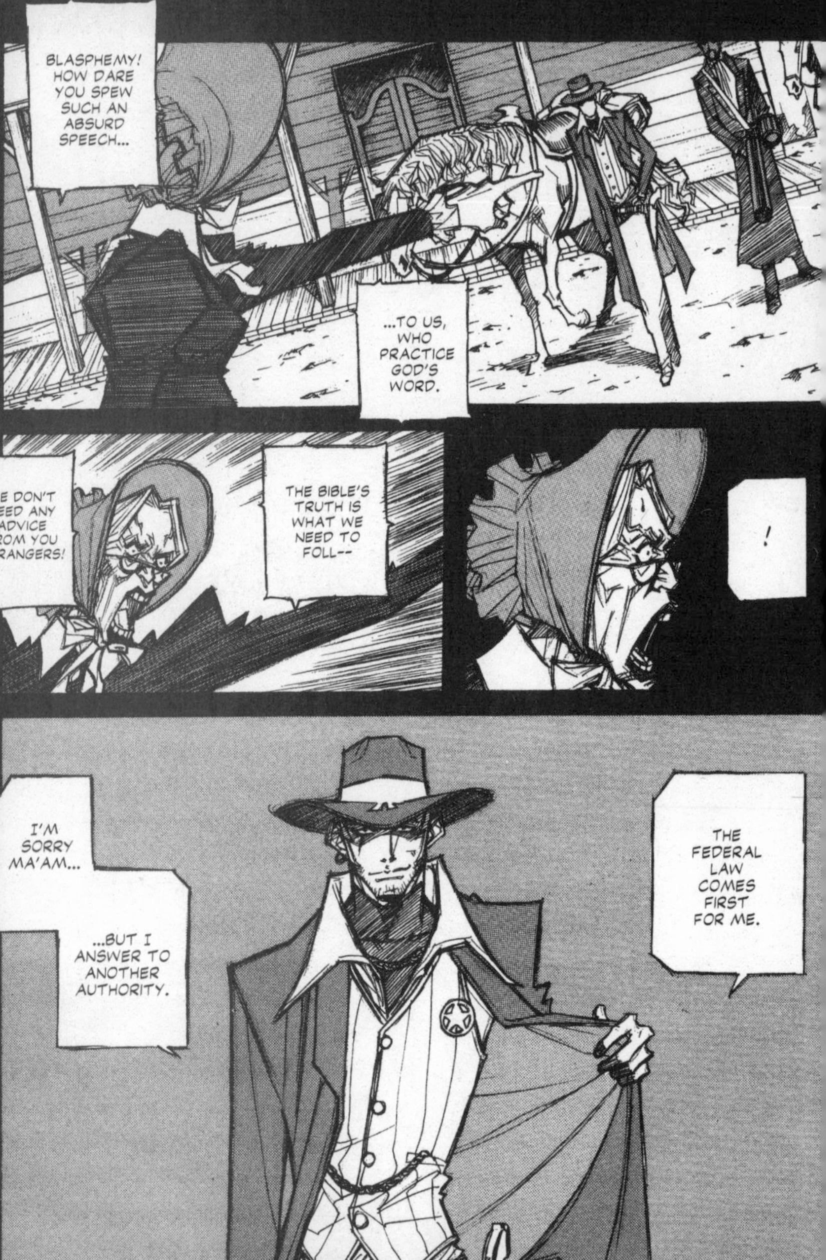
BLASPHEMY! HOW DARE YOU SPEW SUCH AN ABSURD SPEECH...
...TO US, WHO PRACTICE GOD'S WORD.
WE DON'T NEED ANY ADVICE FROM YOU STRANGERS!
THE BIBLE'S TRUTH IS WHAT WE NEED TO FOLL--
!
I'M SORRY MA'AM...
...BUT I ANSWER TO ANOTHER AUTHORITY.
THE FEDERAL LAW COMES FIRST FOR ME.

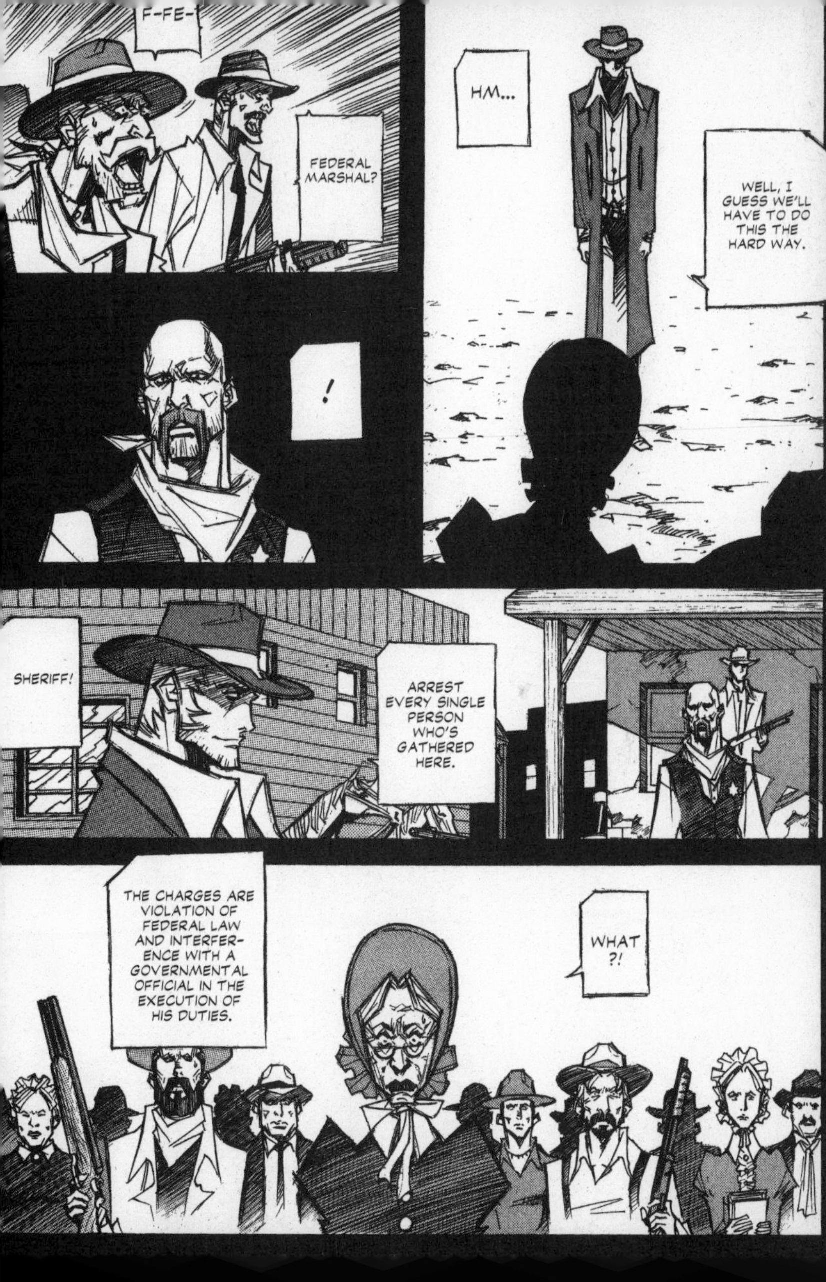
F-FE-
FEDERAL MARSHAL?
HM...
WELL, I GUESS WE'LL HAVE TO DO THIS THE HARD WAY.
!
SHERIFF!
ARREST EVERY SINGLE PERSON WHO'S GATHERED HERE.
THE CHARGES ARE VIOLATION OF FEDERAL LAW AND INTERFERENCE WITH A GOVERNMENTAL OFFICIAL IN THE EXECUTION OF HIS DUTIES.
WHAT?!

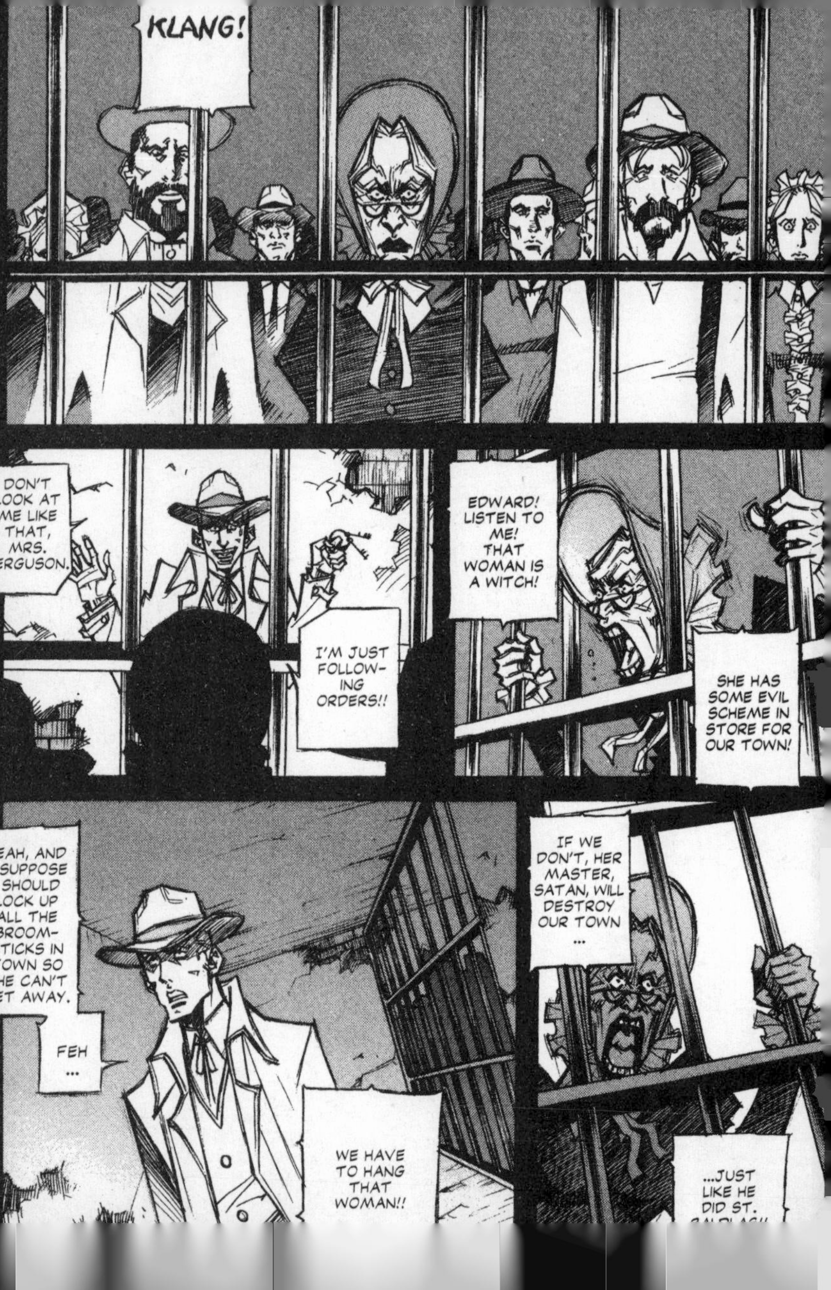
KLANG!
DON'T LOOK AT ME LIKE THAT, MRS. FERGUSON.
I'M JUST FOLLOWING ORDERS!!
EDWARD! LISTEN TO ME! THAT WOMAN IS A WITCH!
SHE HAS SOME EVIL SCHEME IN STORE FOR OUR TOWN!
YEAH, AND I SUPPOSE I SHOULD LOCK UP ALL THE BROOMSTICKS IN TOWN SO SHE CAN'T GET AWAY.
FEH...
WE HAVE TO HANG THAT WOMAN!!
IF WE DON'T, HER MASTER, SATAN, WILL DESTROY OUR TOWN...
...JUST LIKE HE DID ST.

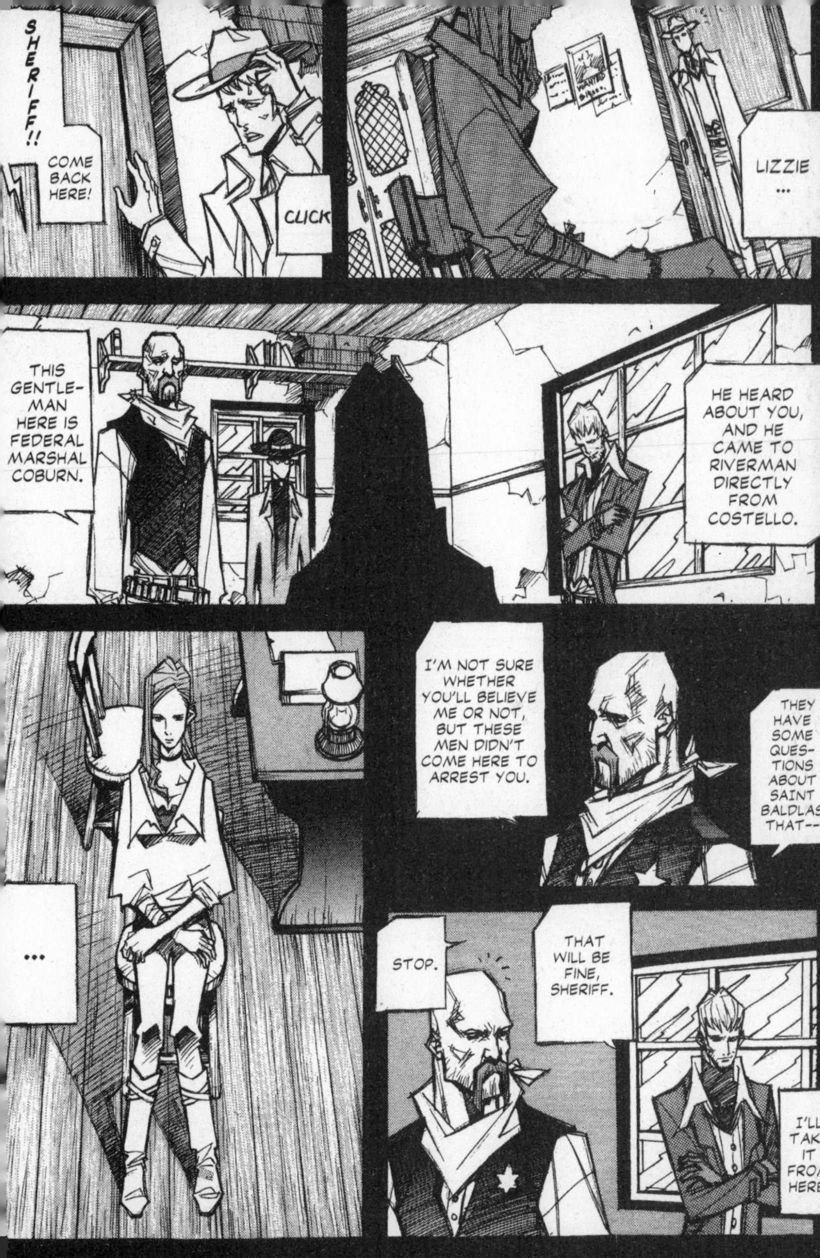
SHERIFF!!
COME BACK HERE!
CLICK
LIZZIE ...
THIS GENTLEMAN HERE IS FEDERAL MARSHAL COBURN.
HE HEARD ABOUT YOU, AND HE CAME TO RIVERMAN DIRECTLY FROM COSTELLO.
...
I'M NOT SURE WHETHER YOU'LL BELIEVE ME OR NOT, BUT THESE MEN DIDN'T COME HERE TO ARREST YOU.
THEY HAVE SOME QUESTIONS ABOUT SAINT BALDLAS THAT--
STOP.
THAT WILL BE FINE, SHERIFF.
I'LL TAKE IT FROM HERE.

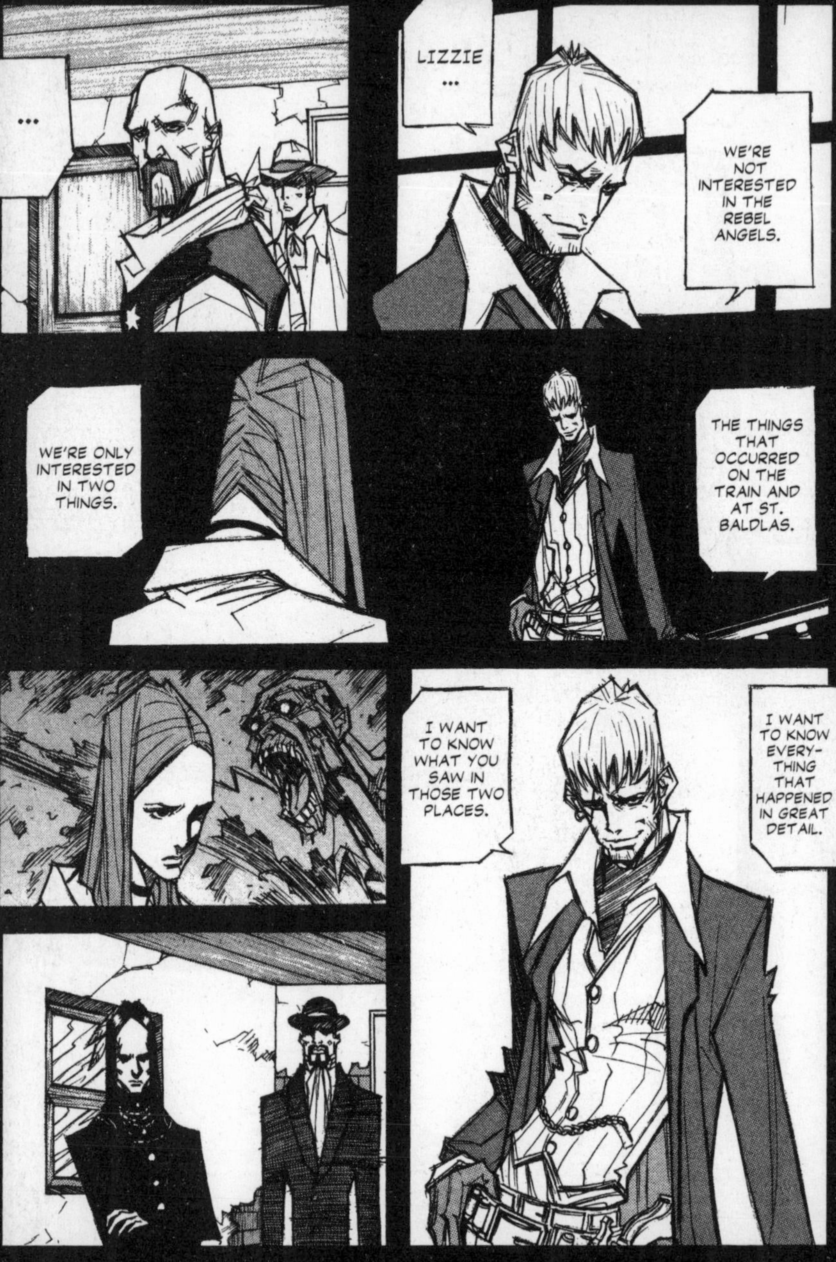
...
LIZZIE ...
WE'RE NOT INTERESTED IN THE REBEL ANGELS.
WE'RE ONLY INTERESTED IN TWO THINGS.
THE THINGS THAT OCCURRED ON THE TRAIN AND AT ST. BALDLAS.
I WANT TO KNOW WHAT YOU SAW IN THOSE TWO PLACES.
I WANT TO KNOW EVERY-THING THAT HAPPENED IN GREAT DETAIL.

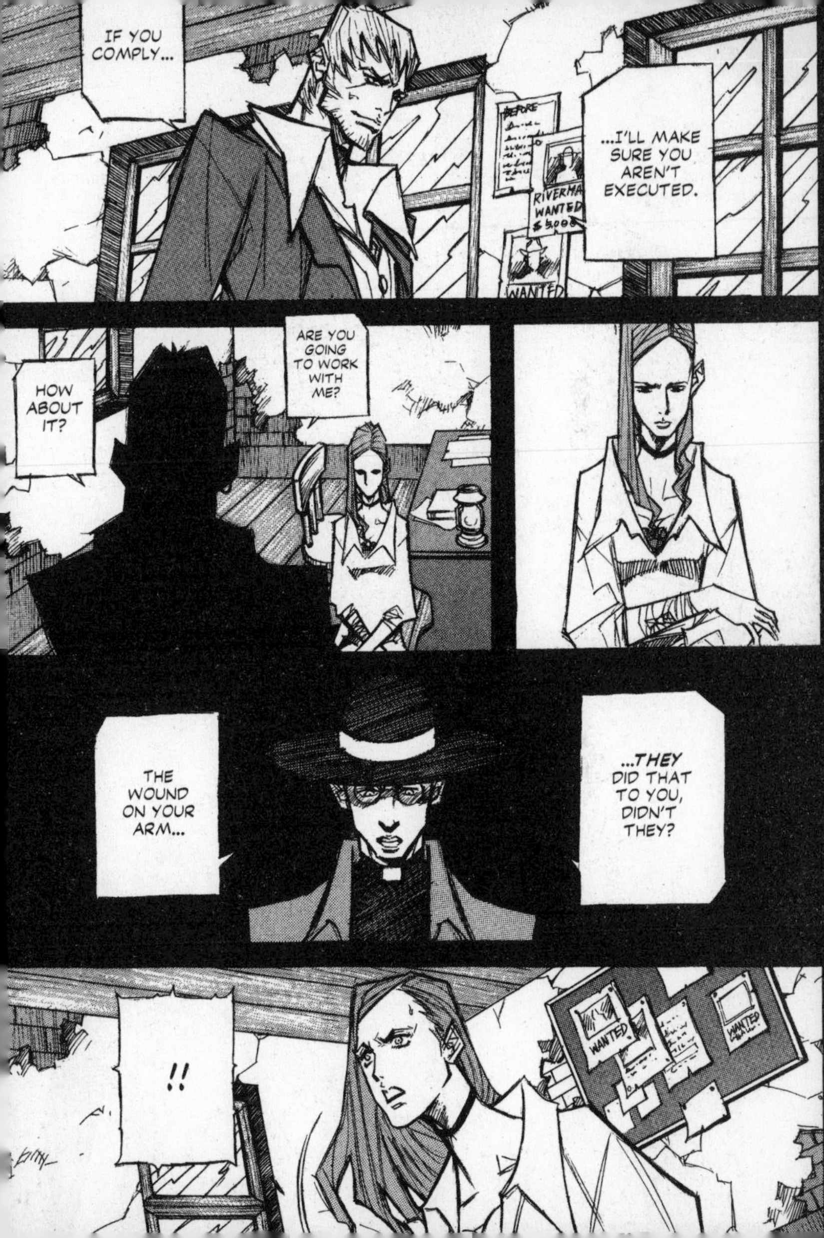
IF YOU COMPLY...
BEFORE
RIVERMA
WANTED
WANTED
...I'LL MAKE SURE YOU AREN'T EXECUTED.
HOW ABOUT IT?
ARE YOU GOING TO WORK WITH ME?
THE WOUND ON YOUR ARM...
...THEY DID THAT TO YOU, DIDN'T THEY?
!!
WANTED
WANTED

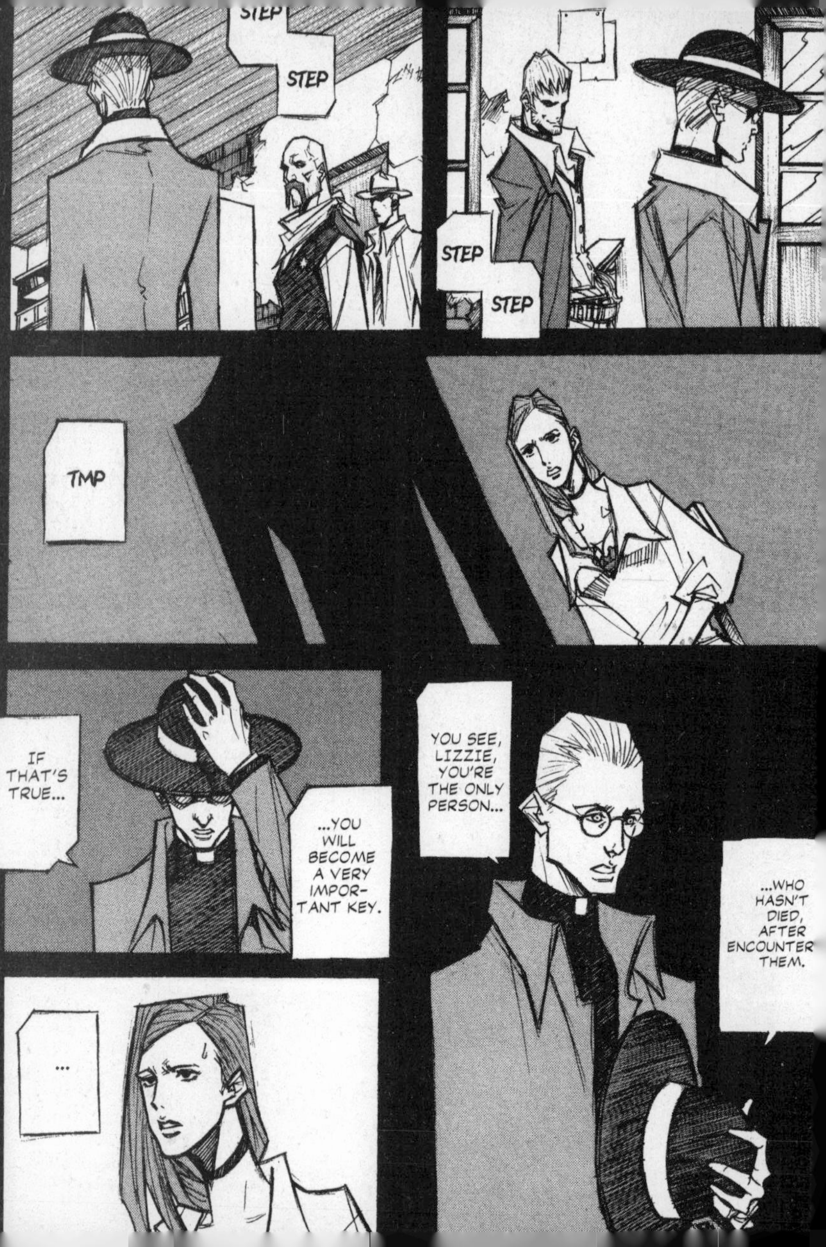
STEP
STEP
STEP
STEP
TMP
IF THAT'S TRUE...
...YOU WILL BECOME A VERY IMPOR-TANT KEY.
YOU SEE, LIZZIE, YOU'RE THE ONLY PERSON...
...WHO HASN'T DIED, AFTER ENCOUNTER THEM.
...

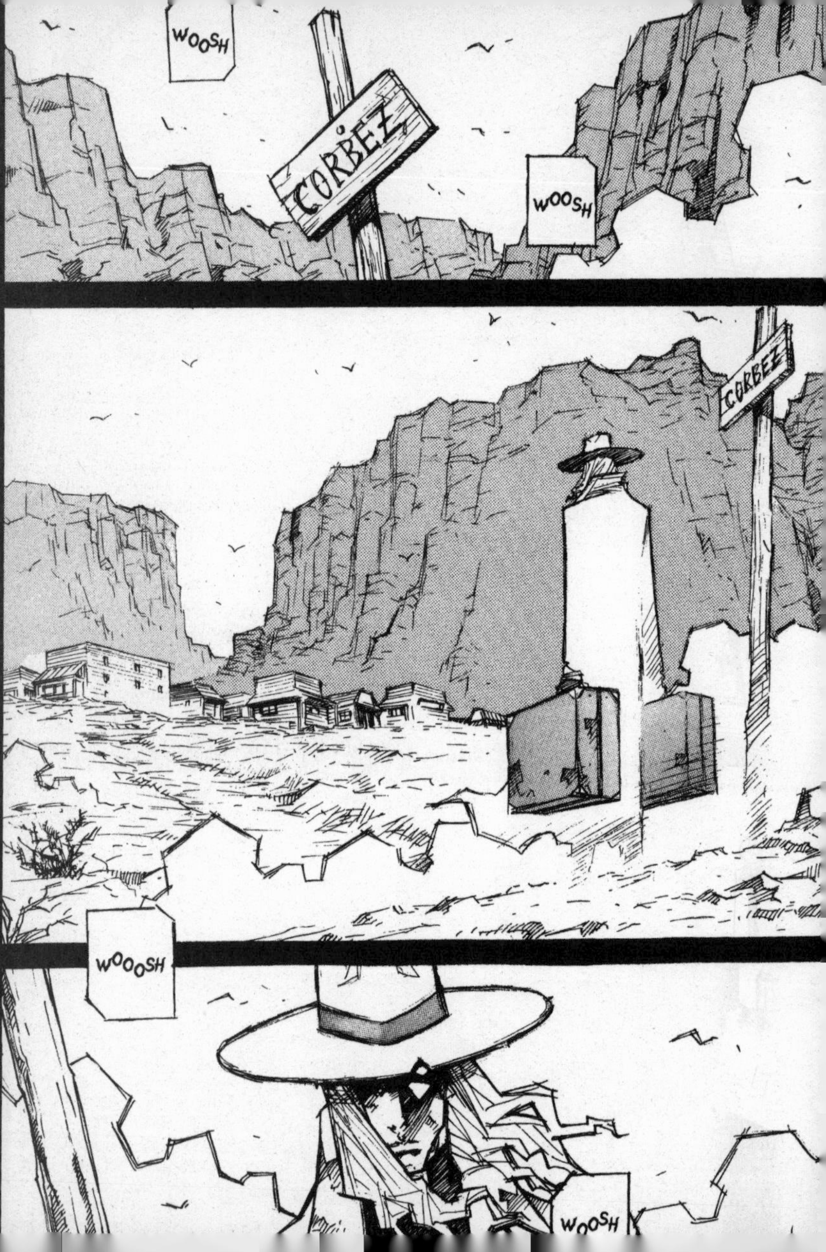
WOOSH
CORBEZ
WOOSH
CORBEZ
WOOOSH
WOOSH

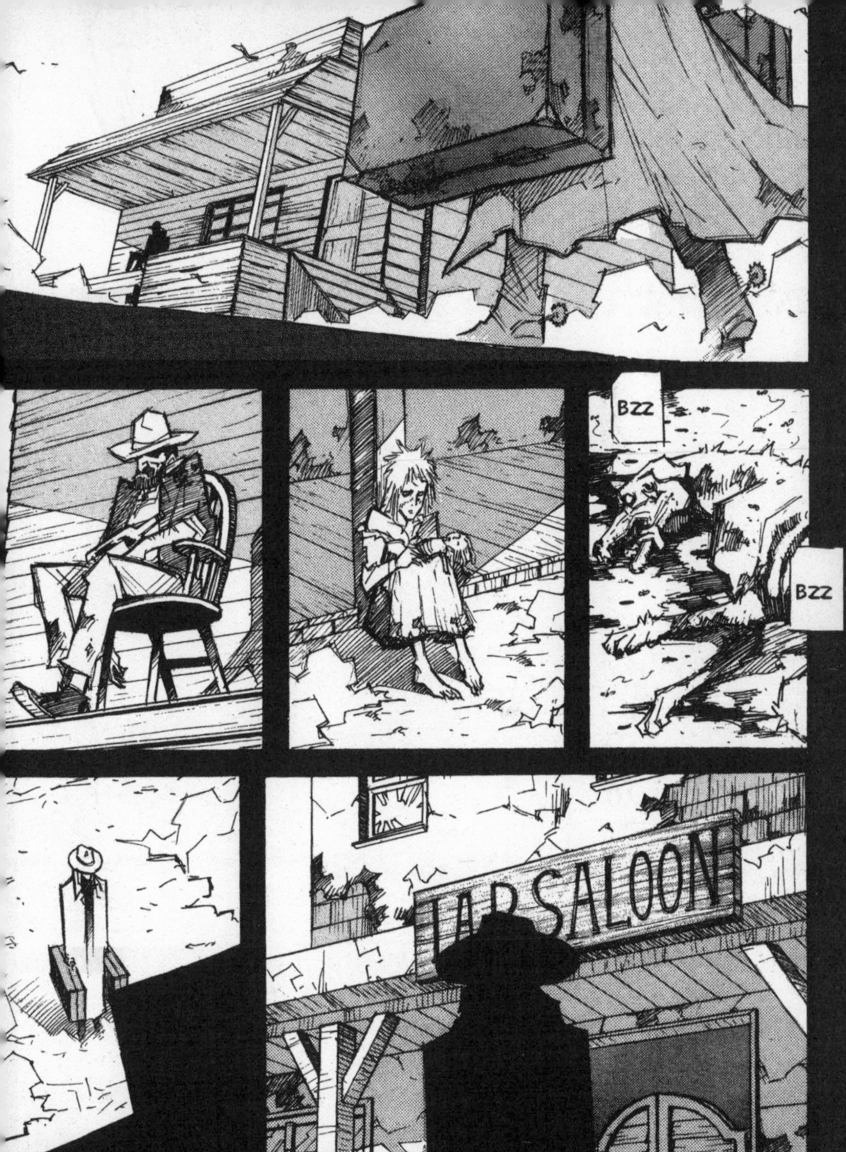
BZZ
BZZ
SALOON

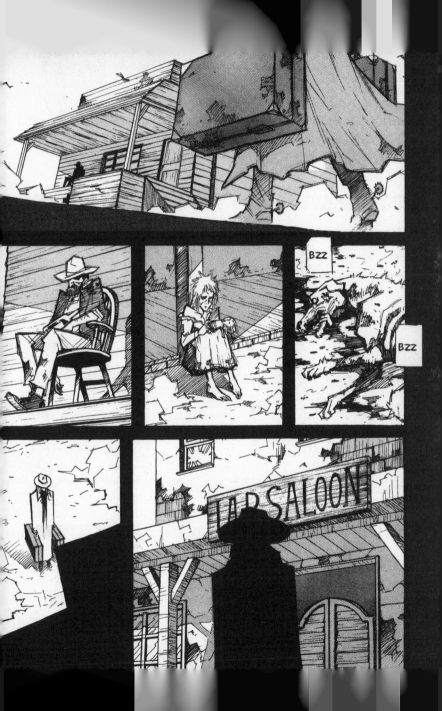

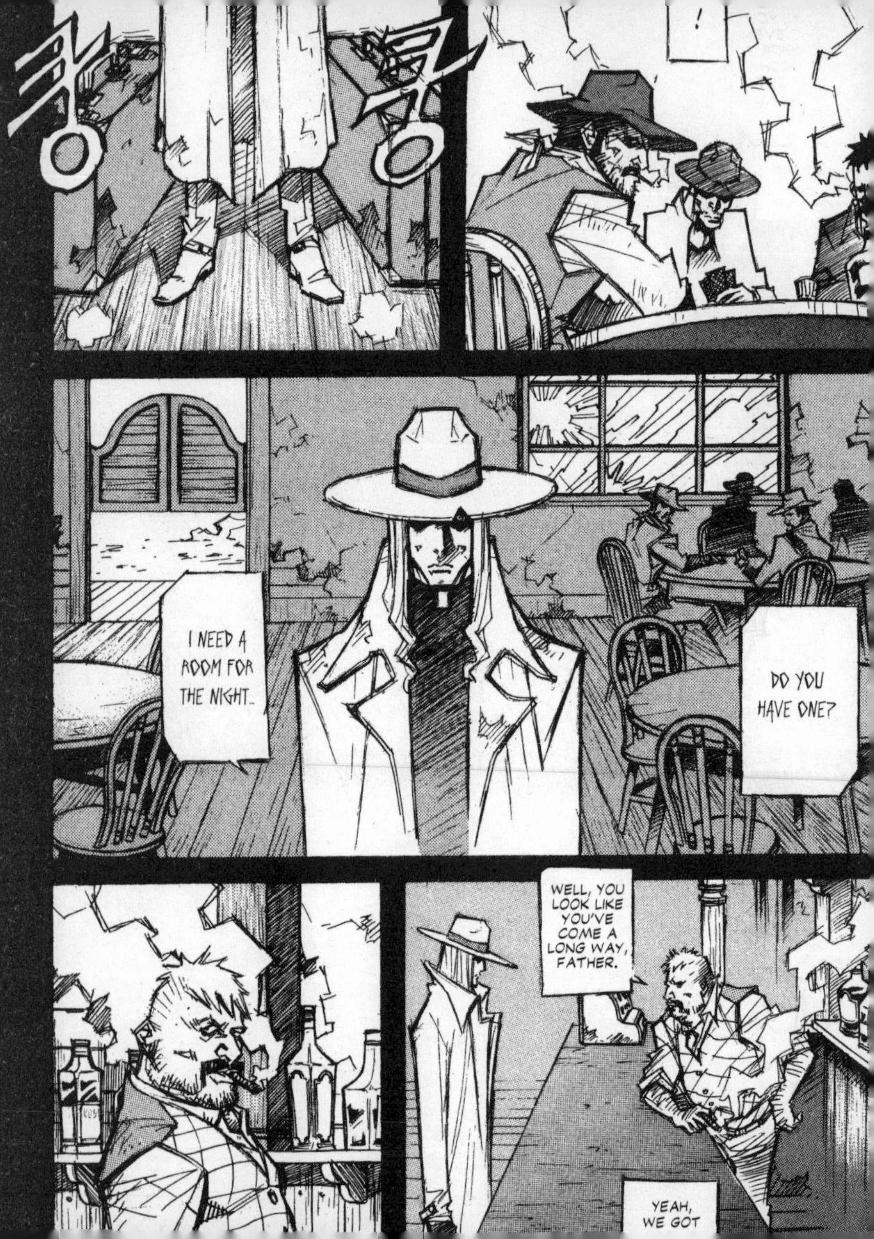

I NEED A ROOM FOR THE NIGHT...
DO YOU HAVE ONE?
WELL, YOU LOOK LIKE YOU'VE COME A LONG WAY, FATHER.
YEAH, WE GOT

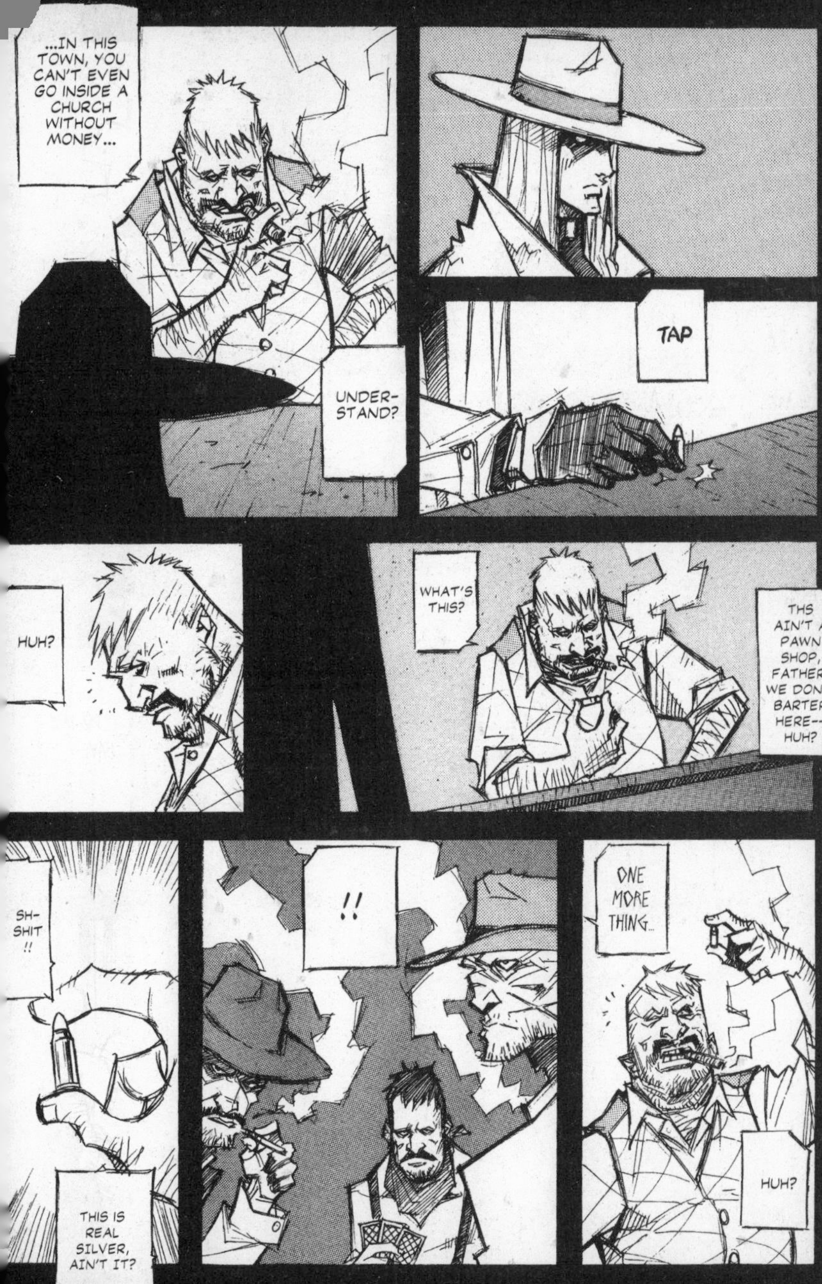
...IN THIS TOWN, YOU CAN'T EVEN GO INSIDE A CHURCH WITHOUT MONEY...
UNDER-STAND?
TAP
HUH?
WHAT'S THIS?
THS AIN'T A PAWN SHOP, FATHER. WE DON'T BARTER HERE-- HUH?
SH-SHIT !!
THIS IS REAL SILVER, AIN'T IT?
!!
ONE MORE THING...
HUH?

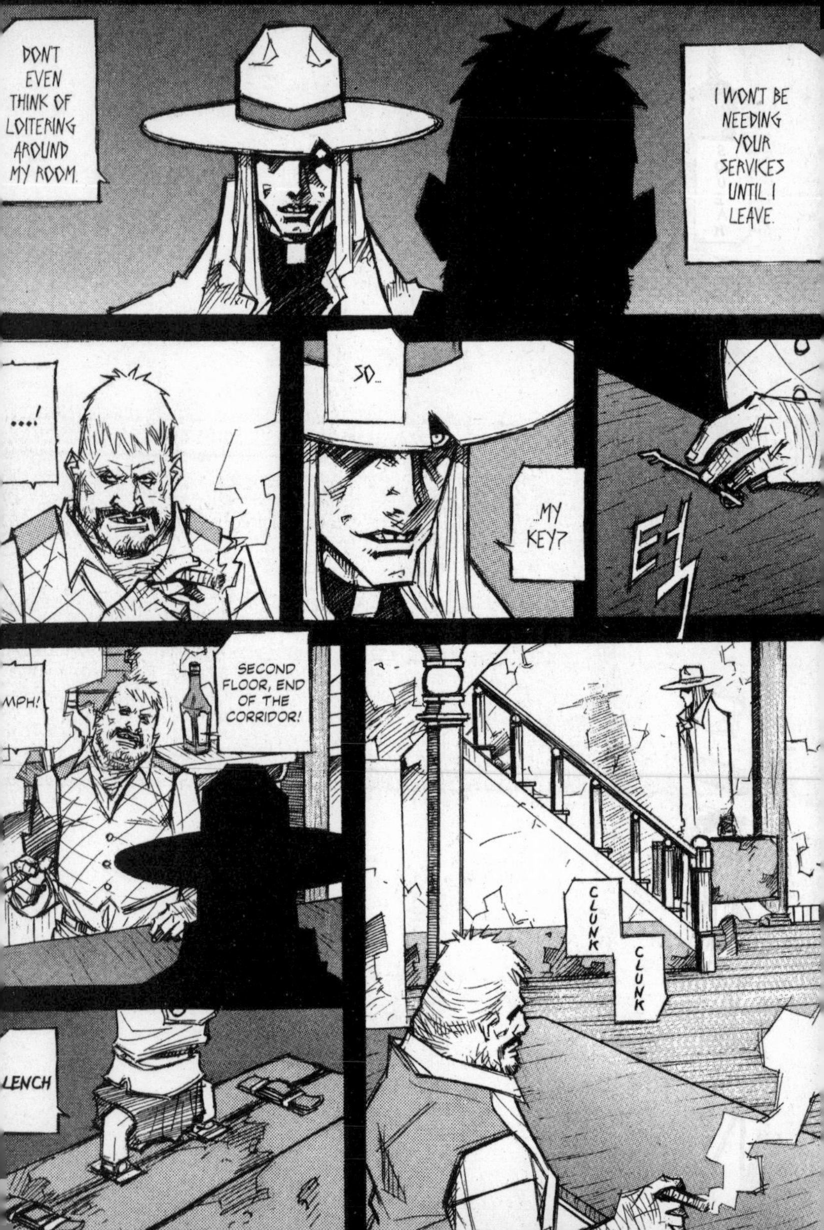
DON'T EVEN THINK OF LOITERING AROUND MY ROOM.
I WON'T BE NEEDING YOUR SERVICES UNTIL I LEAVE.
...!
SO...
...MY KEY?
MPH!
SECOND FLOOR, END OF THE CORRIDOR!
LENCH
CLUNK
CLUNK

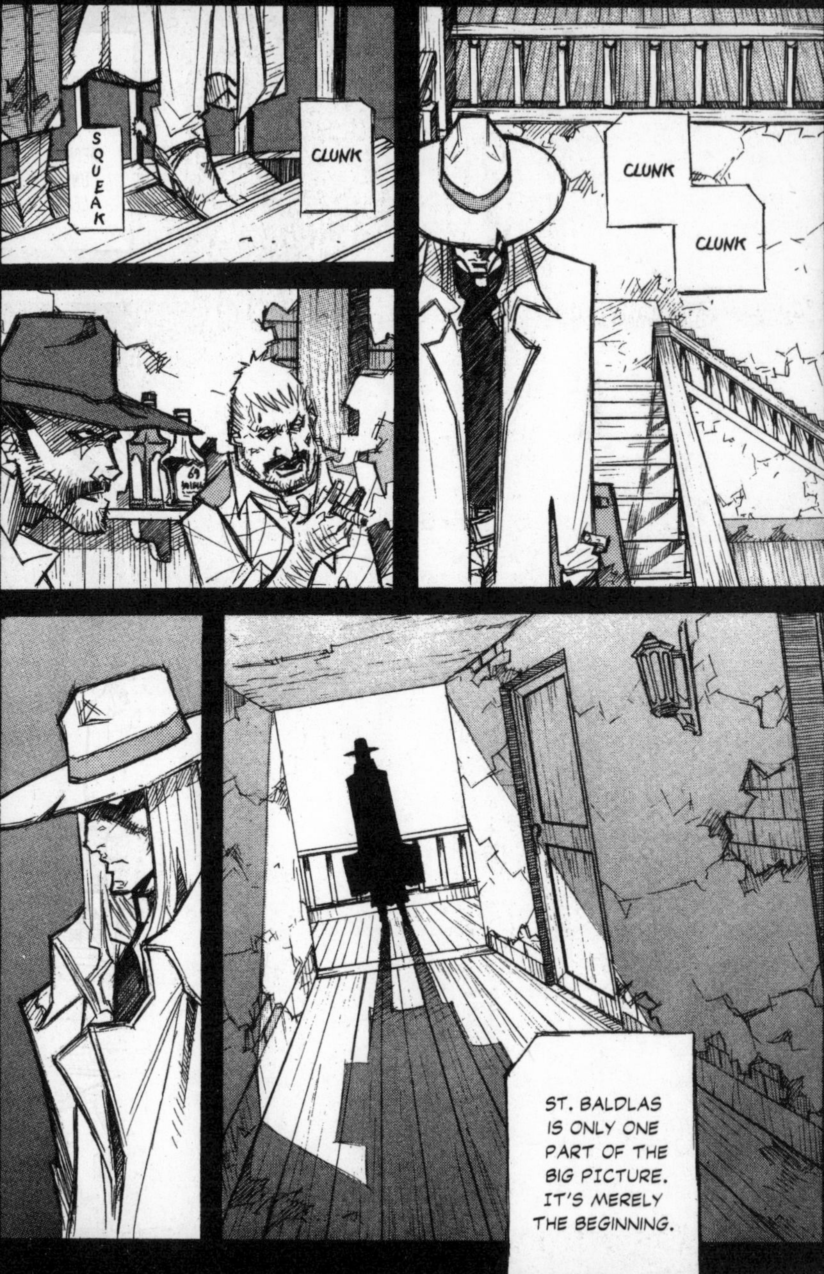
SQUEAK
CLUNK
CLUNK
CLUNK
ST. BALDLAS IS ONLY ONE PART OF THE BIG PICTURE. IT'S MERELY THE BEGINNING.

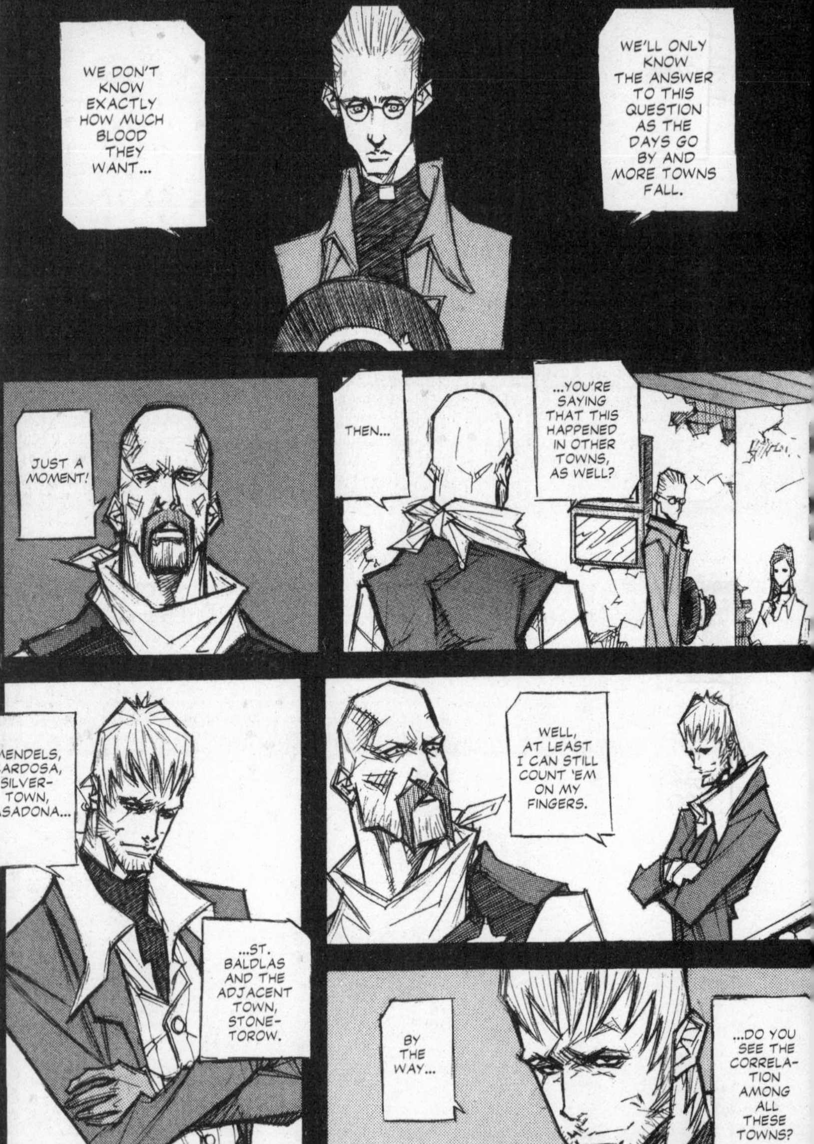
WE DON'T KNOW EXACTLY HOW MUCH BLOOD THEY WANT...
WE'LL ONLY KNOW THE ANSWER TO THIS QUESTION AS THE DAYS GO BY AND MORE TOWNS FALL.
JUST A MOMENT!
THEN...
...YOU'RE SAYING THAT THIS HAPPENED IN OTHER TOWNS, AS WELL?
MENDELS, CARDOSA, SILVER-TOWN, PASADONA...
...ST. BALDLAS AND THE ADJACENT TOWN, STONE-TOROW.
WELL, AT LEAST I CAN STILL COUNT 'EM ON MY FINGERS.
BY THE WAY...
...DO YOU SEE THE CORRELA-TION AMONG ALL THESE TOWNS?

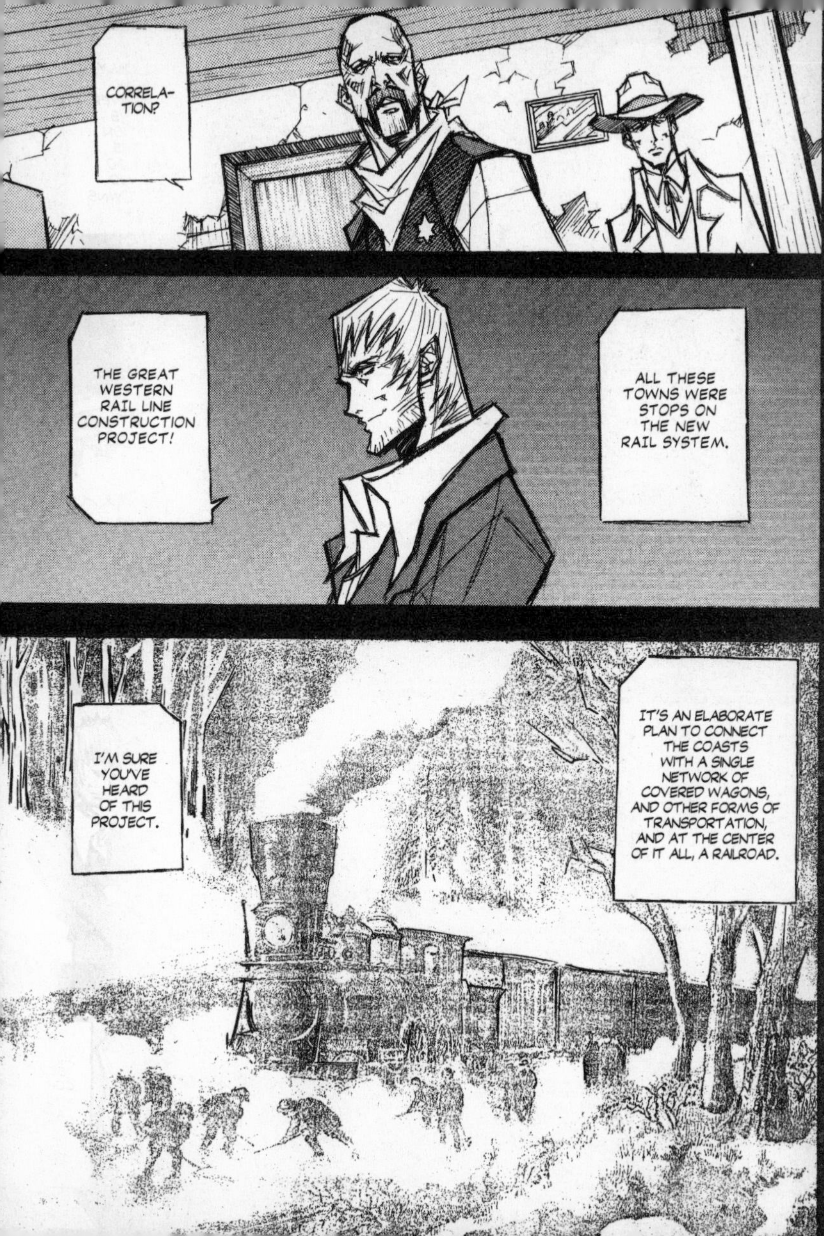
CORRELA-TION?
THE GREAT WESTERN RAIL LINE CONSTRUCTION PROJECT!
ALL THESE TOWNS WERE STOPS ON THE NEW RAIL SYSTEM.
I'M SURE YOU'VE HEARD OF THIS PROJECT.
IT'S AN ELABORATE PLAN TO CONNECT THE COASTS WITH A SINGLE NETWORK OF COVERED WAGONS, AND OTHER FORMS OF TRANSPORTATION, AND AT THE CENTER OF IT ALL, A RAILROAD.

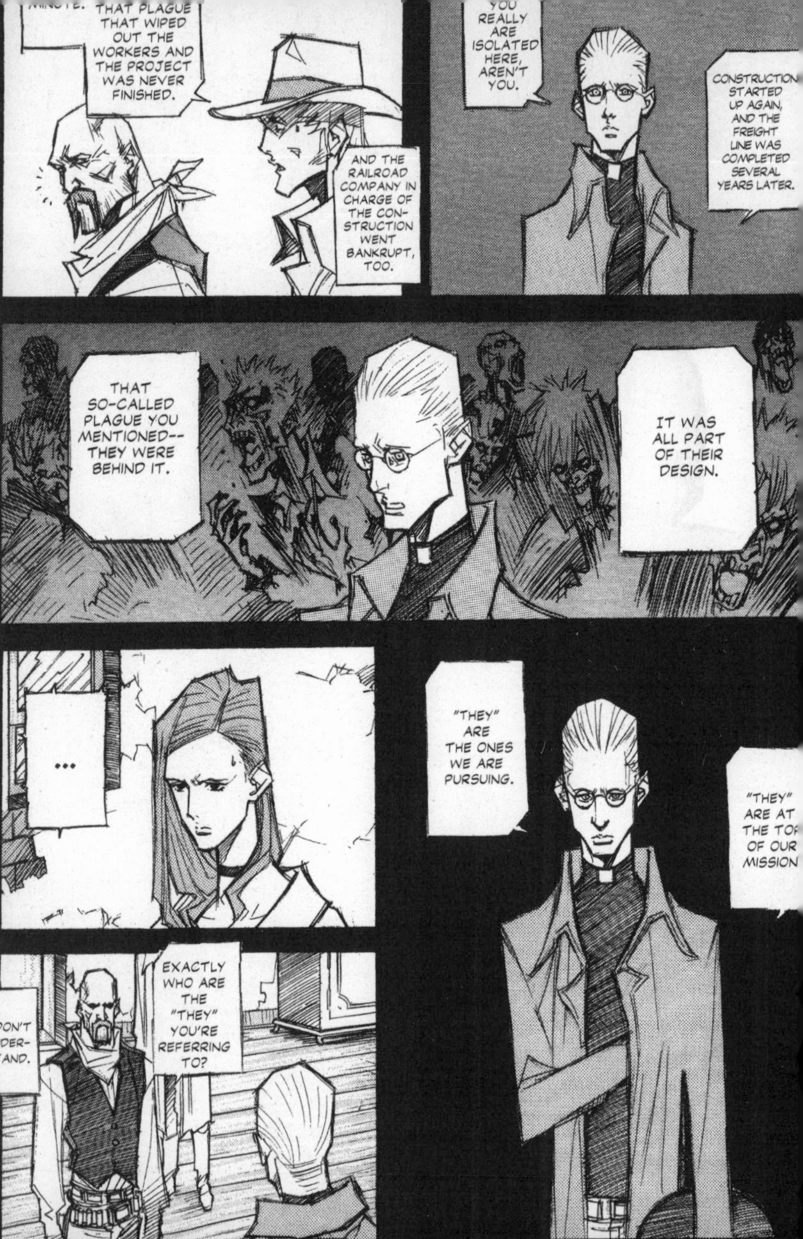
THAT PLAGUE THAT WIPED OUT THE WORKERS AND THE PROJECT WAS NEVER FINISHED.
AND THE RAILROAD COMPANY IN CHARGE OF THE CON-STRUCTION WENT BANKRUPT, TOO.
YOU REALLY ARE ISOLATED HERE, AREN'T YOU.
CONSTRUCTION STARTED UP AGAIN, AND THE FREIGHT LINE WAS COMPLETED SEVERAL YEARS LATER.
THAT SO-CALLED PLAGUE YOU MENTIONED--THEY WERE BEHIND IT.
IT WAS ALL PART OF THEIR DESIGN.
...
I DON'T UNDER-STAND.
EXACTLY WHO ARE THE "THEY" YOU'RE REFERRING TO?
"THEY" ARE THE ONES WE ARE PURSUING.
"THEY" ARE AT THE TOP OF OUR MISSION

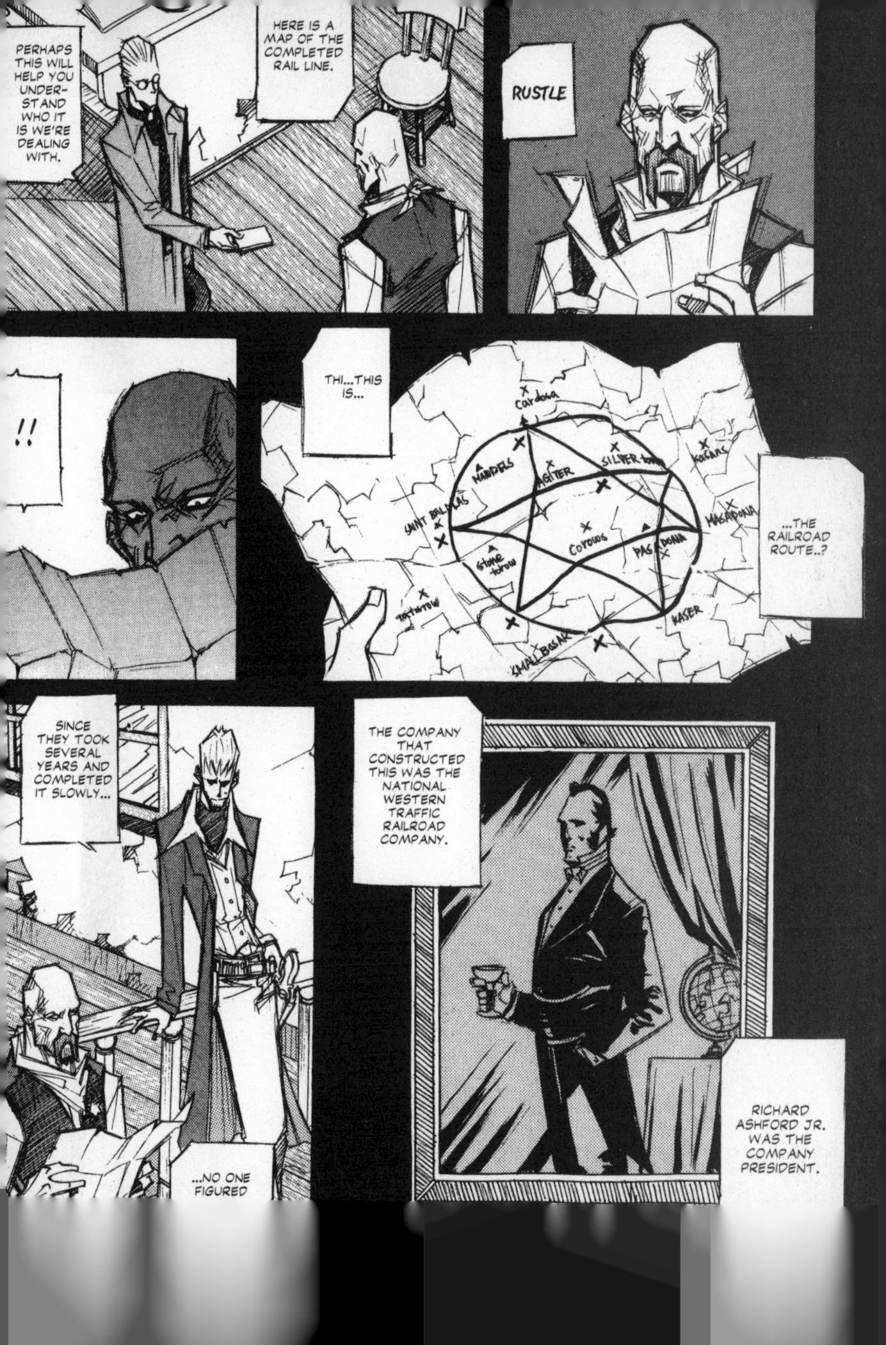
PERHAPS THIS WILL HELP YOU UNDER-STAND WHO IT IS WE'RE DEALING WITH.
HERE IS A MAP OF THE COMPLETED RAIL LINE.
RUSTLE
!!
THI...THIS IS...
cardona
MANDELS
AGITER
SILVER
kasans
MASADONA
Corows
stone town
KASER
SMALL BOSAK
...THE RAILROAD ROUTE..?
SINCE THEY TOOK SEVERAL YEARS AND COMPLETED IT SLOWLY...
...NO ONE FIGURED
THE COMPANY THAT CONSTRUCTED THIS WAS THE NATIONAL WESTERN TRAFFIC RAILROAD COMPANY.
RICHARD ASHFORD JR. WAS THE COMPANY PRESIDENT.

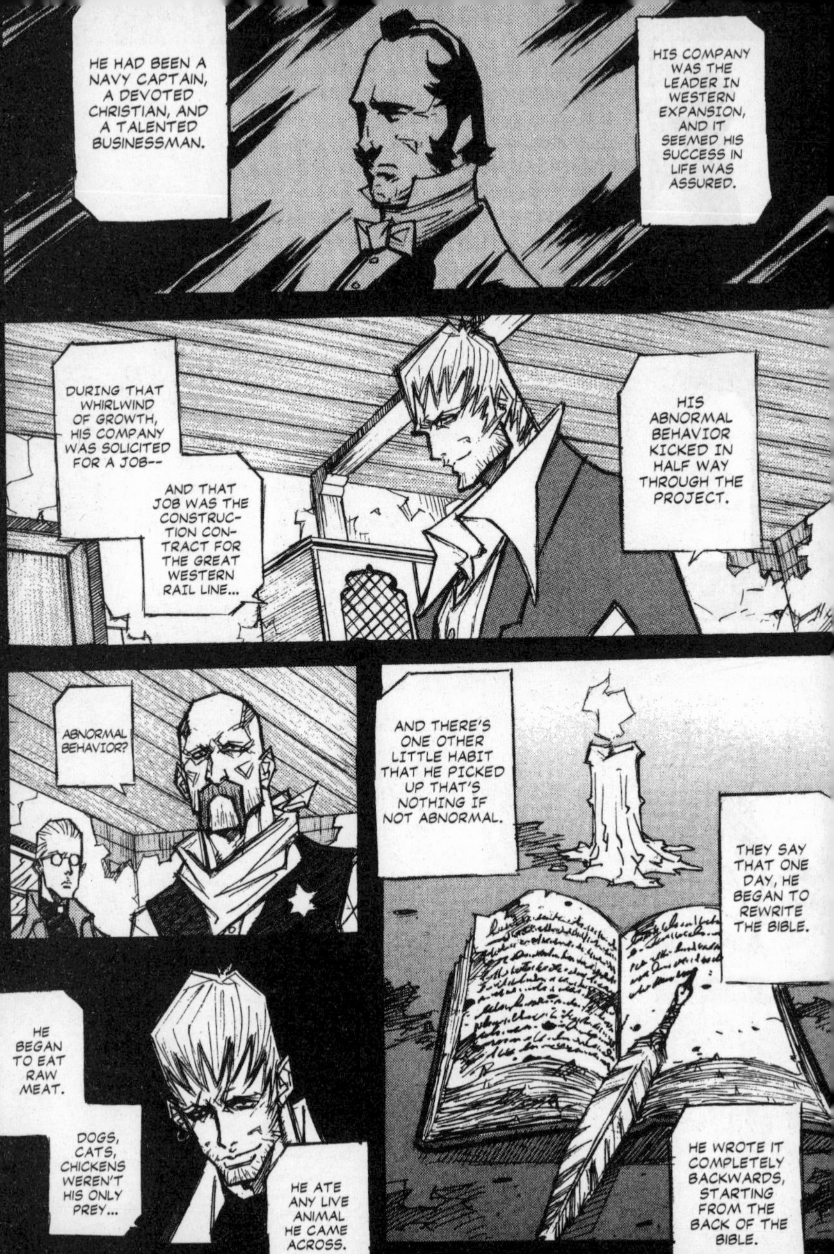
HE HAD BEEN A NAVY CAPTAIN, A DEVOTED CHRISTIAN, AND A TALENTED BUSINESSMAN.
HIS COMPANY WAS THE LEADER IN WESTERN EXPANSION, AND IT SEEMED HIS SUCCESS IN LIFE WAS ASSURED.
DURING THAT WHIRLWIND OF GROWTH, HIS COMPANY WAS SOLICITED FOR A JOB--
AND THAT JOB WAS THE CONSTRUCTION CONTRACT FOR THE GREAT WESTERN RAIL LINE...
HIS ABNORMAL BEHAVIOR KICKED IN HALF WAY THROUGH THE PROJECT.
ABNORMAL BEHAVIOR?
HE BEGAN TO EAT RAW MEAT.
DOGS, CATS, CHICKENS WEREN'T HIS ONLY PREY...
HE ATE ANY LIVE ANIMAL HE CAME ACROSS.
AND THERE'S ONE OTHER LITTLE HABIT THAT HE PICKED UP THAT'S NOTHING IF NOT ABNORMAL.
THEY SAY THAT ONE DAY, HE BEGAN TO REWRITE THE BIBLE.
HE WROTE IT COMPLETELY BACKWARDS, STARTING FROM THE BACK OF THE BIBLE.

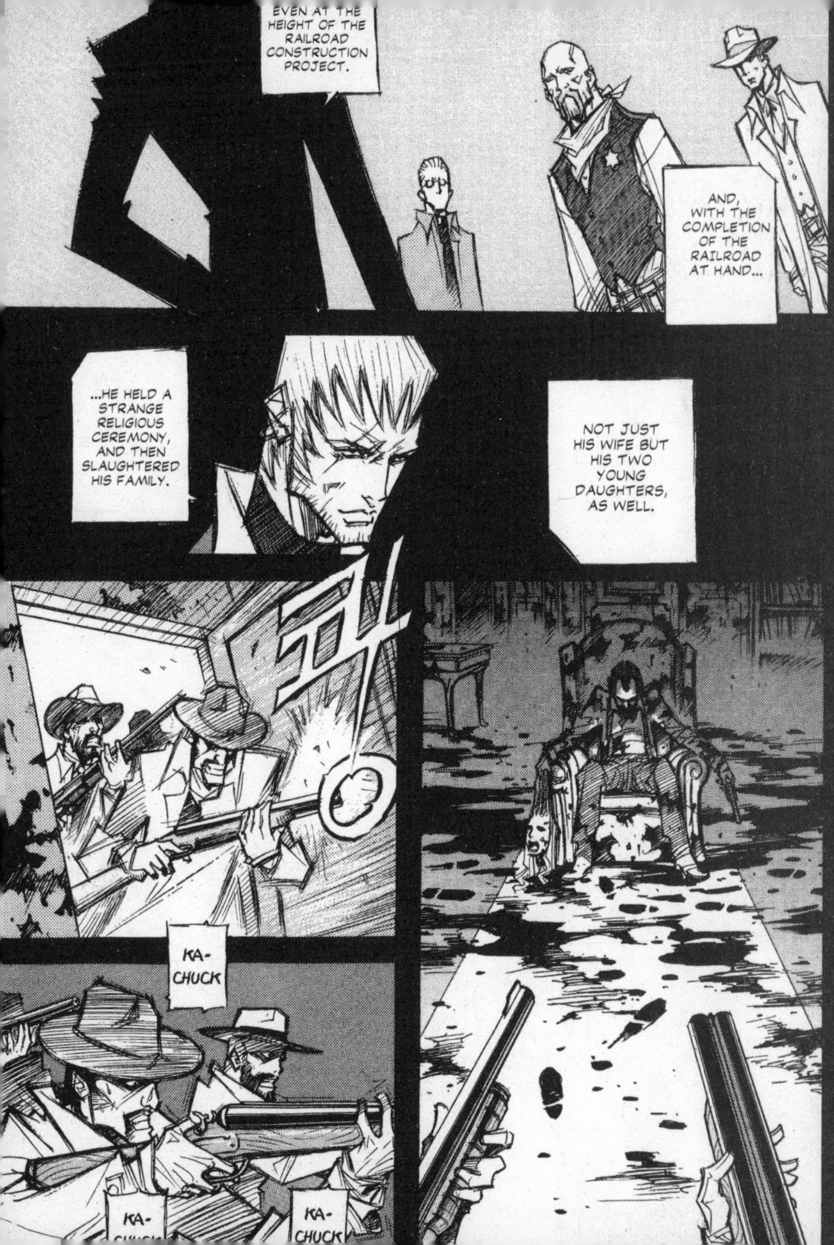
EVEN AT THE HEIGHT OF THE RAILROAD CONSTRUCTION PROJECT.
AND, WITH THE COMPLETION OF THE RAILROAD AT HAND...
...HE HELD A STRANGE RELIGIOUS CEREMONY, AND THEN SLAUGHTERED HIS FAMILY.
NOT JUST HIS WIFE BUT HIS TWO YOUNG DAUGHTERS, AS WELL.
KA-CHUCK
KA-
KA-CHUCK

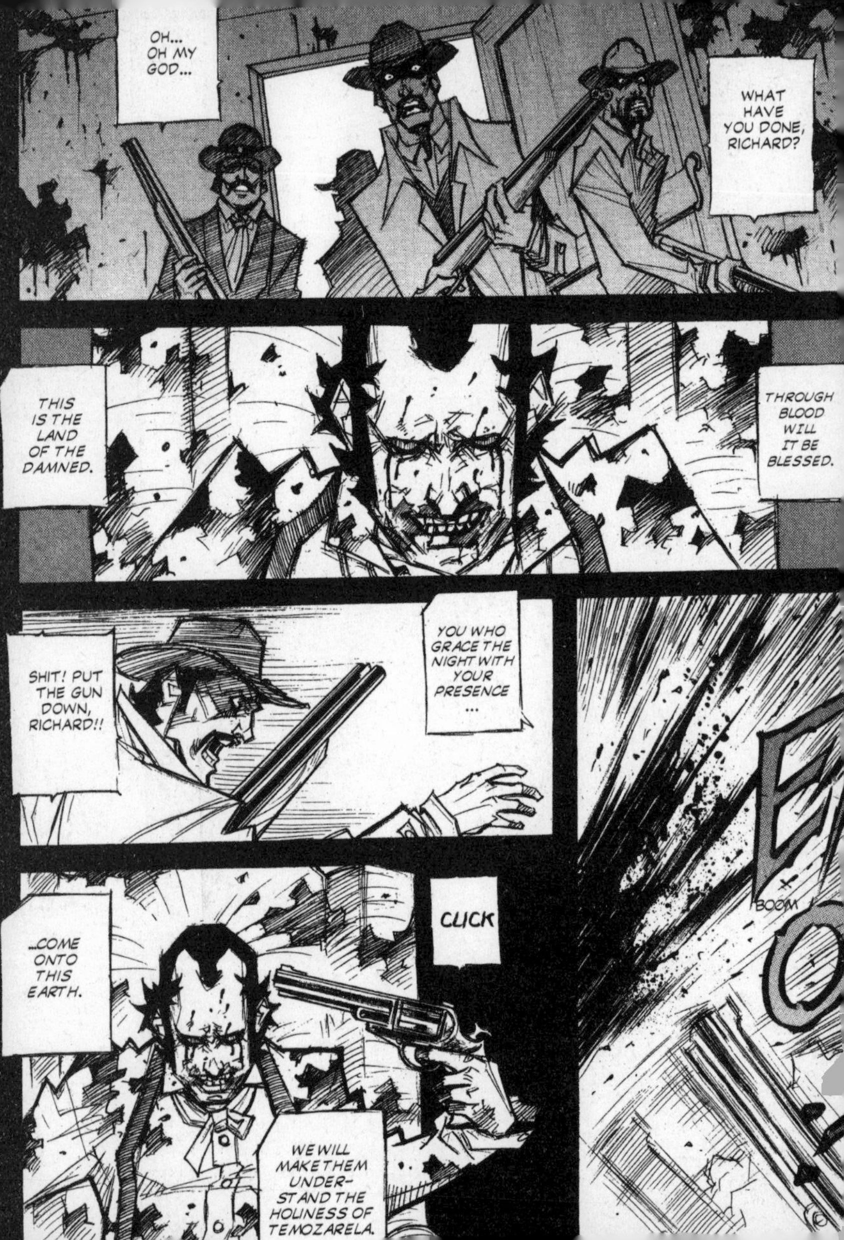
OH... OH MY GOD...
WHAT HAVE YOU DONE, RICHARD?
THIS IS THE LAND OF THE DAMNED.
THROUGH BLOOD WILL IT BE BLESSED.
SHIT! PUT THE GUN DOWN, RICHARD!!
YOU WHO GRACE THE NIGHT WITH YOUR PRESENCE...
...COME ONTO THIS EARTH.
CLICK
WE WILL MAKE THEM UNDER-STAND THE HOLINESS OF TEMOZARELA.
BOOM

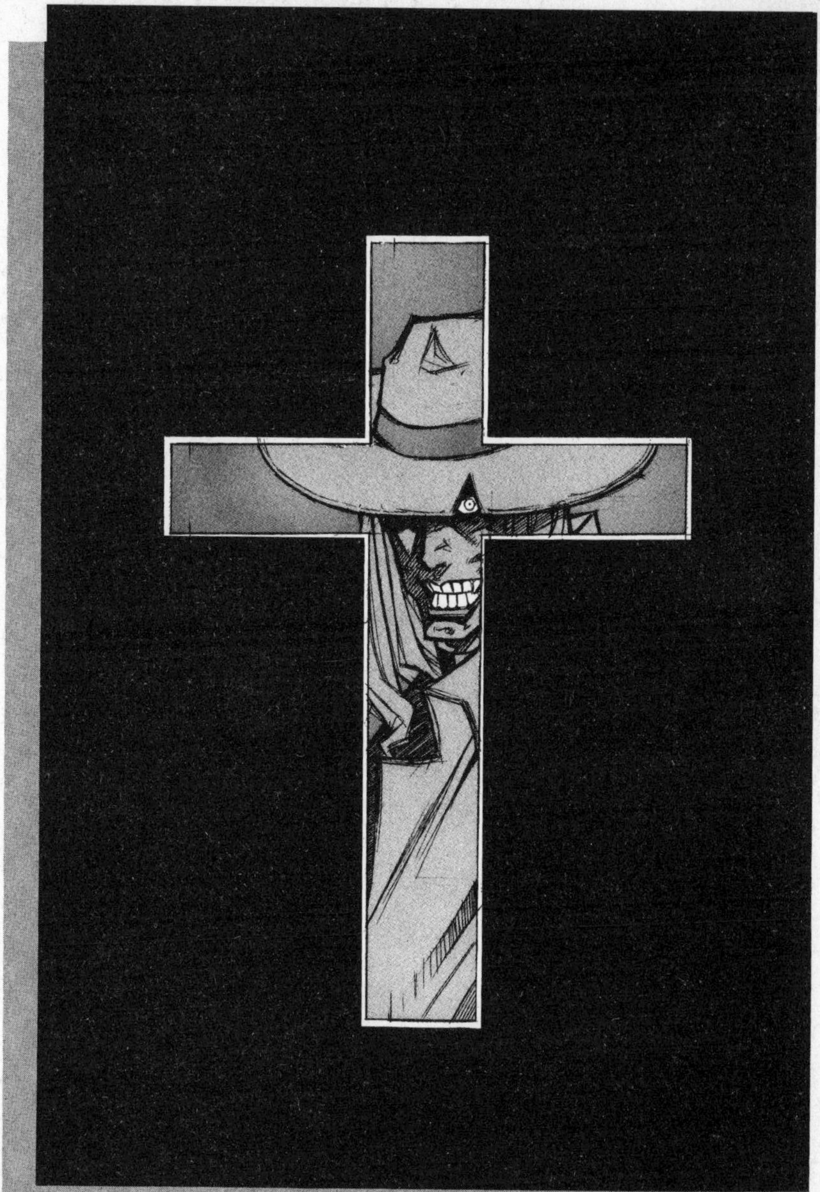

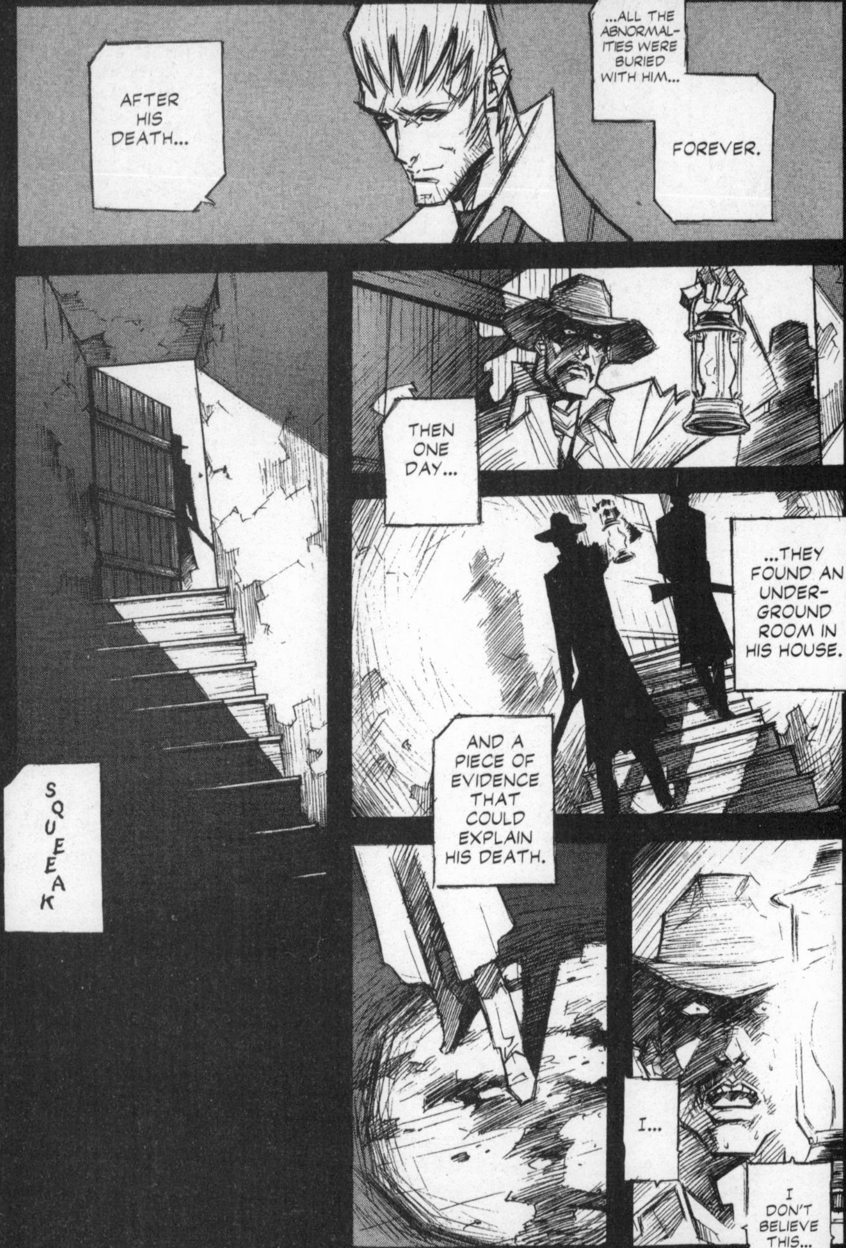
AFTER HIS DEATH...
...ALL THE ABNORMAL-ITIES WERE BURIED WITH HIM...
FOREVER.
SQUEEAK
THEN ONE DAY...
...THEY FOUND AN UNDER-GROUND ROOM IN HIS HOUSE.
AND A PIECE OF EVIDENCE THAT COULD EXPLAIN HIS DEATH.
I...
I DON'T BELIEVE THIS...

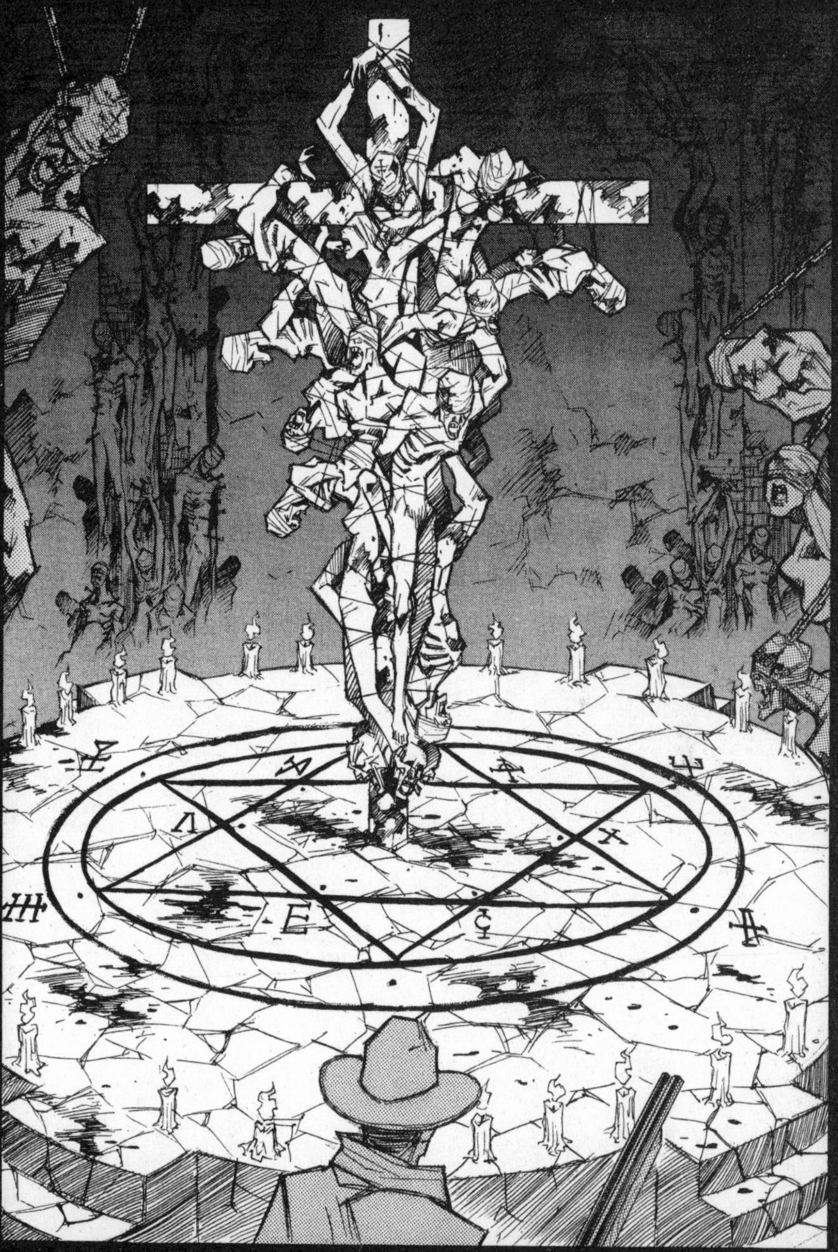

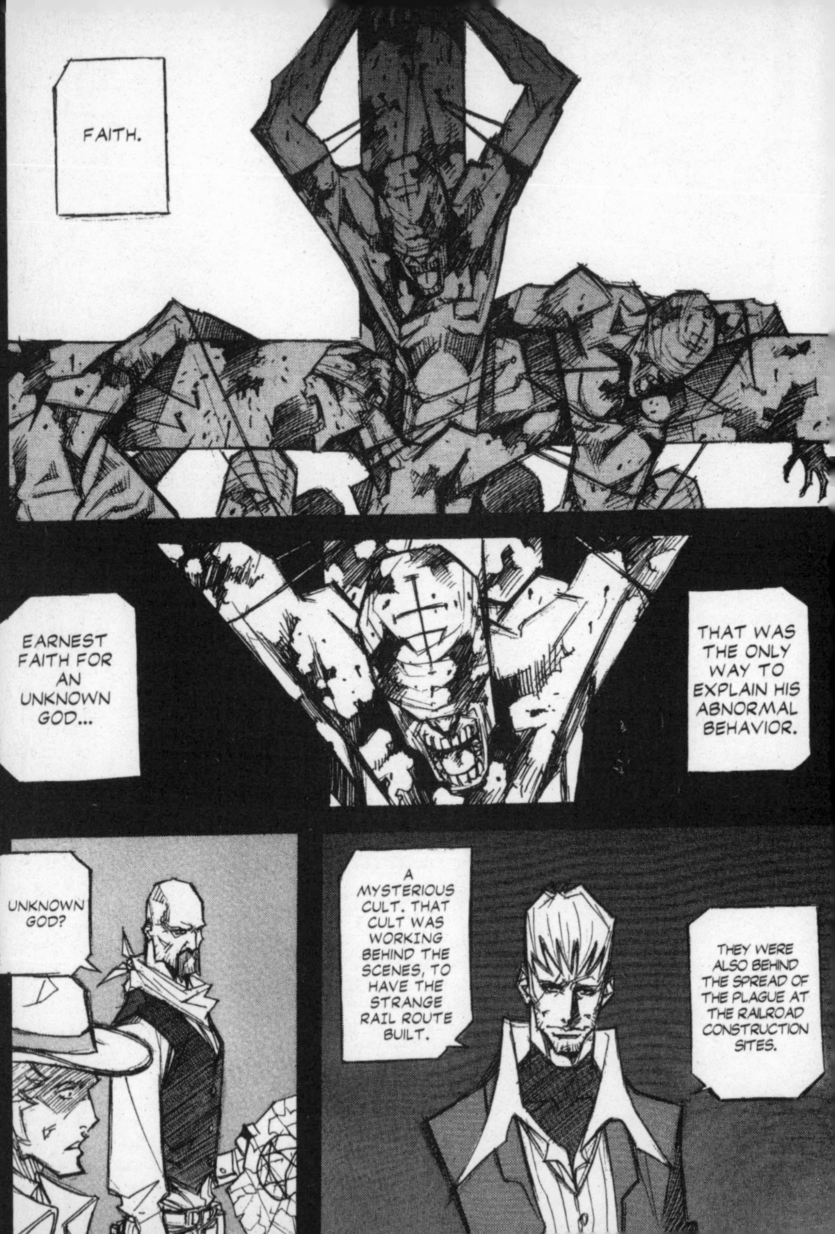
FAITH.
EARNEST FAITH FOR AN UNKNOWN GOD...
THAT WAS THE ONLY WAY TO EXPLAIN HIS ABNORMAL BEHAVIOR.
UNKNOWN GOD?
A MYSTERIOUS CULT. THAT CULT WAS WORKING BEHIND THE SCENES, TO HAVE THE STRANGE RAIL ROUTE BUILT.
THEY WERE ALSO BEHIND THE SPREAD OF THE PLAGUE AT THE RAILROAD CONSTRUCTION SITES.

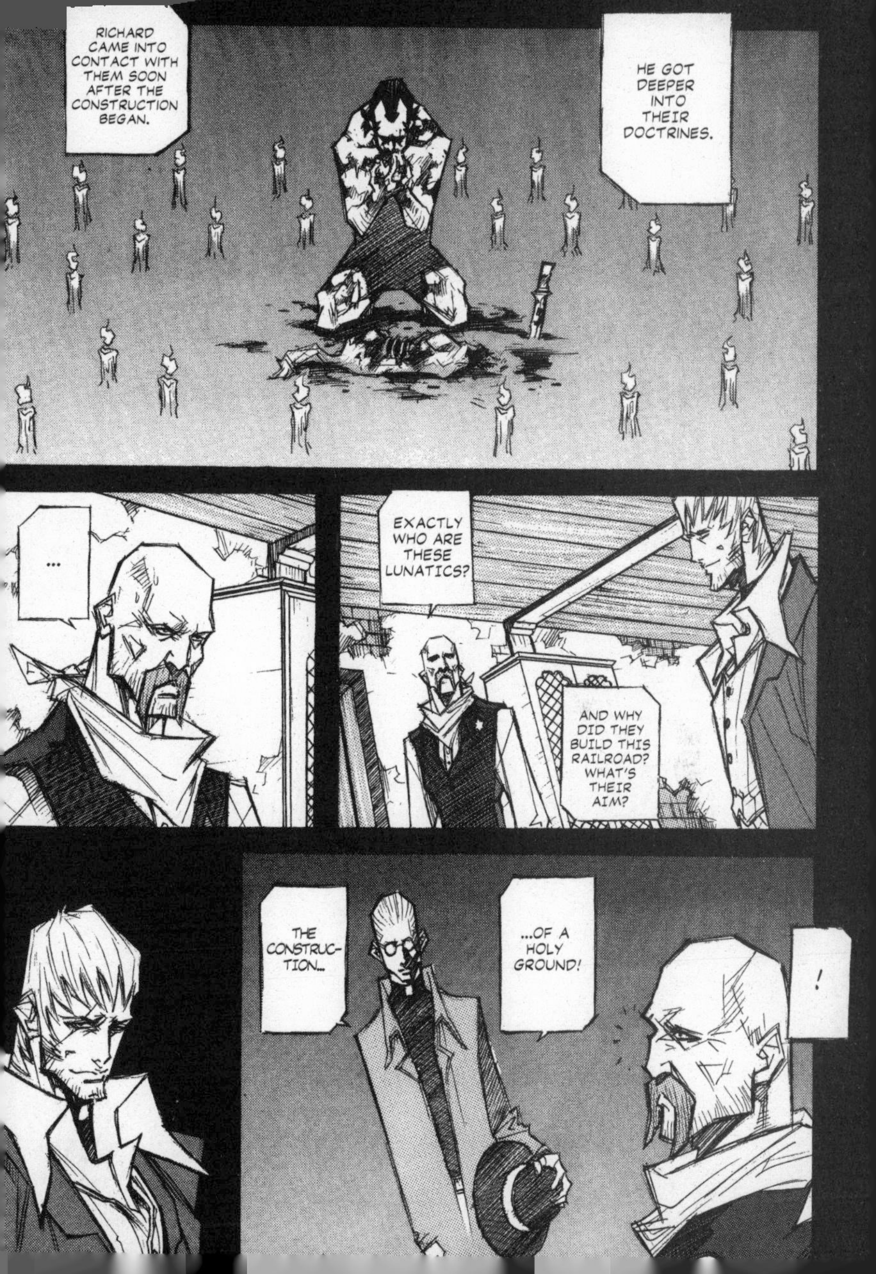
RICHARD CAME INTO CONTACT WITH THEM SOON AFTER THE CONSTRUCTION BEGAN.
HE GOT DEEPER INTO THEIR DOCTRINES.
...
EXACTLY WHO ARE THESE LUNATICS?
AND WHY DID THEY BUILD THIS RAILROAD? WHAT'S THEIR AIM?
THE CONSTRUCTION...
...OF A HOLY GROUND!
!

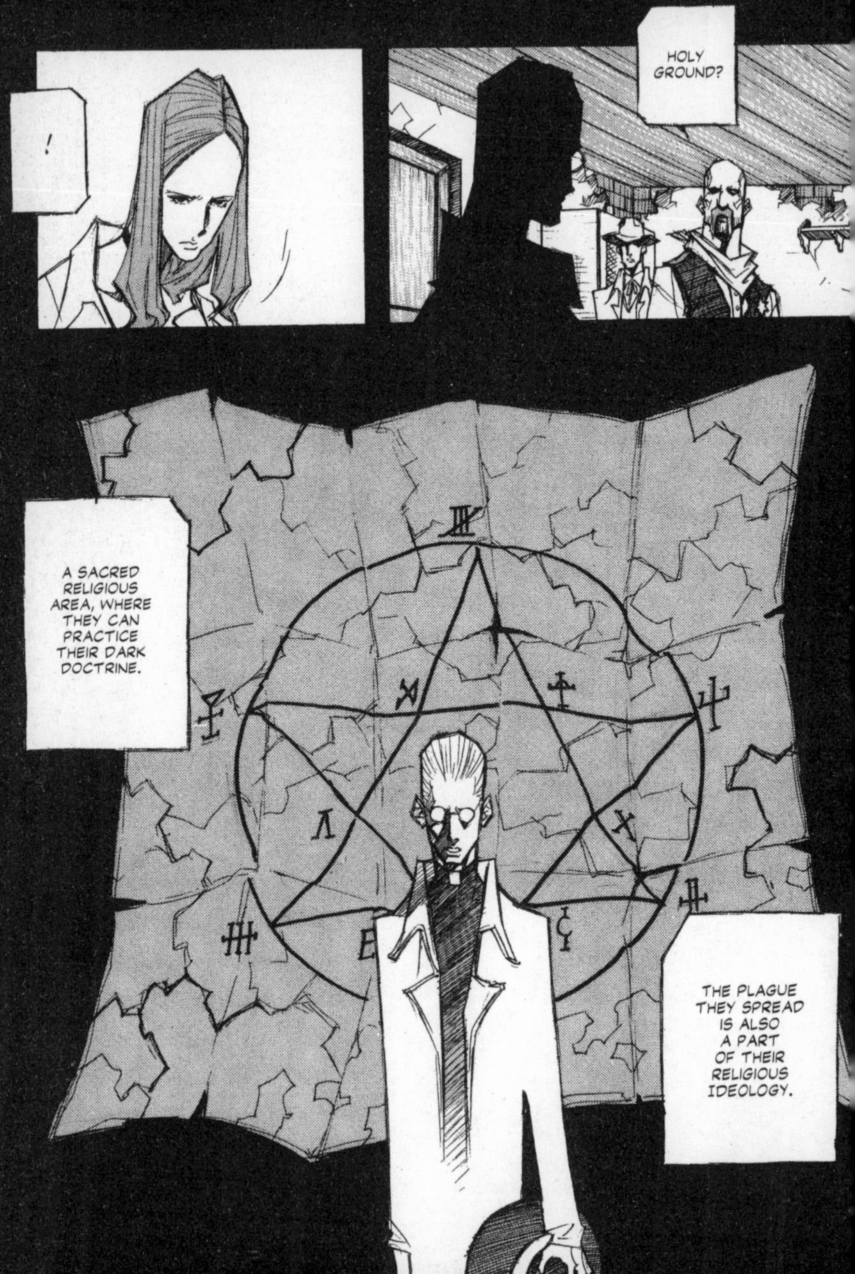
!
HOLY GROUND?
A SACRED RELIGIOUS AREA, WHERE THEY CAN PRACTICE THEIR DARK DOCTRINE.
THE PLAGUE THEY SPREAD IS ALSO A PART OF THEIR RELIGIOUS IDEOLOGY.

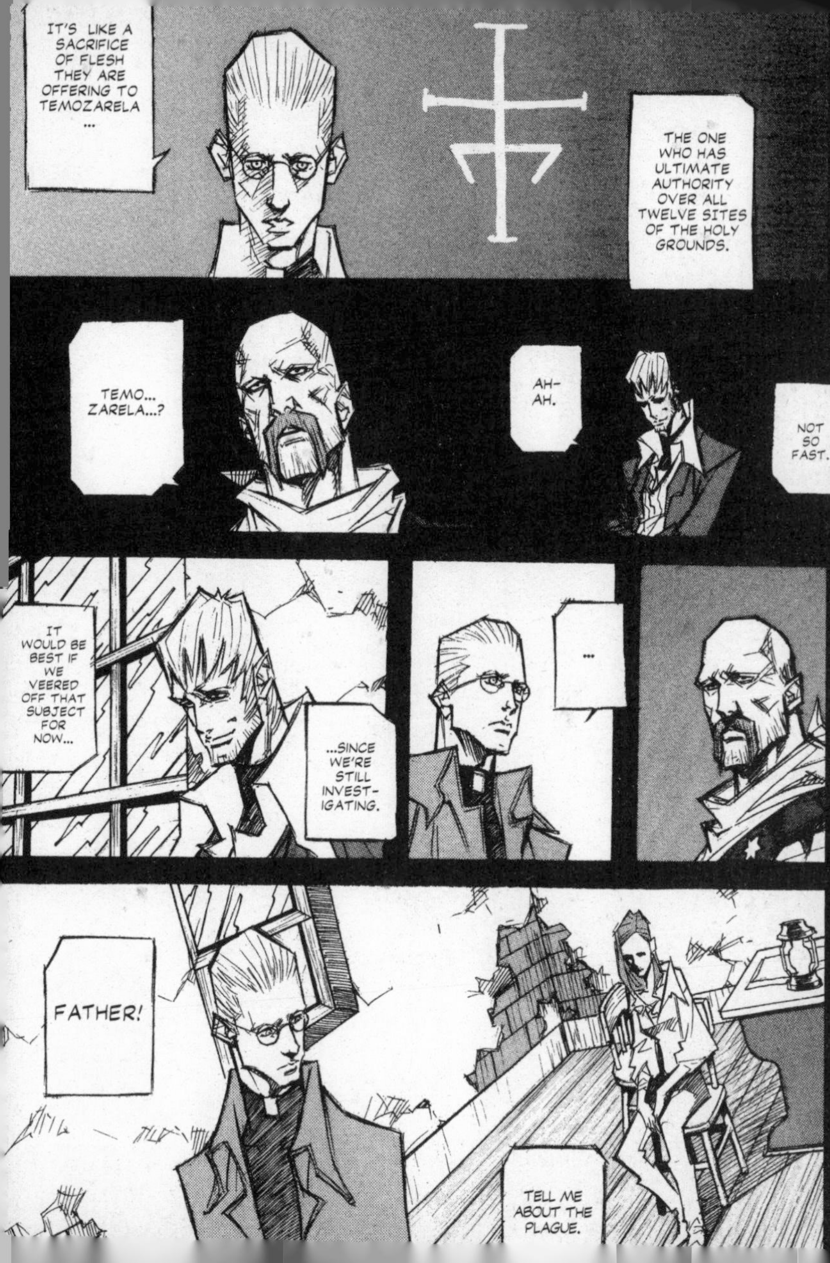

IT'S LIKE A SACRIFICE OF FLESH THEY ARE OFFERING TO TEMOZARELA ...
THE ONE WHO HAS ULTIMATE AUTHORITY OVER ALL TWELVE SITES OF THE HOLY GROUNDS.
TEMO... ZARELA...?
AH-AH.
NOT SO FAST.
IT WOULD BE BEST IF WE VEERED OFF THAT SUBJECT FOR NOW...
...SINCE WE'RE STILL INVEST-IGATING.
...
FATHER!
TELL ME ABOUT THE PLAGUE.

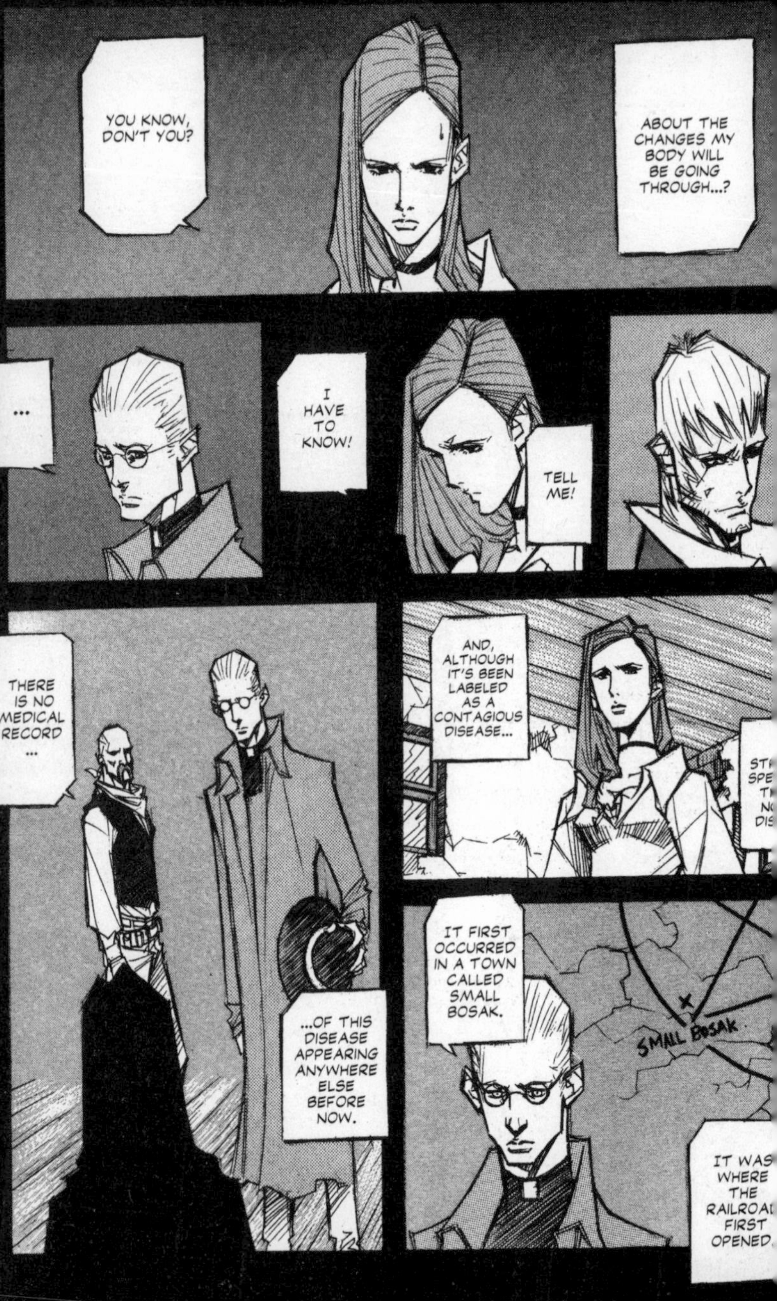
YOU KNOW, DON'T YOU?
ABOUT THE CHANGES MY BODY WILL BE GOING THROUGH...?
...
I HAVE TO KNOW!
TELL ME!
THERE IS NO MEDICAL RECORD ...
...OF THIS DISEASE APPEARING ANYWHERE ELSE BEFORE NOW.
AND, ALTHOUGH IT'S BEEN LABELED AS A CONTAGIOUS DISEASE...
IT FIRST OCCURRED IN A TOWN CALLED SMALL BOSAK.
SMALL BOSAK
IT WAS WHERE THE RAILROA FIRST OPENED

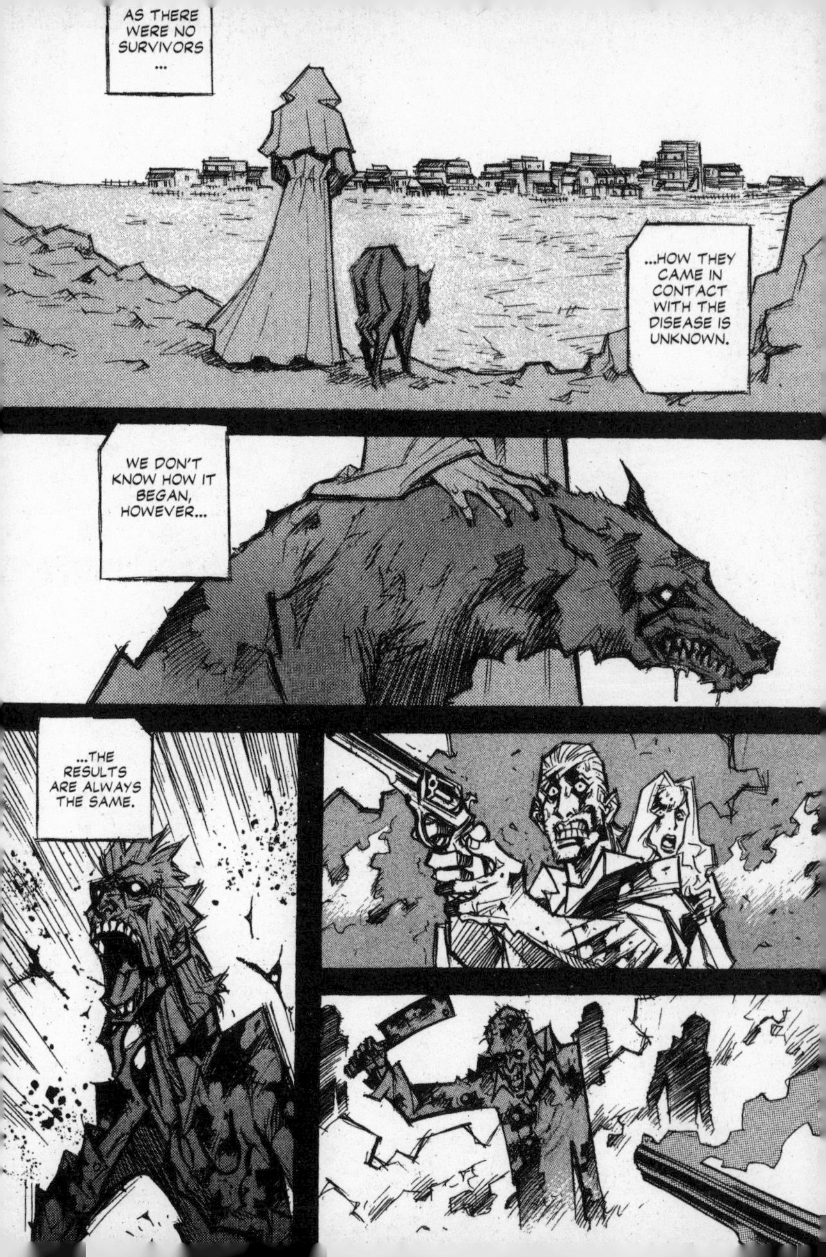
AS THERE WERE NO SURVIVORS ...
...HOW THEY CAME IN CONTACT WITH THE DISEASE IS UNKNOWN.
WE DON'T KNOW HOW IT BEGAN, HOWEVER...
...THE RESULTS ARE ALWAYS THE SAME.

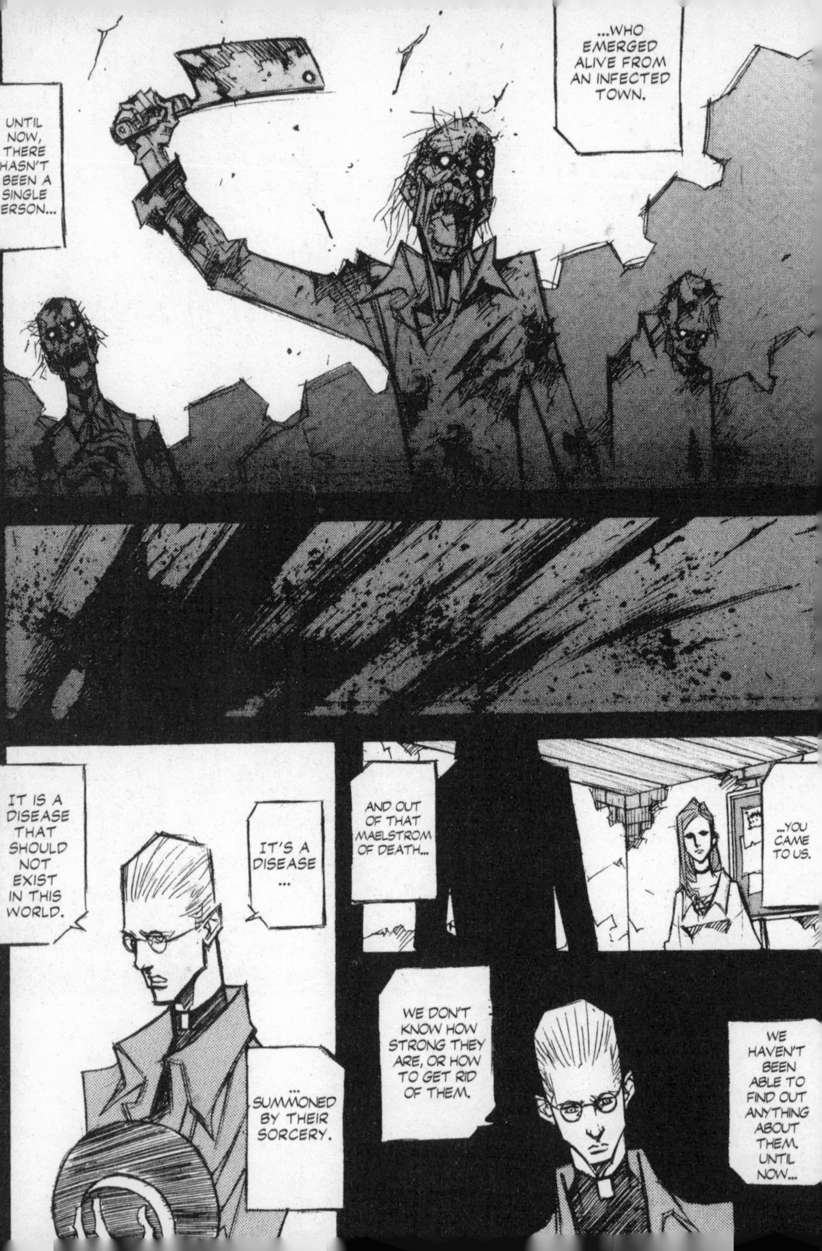
UNTIL NOW, THERE HASN'T BEEN A SINGLE PERSON...
...WHO EMERGED ALIVE FROM AN INFECTED TOWN.
IT IS A DISEASE THAT SHOULD NOT EXIST IN THIS WORLD.
IT'S A DISEASE ...
...SUMMONED BY THEIR SORCERY.
AND OUT OF THAT MAELSTROM OF DEATH...
...YOU CAME TO US.
WE DON'T KNOW HOW STRONG THEY ARE, OR HOW TO GET RID OF THEM.
WE HAVEN'T BEEN ABLE TO FIND OUT ANYTHING ABOUT THEM. UNTIL NOW...

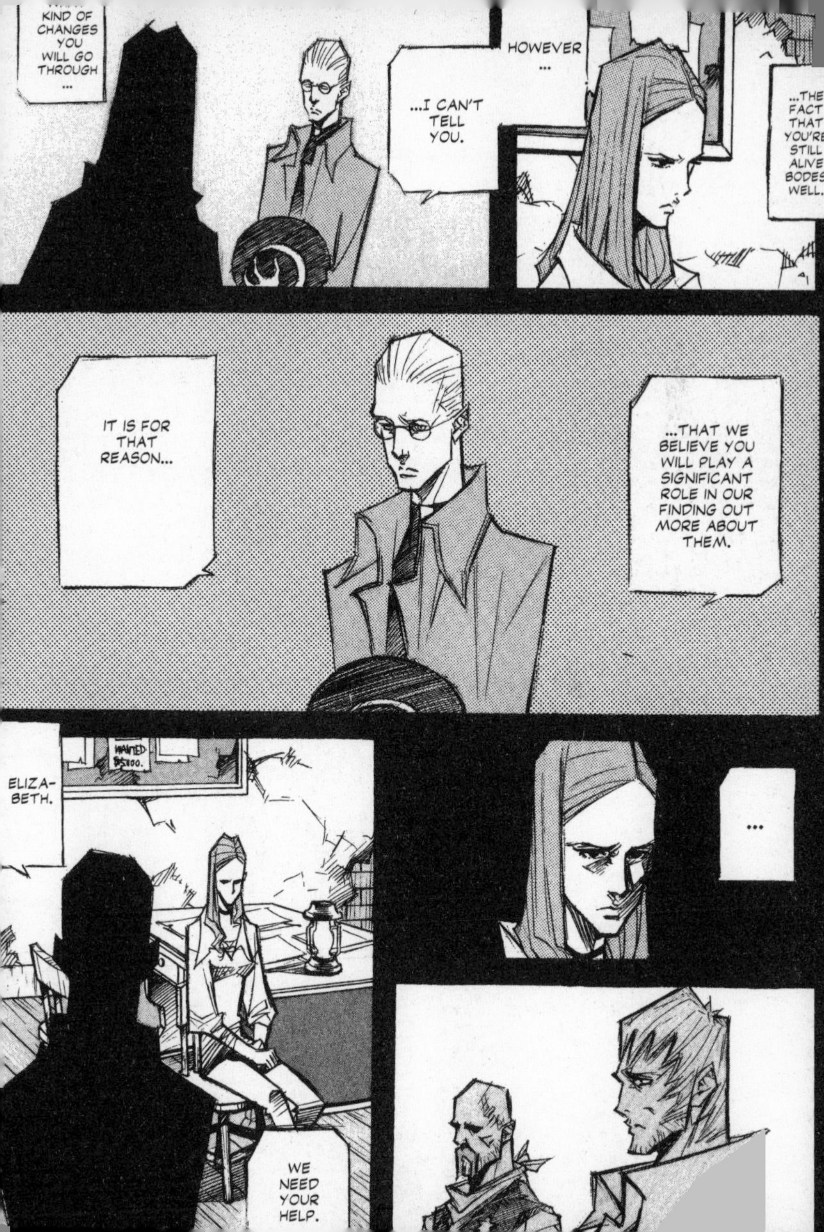
KIND OF CHANGES YOU WILL GO THROUGH ...
...I CAN'T TELL YOU.
HOWEVER ...
...THE FACT THAT YOU'RE STILL ALIVE BODES WELL.
IT IS FOR THAT REASON...
...THAT WE BELIEVE YOU WILL PLAY A SIGNIFICANT ROLE IN OUR FINDING OUT MORE ABOUT THEM.
ELIZA-BETH.
WE NEED YOUR HELP.
...

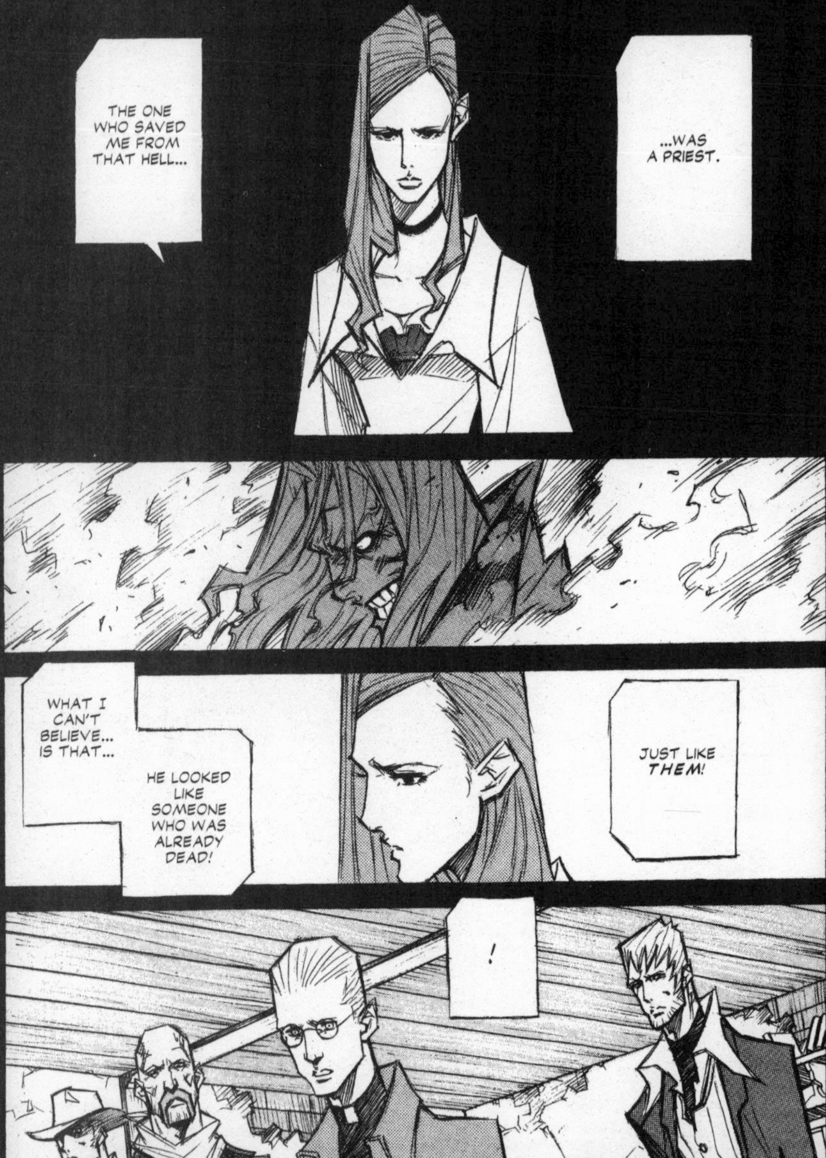
THE ONE WHO SAVED ME FROM THAT HELL...
...WAS A PRIEST.
WHAT I CAN'T BELIEVE... IS THAT...
HE LOOKED LIKE SOMEONE WHO WAS ALREADY DEAD!
JUST LIKE *THEM!*
!

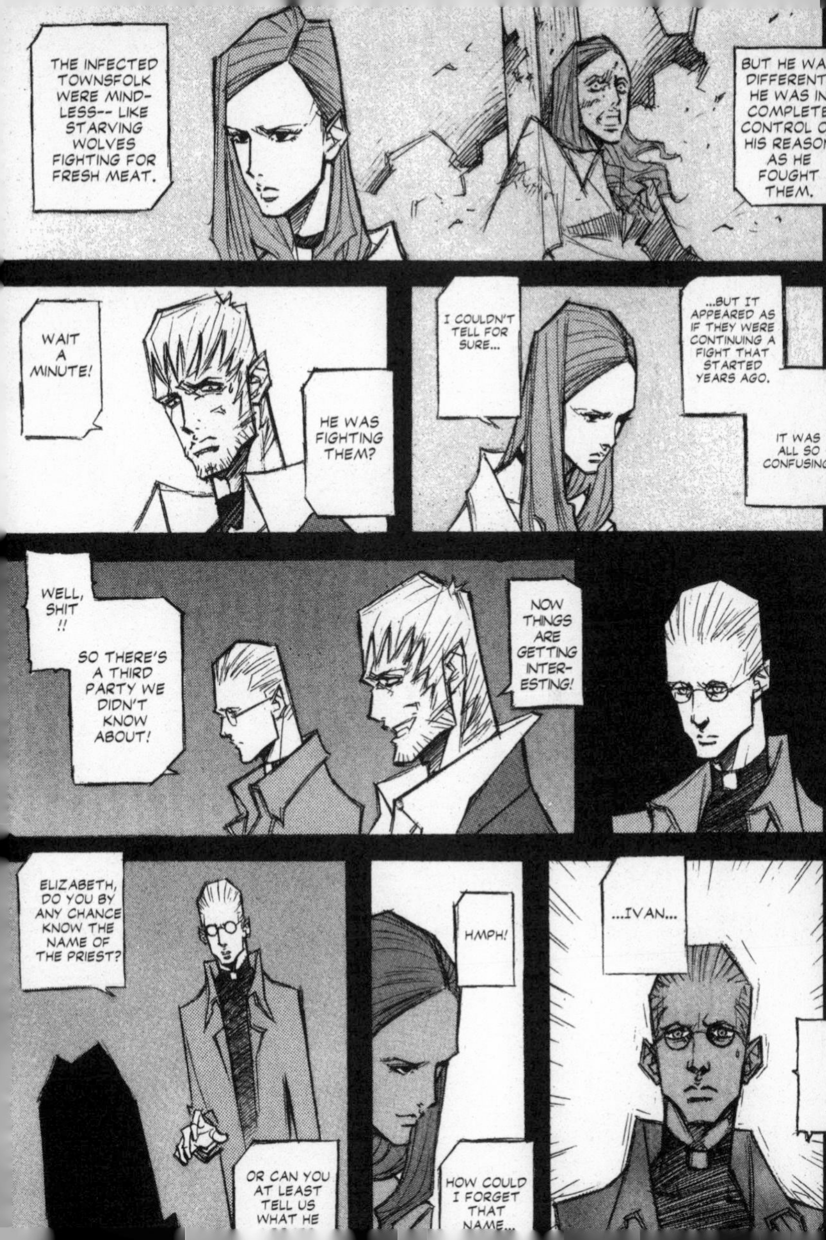
THE INFECTED TOWNSFOLK WERE MINDLESS-- LIKE STARVING WOLVES FIGHTING FOR FRESH MEAT.
BUT HE WAS DIFFERENT. HE WAS IN COMPLETE CONTROL OF HIS REASON AS HE FOUGHT THEM.
WAIT A MINUTE!
HE WAS FIGHTING THEM?
I COULDN'T TELL FOR SURE...
...BUT IT APPEARED AS IF THEY WERE CONTINUING A FIGHT THAT STARTED YEARS AGO.
IT WAS ALL SO CONFUSING.
WELL, SHIT!!
SO THERE'S A THIRD PARTY WE DIDN'T KNOW ABOUT!
NOW THINGS ARE GETTING INTERESTING!
ELIZABETH, DO YOU BY ANY CHANCE KNOW THE NAME OF THE PRIEST?
OR CAN YOU AT LEAST TELL US WHAT HE
HMPH!
HOW COULD I FORGET THAT NAME...
...IVAN...
!

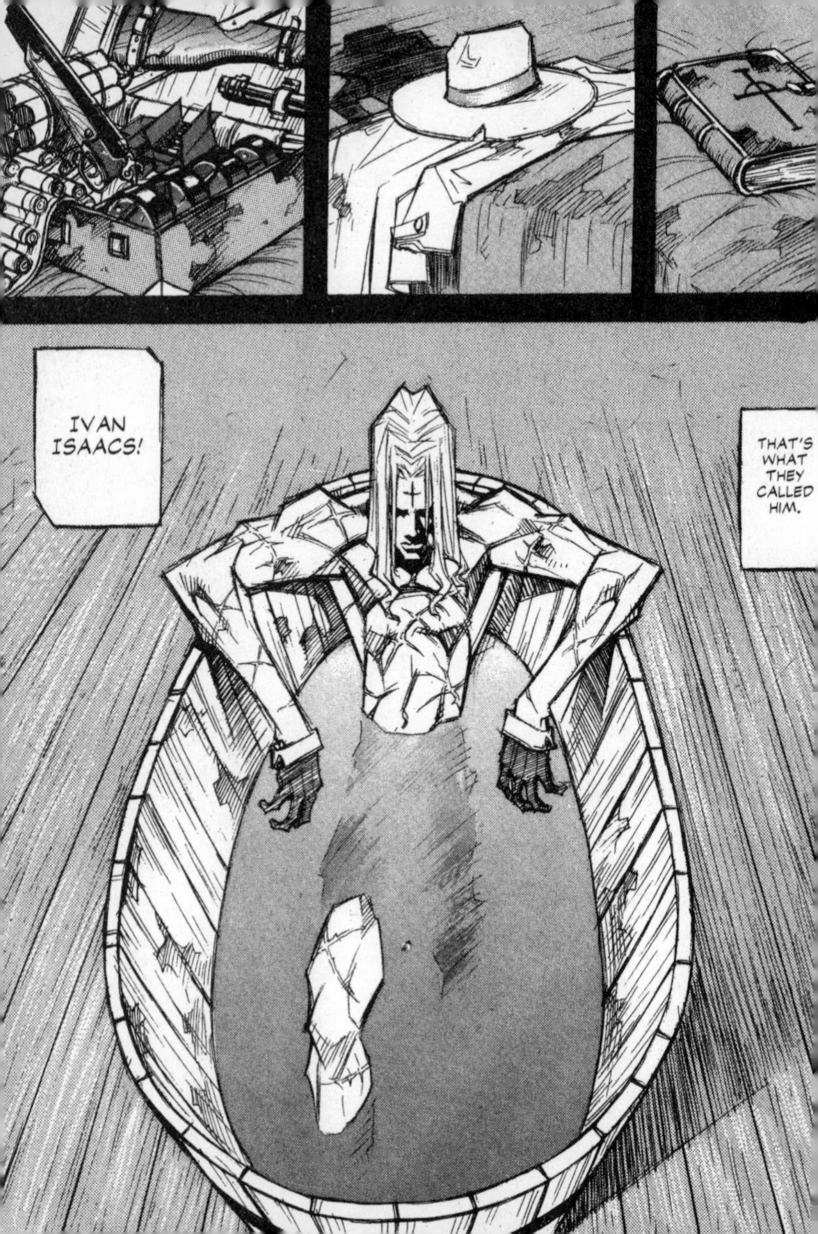
IVAN ISAACS!
THAT'S WHAT THEY CALLED HIM.

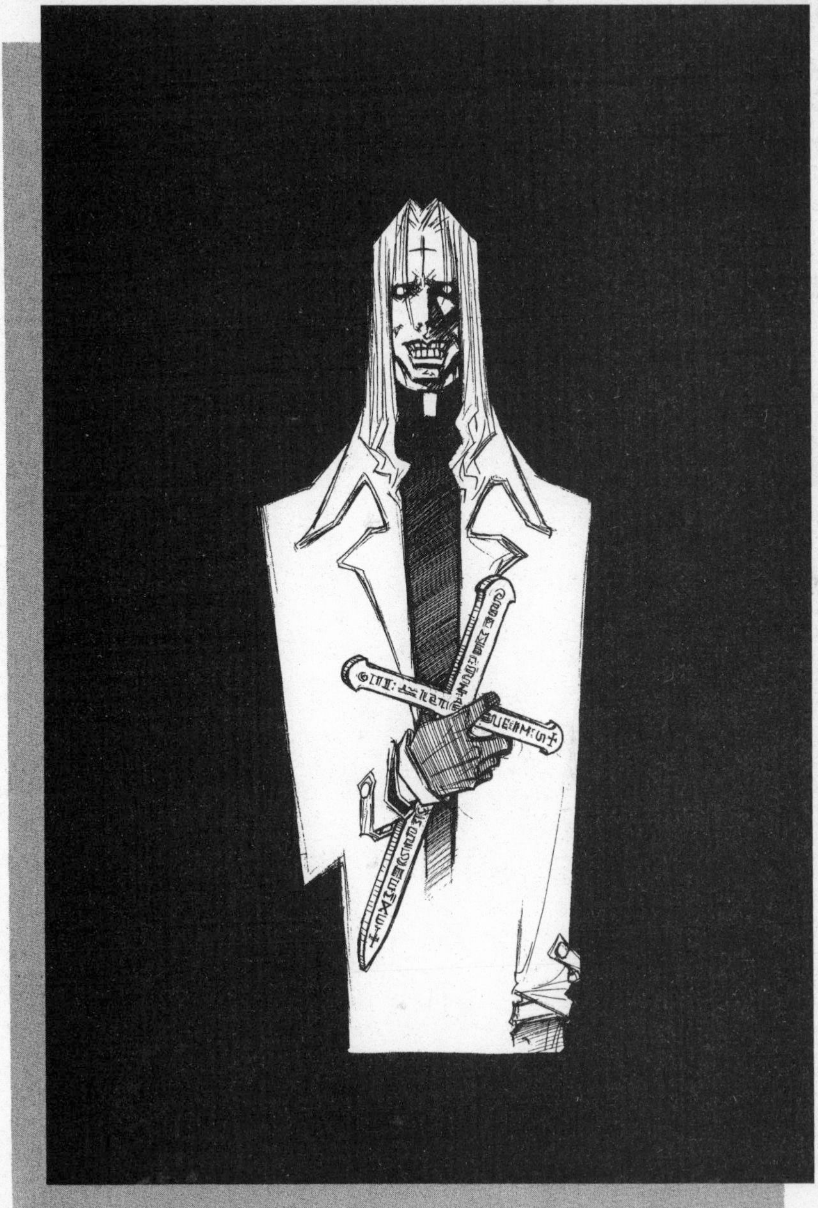

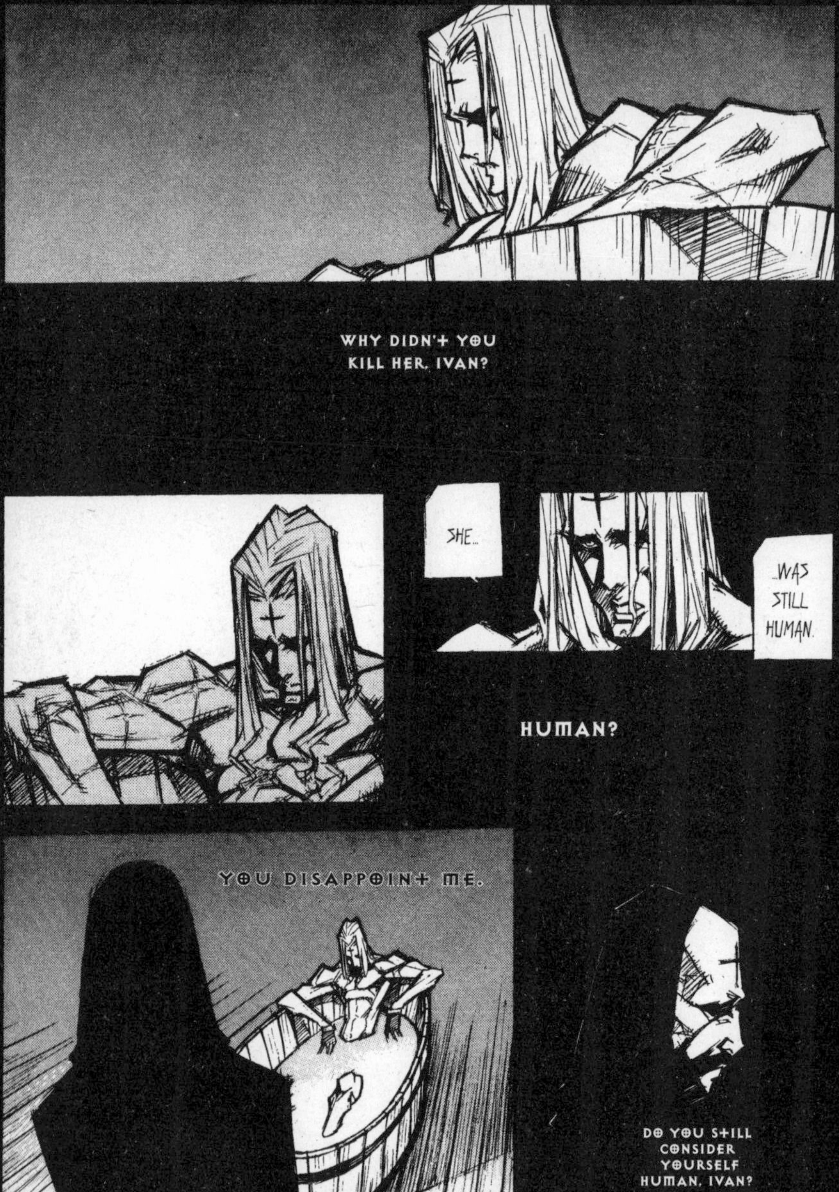
WHY DIDN'T YOU KILL HER, IVAN?
SHE...
...WAS STILL HUMAN.
HUMAN?
YOU DISAPPOINT ME.
DO YOU STILL CONSIDER YOURSELF HUMAN, IVAN?

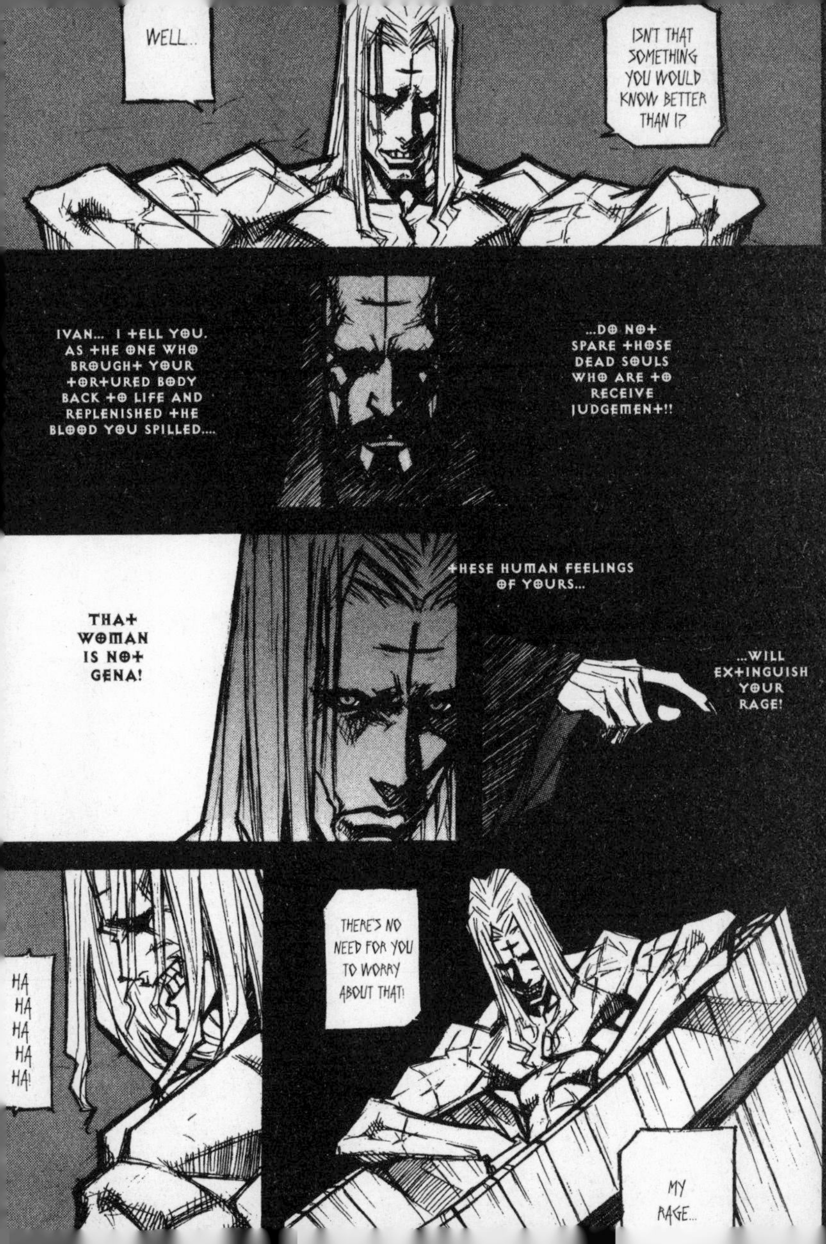
WELL...
ISN'T THAT SOMETHING YOU WOULD KNOW BETTER THAN I?
IVAN... I TELL YOU. AS THE ONE WHO BROUGHT YOUR TORTURED BODY BACK TO LIFE AND REPLENISHED THE BLOOD YOU SPILLED....
...DO NOT SPARE THOSE DEAD SOULS WHO ARE TO RECEIVE JUDGEMENT!!
THAT WOMAN IS NOT GENA!
THESE HUMAN FEELINGS OF YOURS...
...WILL EXTINGUISH YOUR RAGE!
HA HA HA HA HA!
THERE'S NO NEED FOR YOU TO WORRY ABOUT THAT!
MY RAGE...

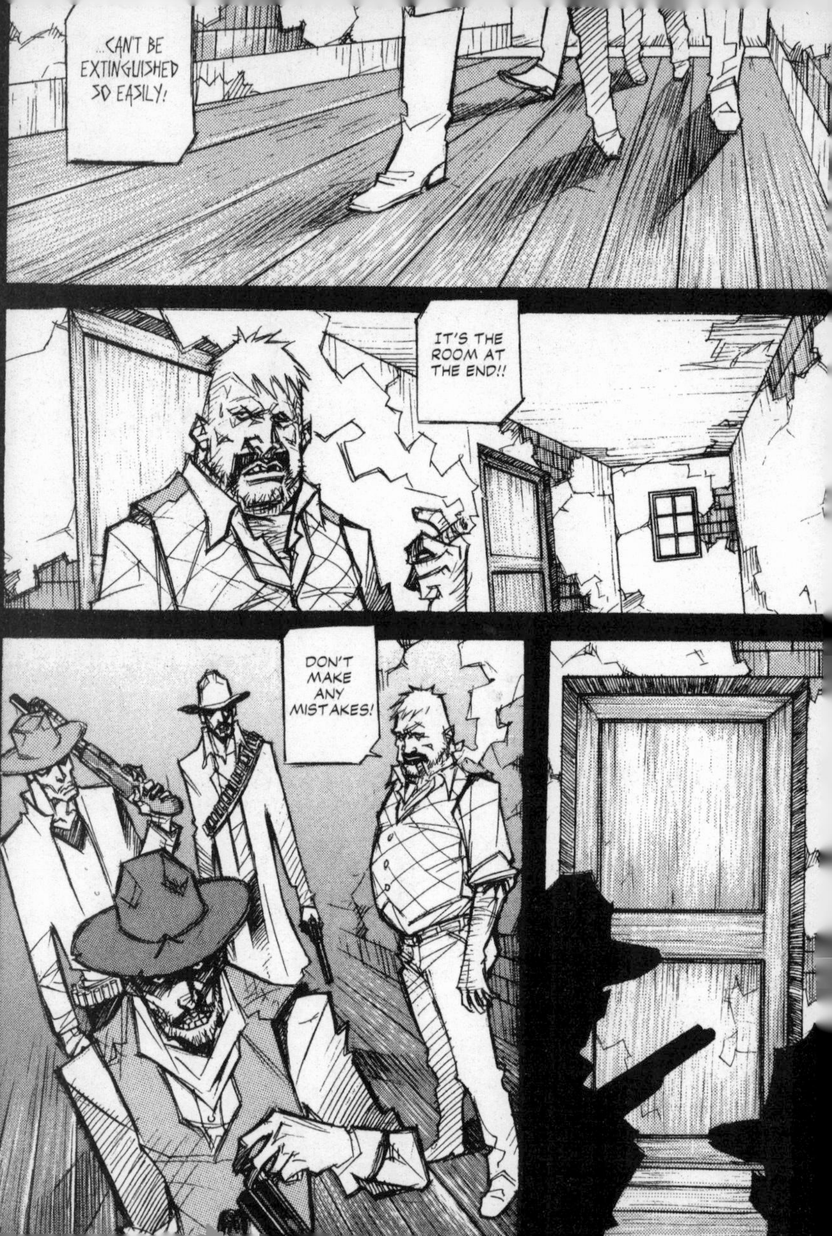
...CAN'T BE EXTINGUISHED SO EASILY!
IT'S THE ROOM AT THE END!!
DON'T MAKE ANY MISTAKES!

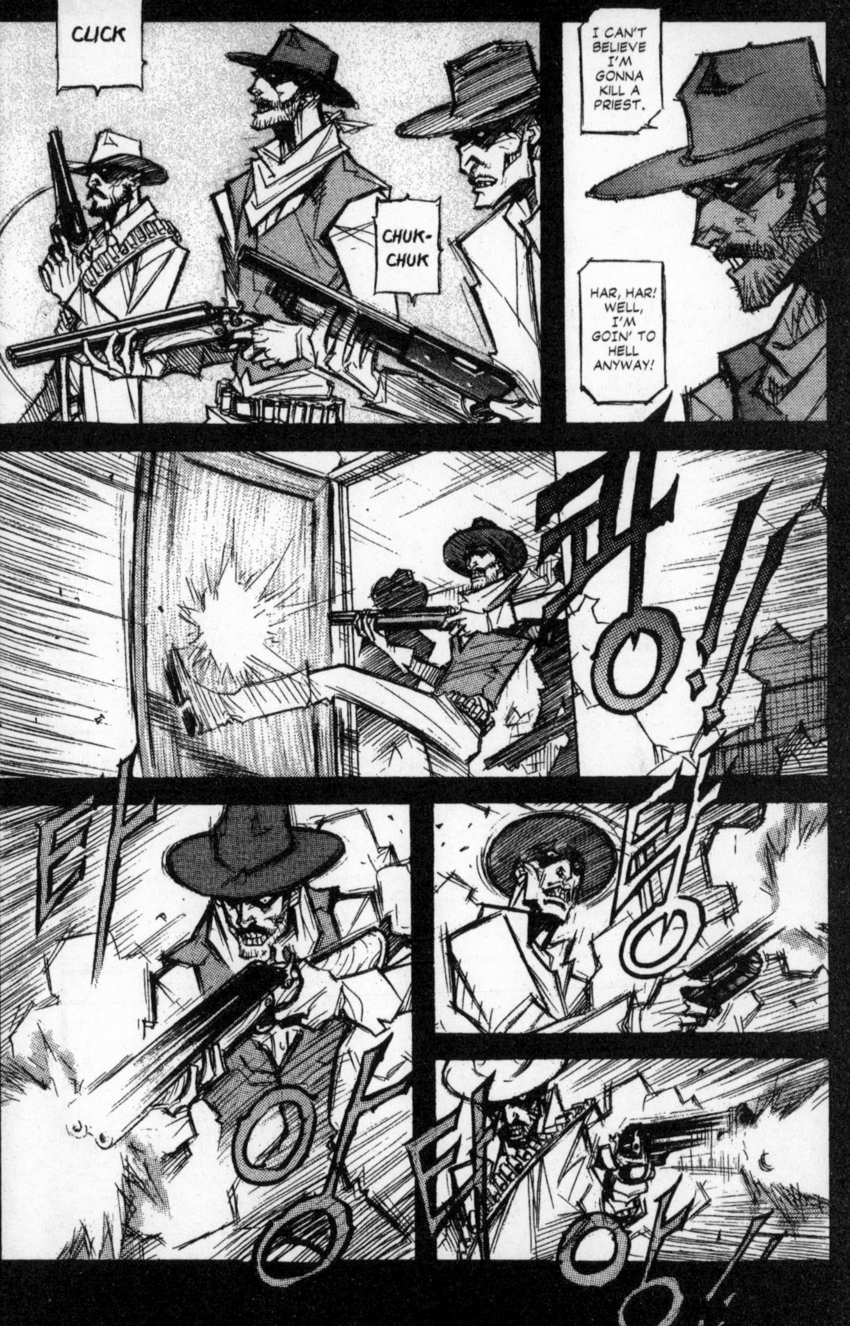
CLICK
CHUK-CHUK
I CAN'T BELIEVE I'M GONNA KILL A PRIEST.
HAR, HAR! WELL, I'M GOIN' TO HELL ANYWAY!

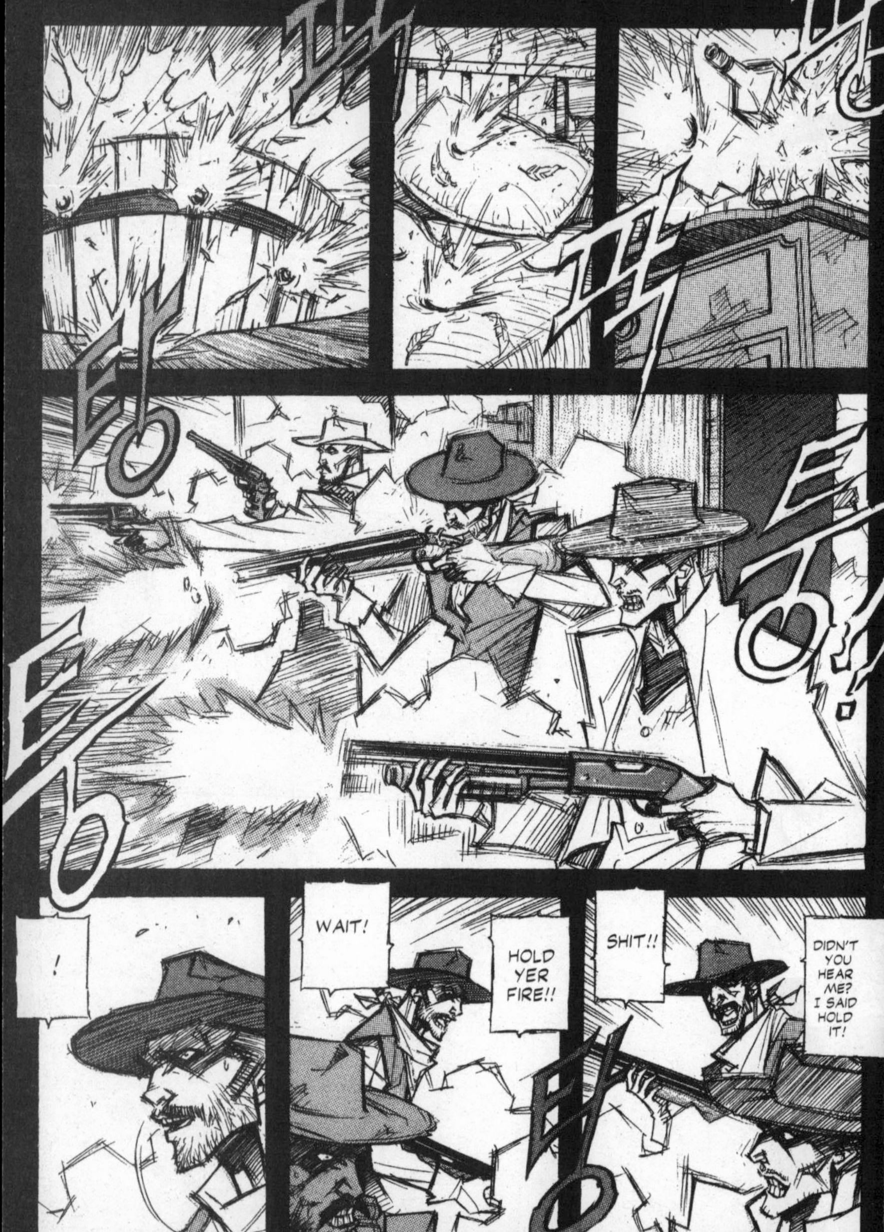
!
WAIT!
HOLD YER FIRE!!
SHIT!!
DIDN'T YOU HEAR ME? I SAID HOLD IT!

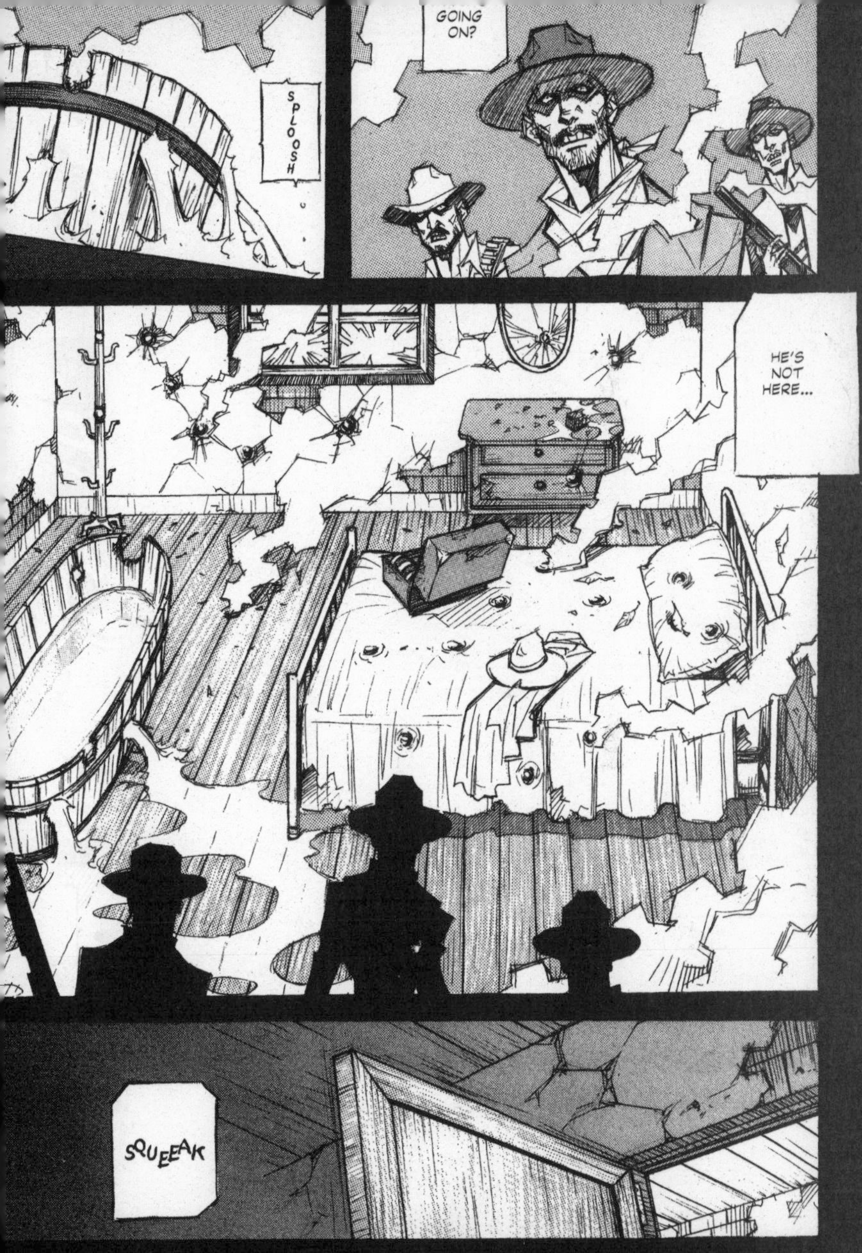
SPLOOSH
GOING ON?
HE'S NOT HERE...
SQUEEAK

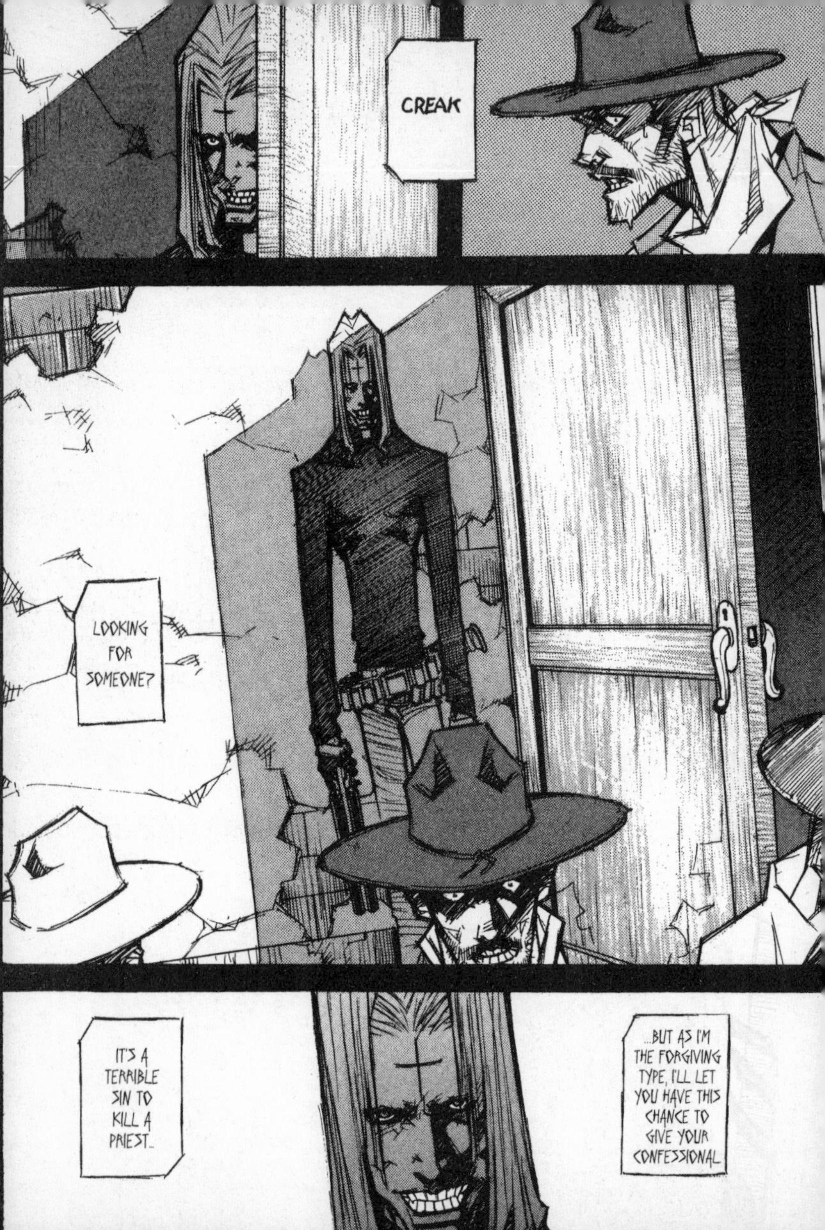
CREAK
LOOKING FOR SOMEONE?
IT'S A TERRIBLE SIN TO KILL A PRIEST...
...BUT AS I'M THE FORGIVING TYPE, I'LL LET YOU HAVE THIS CHANCE TO GIVE YOUR CONFESSIONAL.

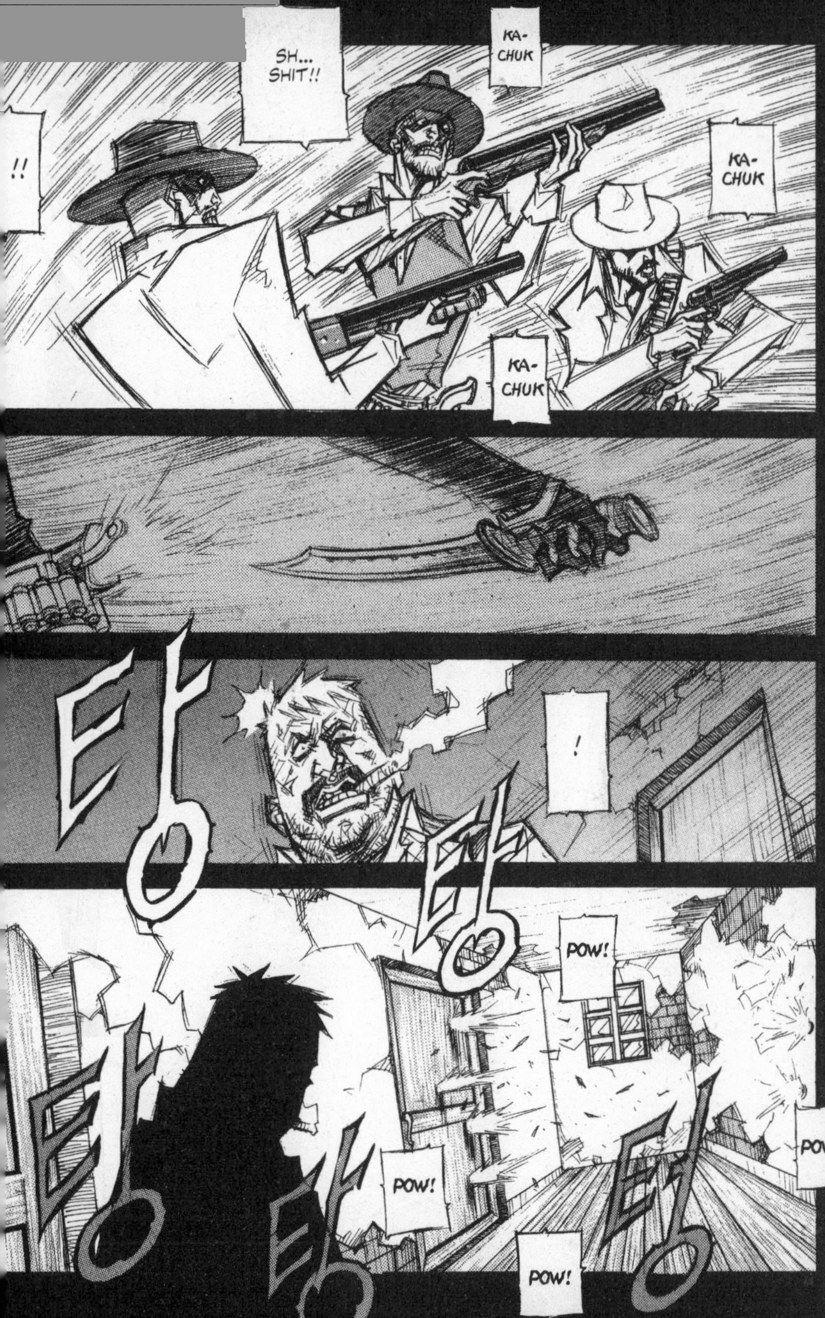
!!
SH... SHIT!!
KA-CHUK
KA-CHUK
KA-CHUK
탕
!
탕
탕
POW!
탕
POW!
POW!
탕
POW!

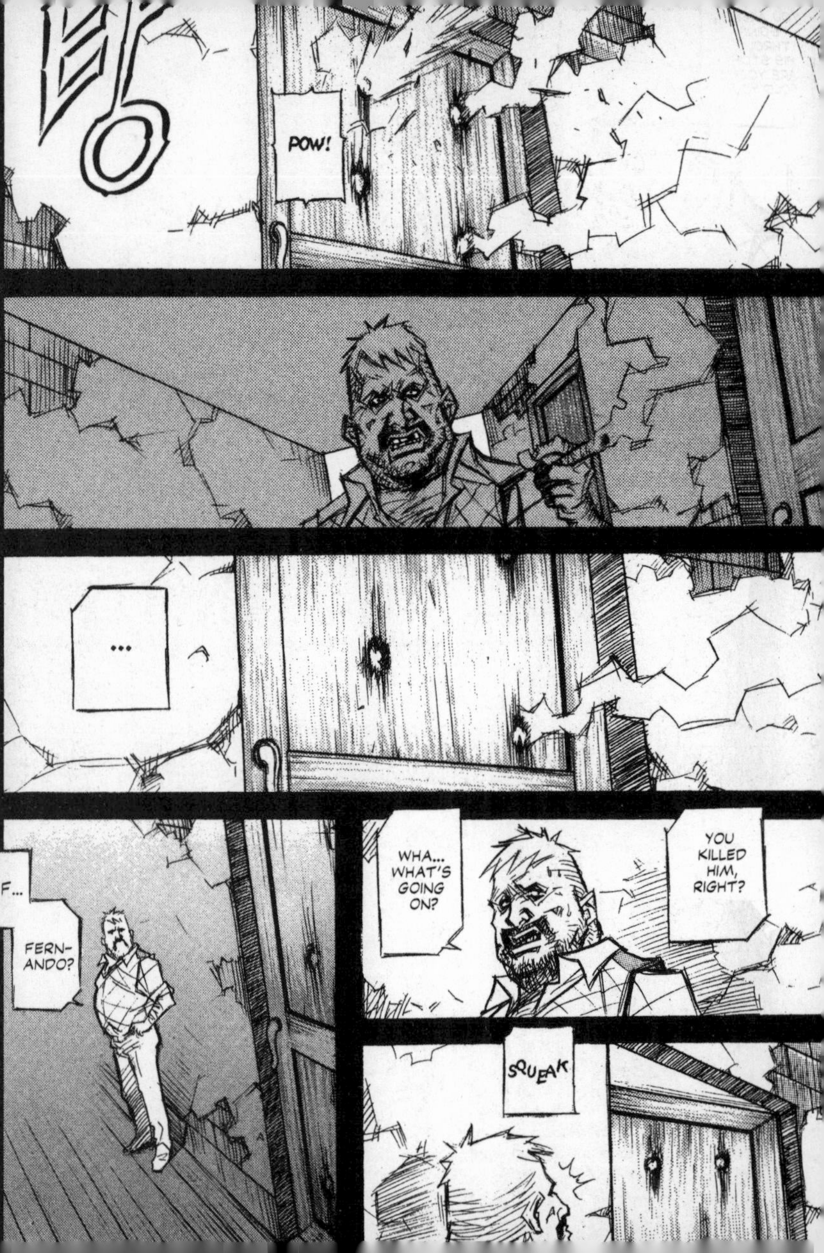
POW!
...
F...
FERN-ANDO?
WHA... WHAT'S GOING ON?
YOU KILLED HIM, RIGHT?
SQUEAK

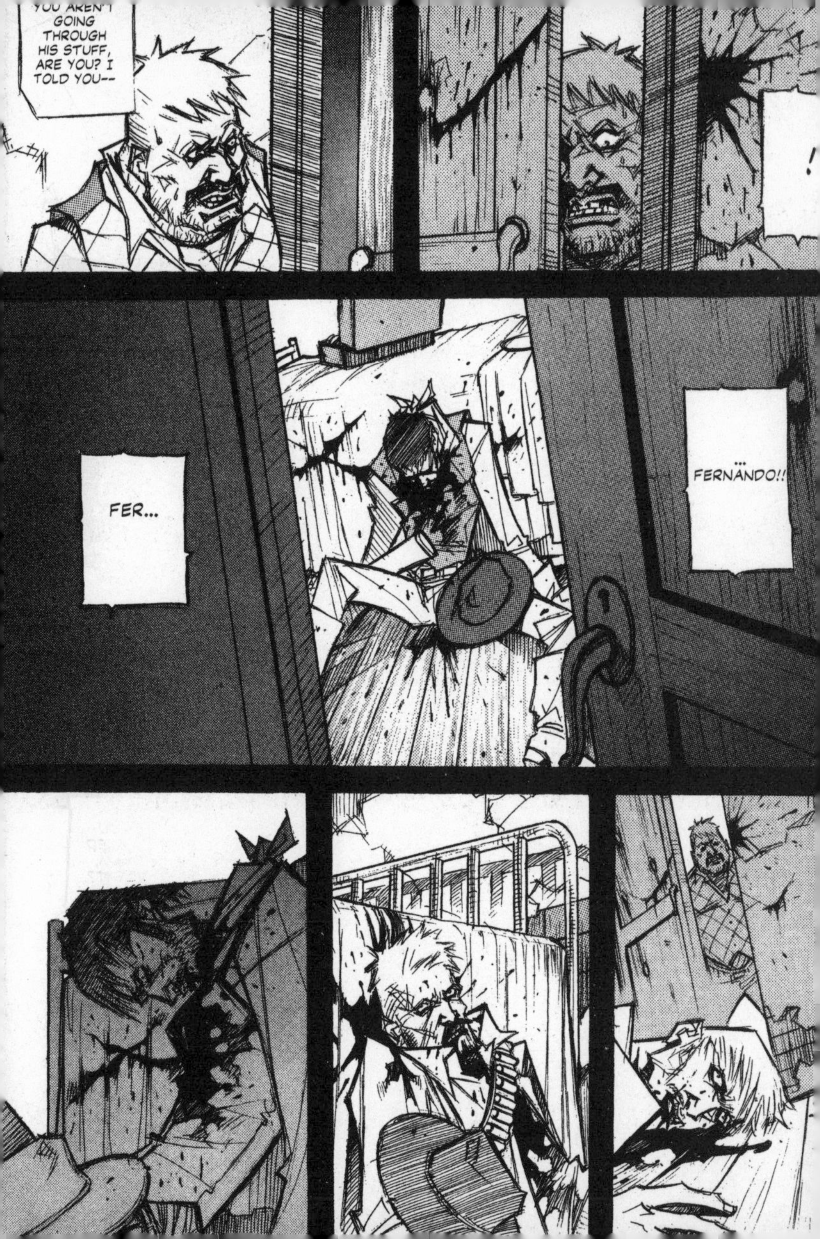
YOU AREN'T GOING THROUGH HIS STUFF, ARE YOU? I TOLD YOU--
!
FER...
... FERNANDO!!

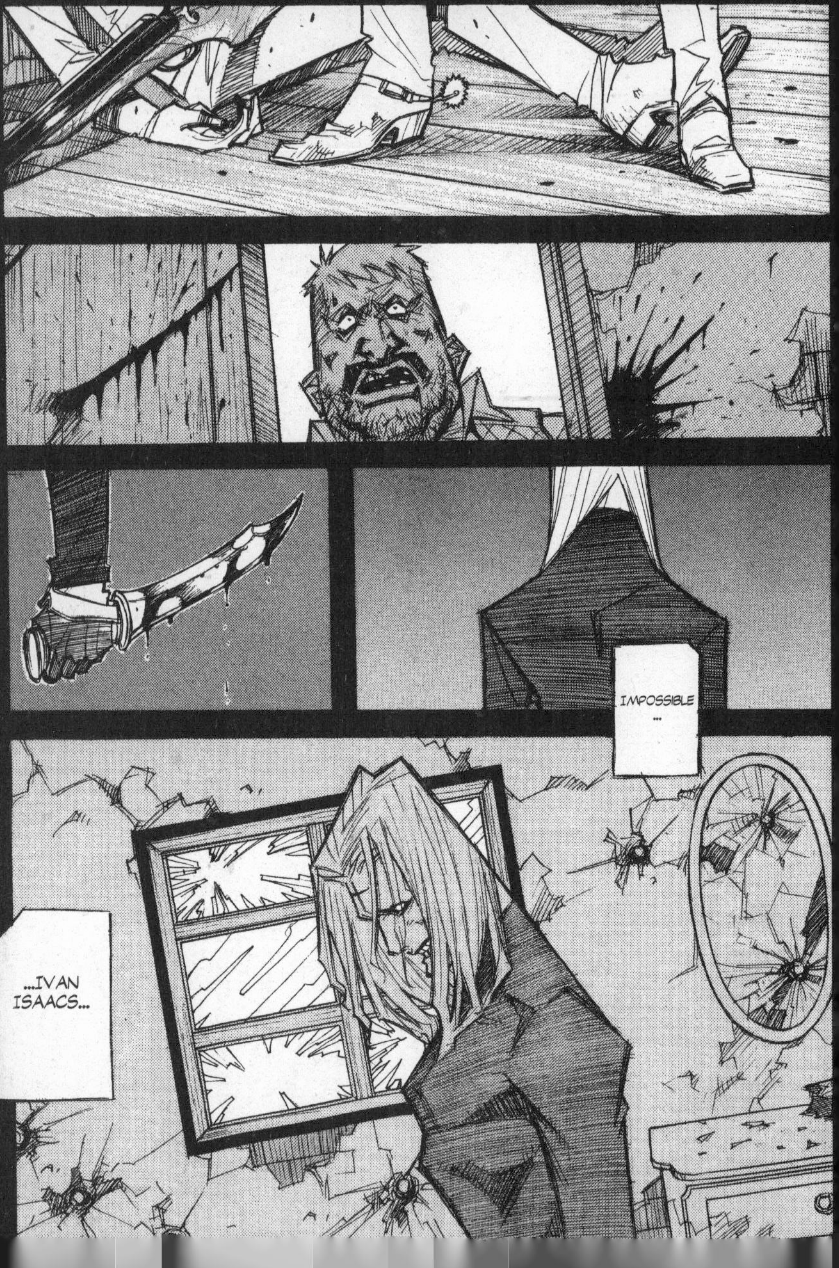
IMPOSSIBLE ...
...IVAN ISAACS...

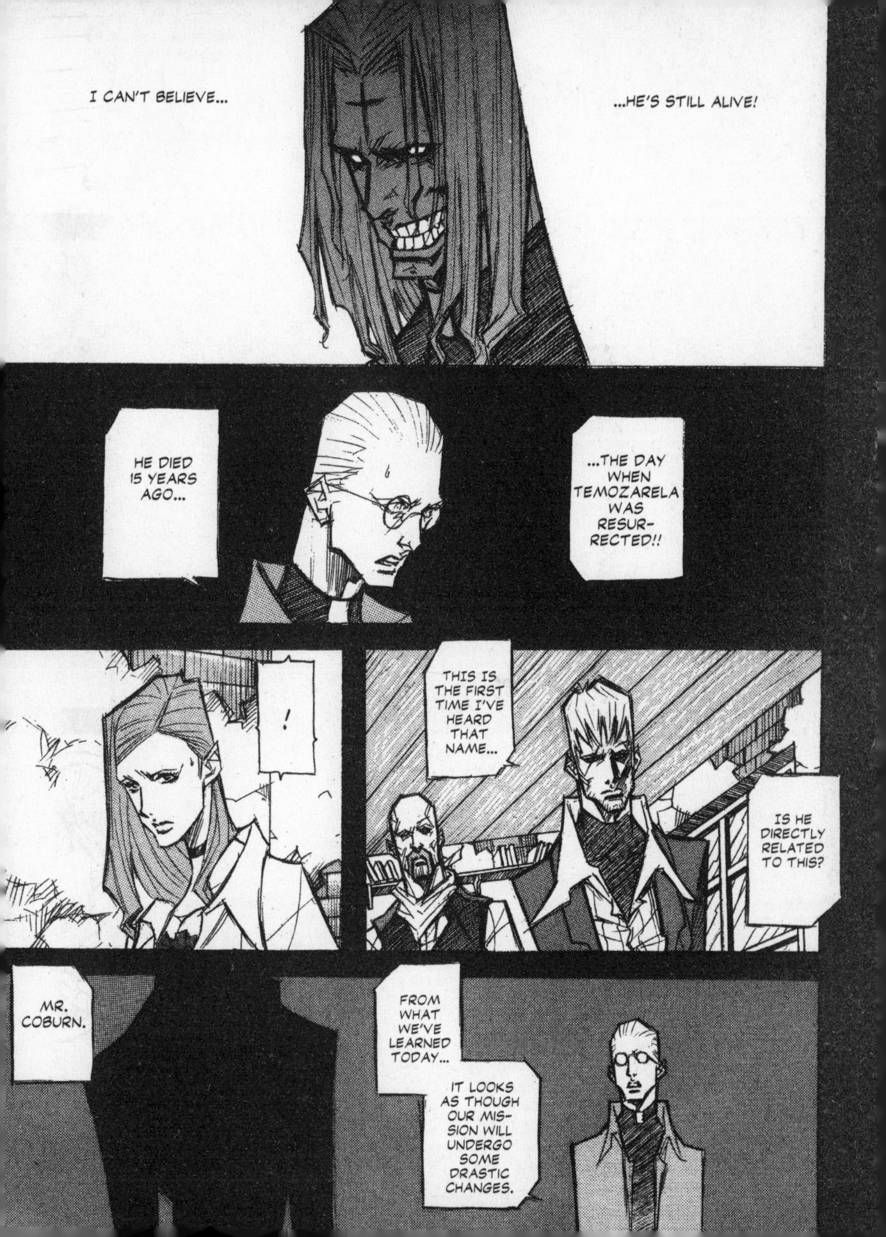
I CAN'T BELIEVE...
...HE'S STILL ALIVE!
HE DIED 15 YEARS AGO...
...THE DAY WHEN TEMOZARELA WAS RESURRECTED!!
!
THIS IS THE FIRST TIME I'VE HEARD THAT NAME...
IS HE DIRECTLY RELATED TO THIS?
MR. COBURN.
FROM WHAT WE'VE LEARNED TODAY...
IT LOOKS AS THOUGH OUR MISSION WILL UNDERGO SOME DRASTIC CHANGES.

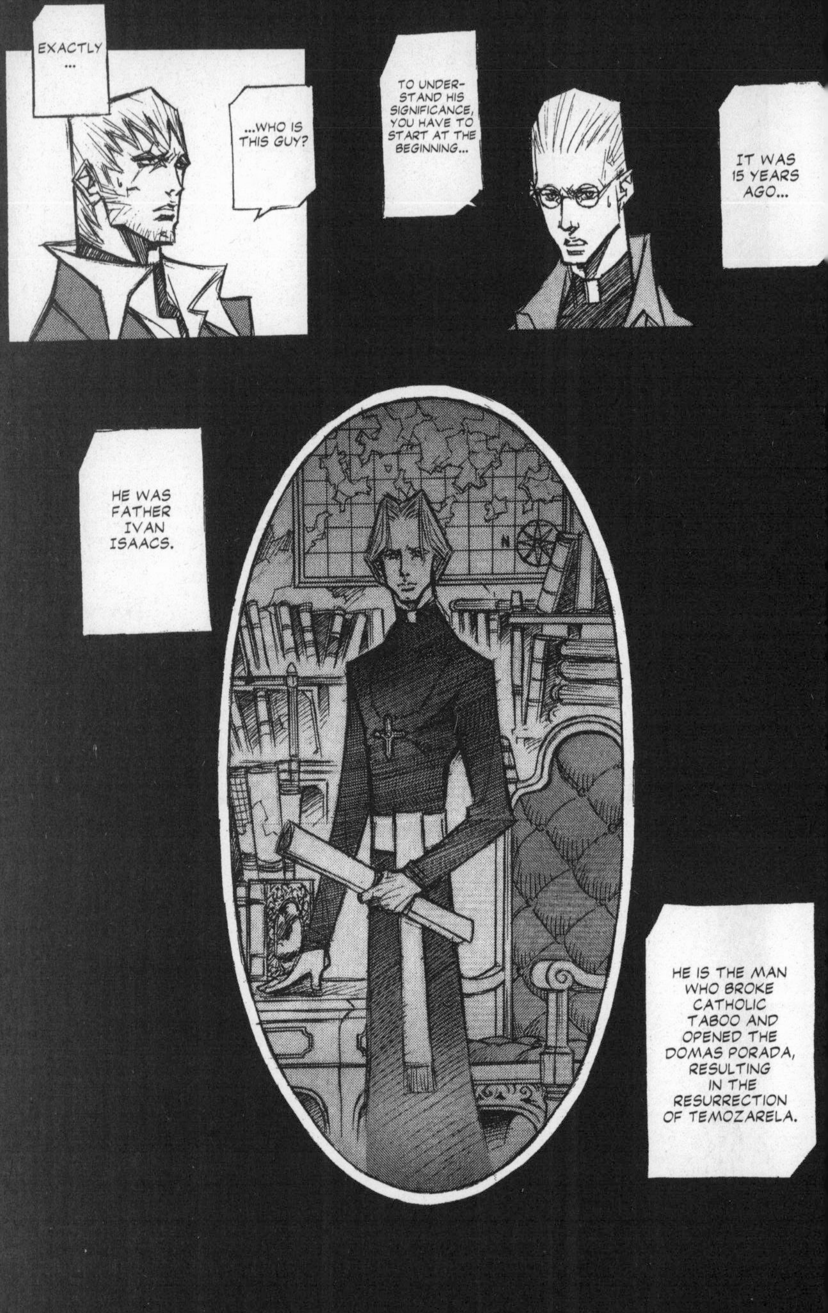
EXACTLY ...
...WHO IS THIS GUY?
TO UNDER-STAND HIS SIGNIFICANCE, YOU HAVE TO START AT THE BEGINNING...
IT WAS 15 YEARS AGO...
HE WAS FATHER IVAN ISAACS.
N
HE IS THE MAN WHO BROKE CATHOLIC TABOO AND OPENED THE DOMAS PORADA, RESULTING IN THE RESURRECTION OF TEMOZARELA.

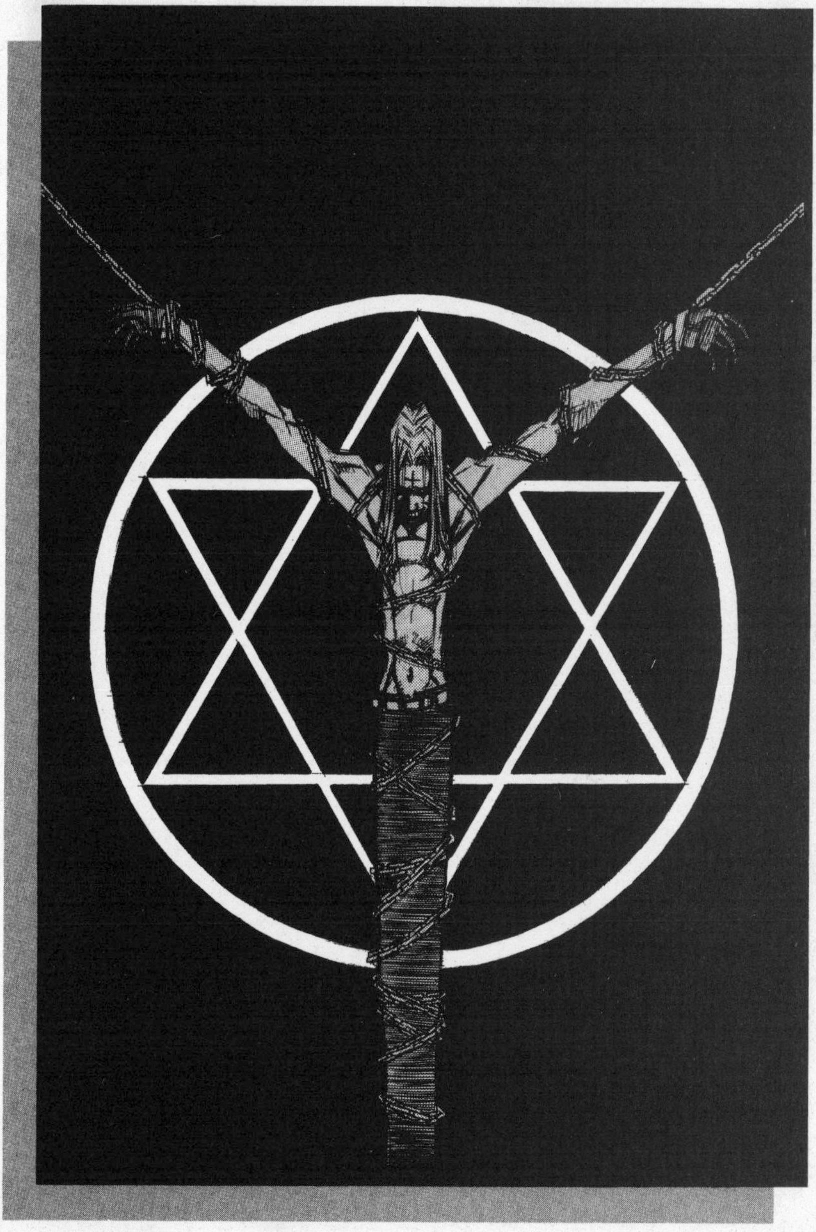

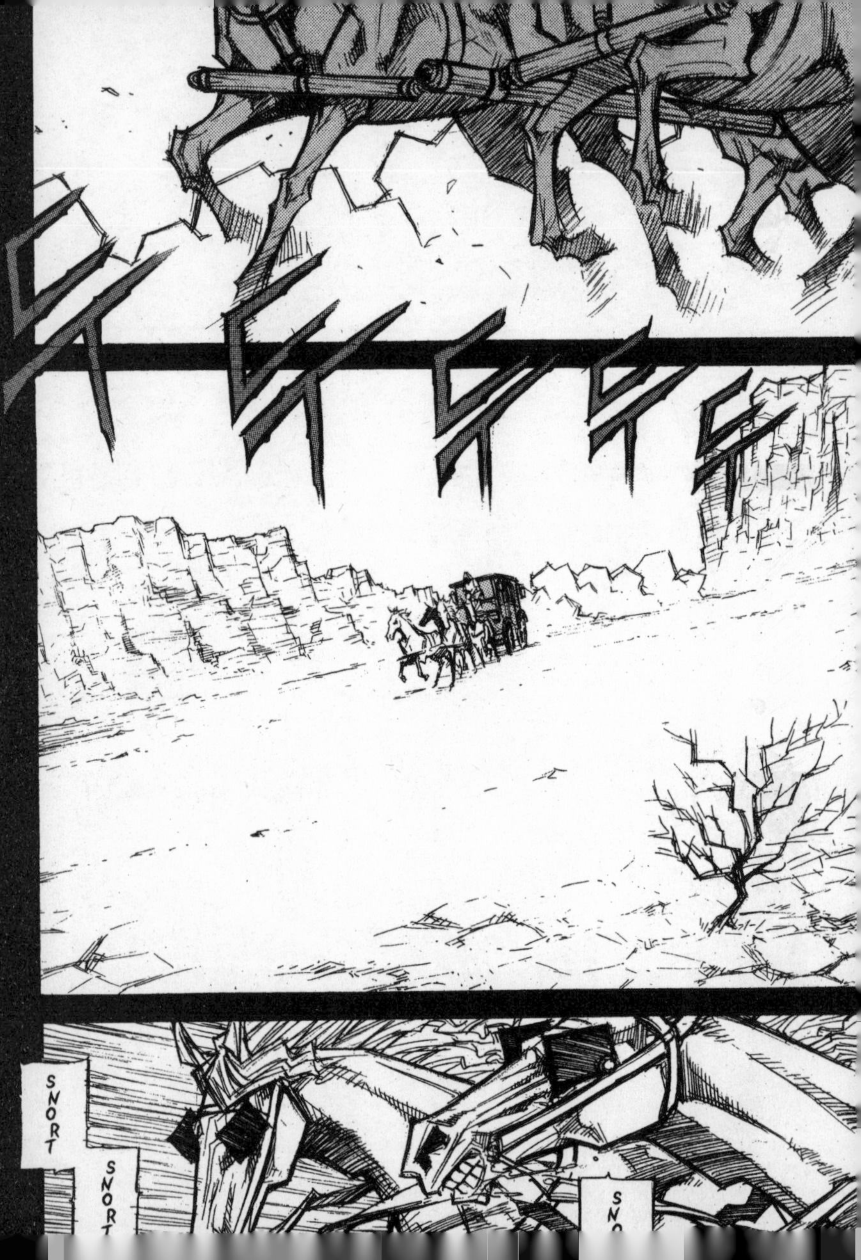
SNORT
SNORT
SNO

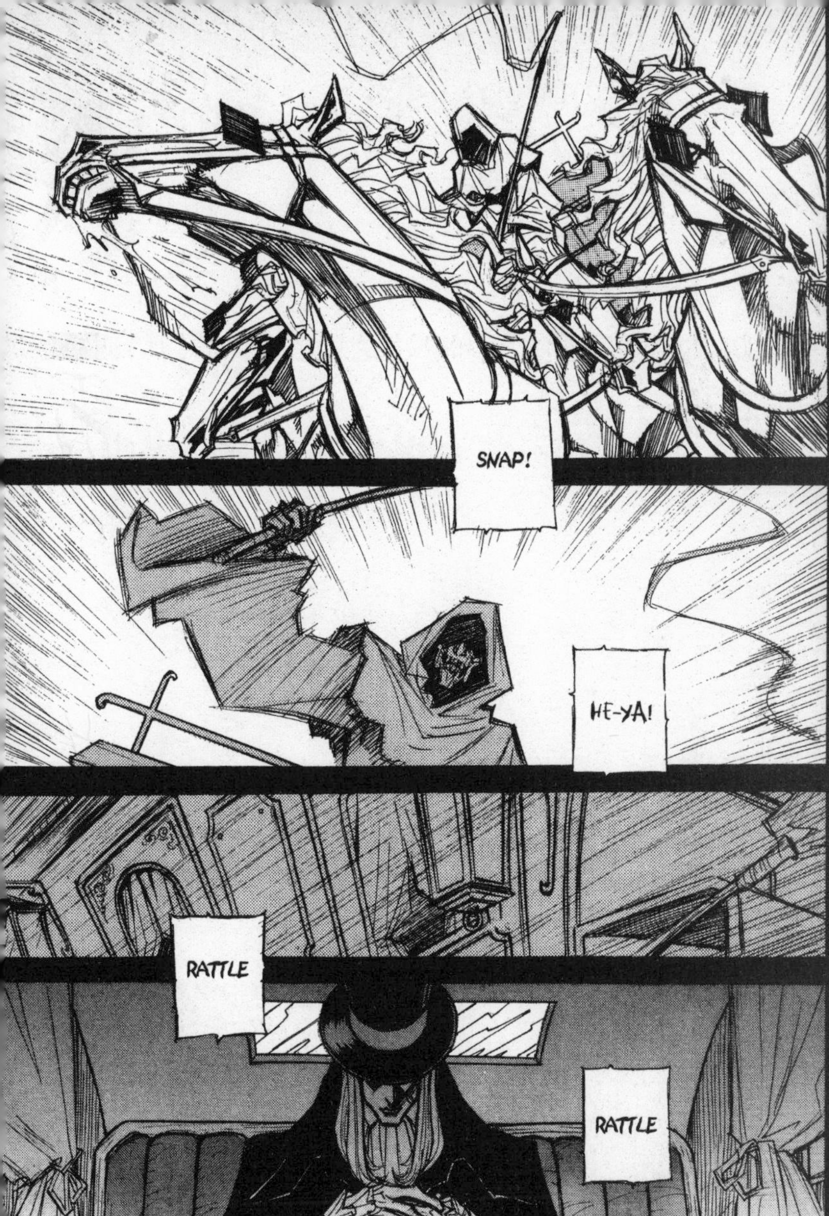
SNAP!
HE-YA!
RATTLE
RATTLE

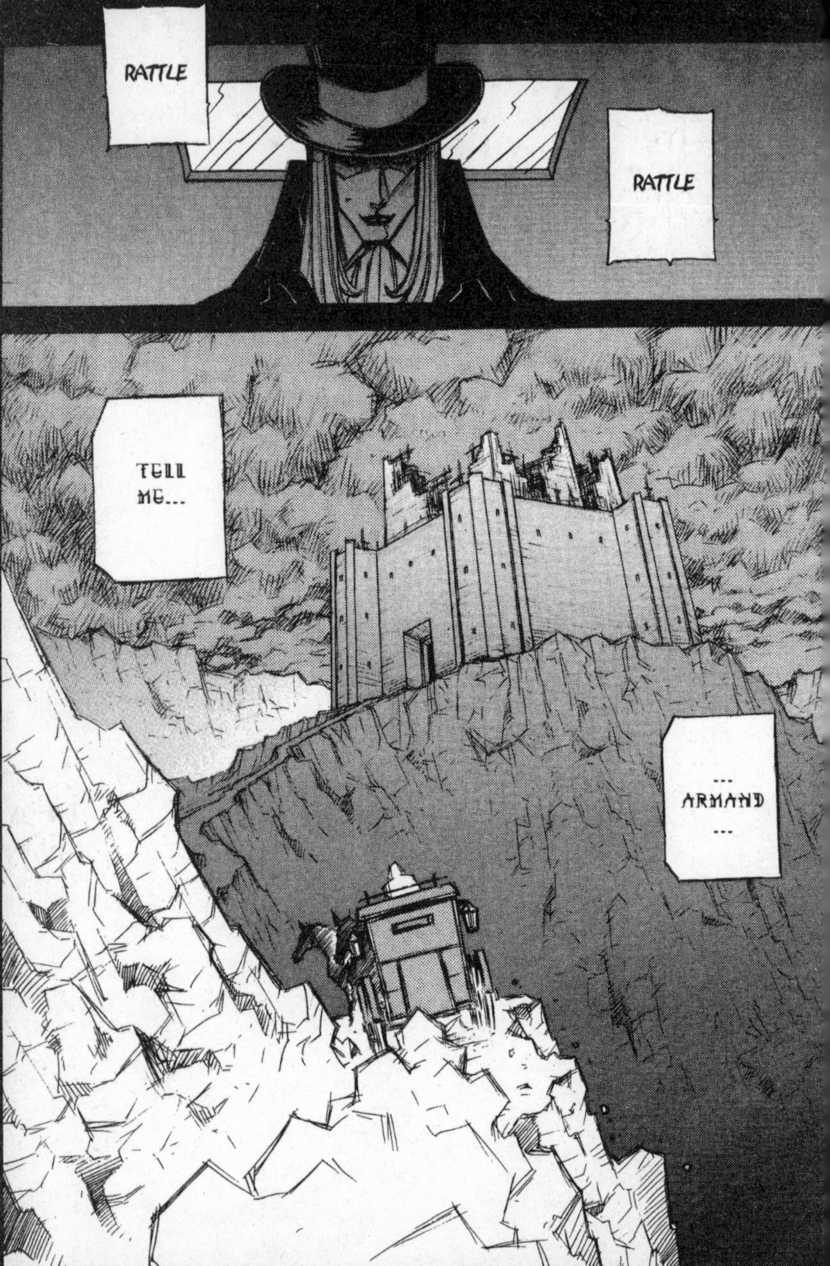
RATTLE
RATTLE
TELL ME...
...ARMAND...

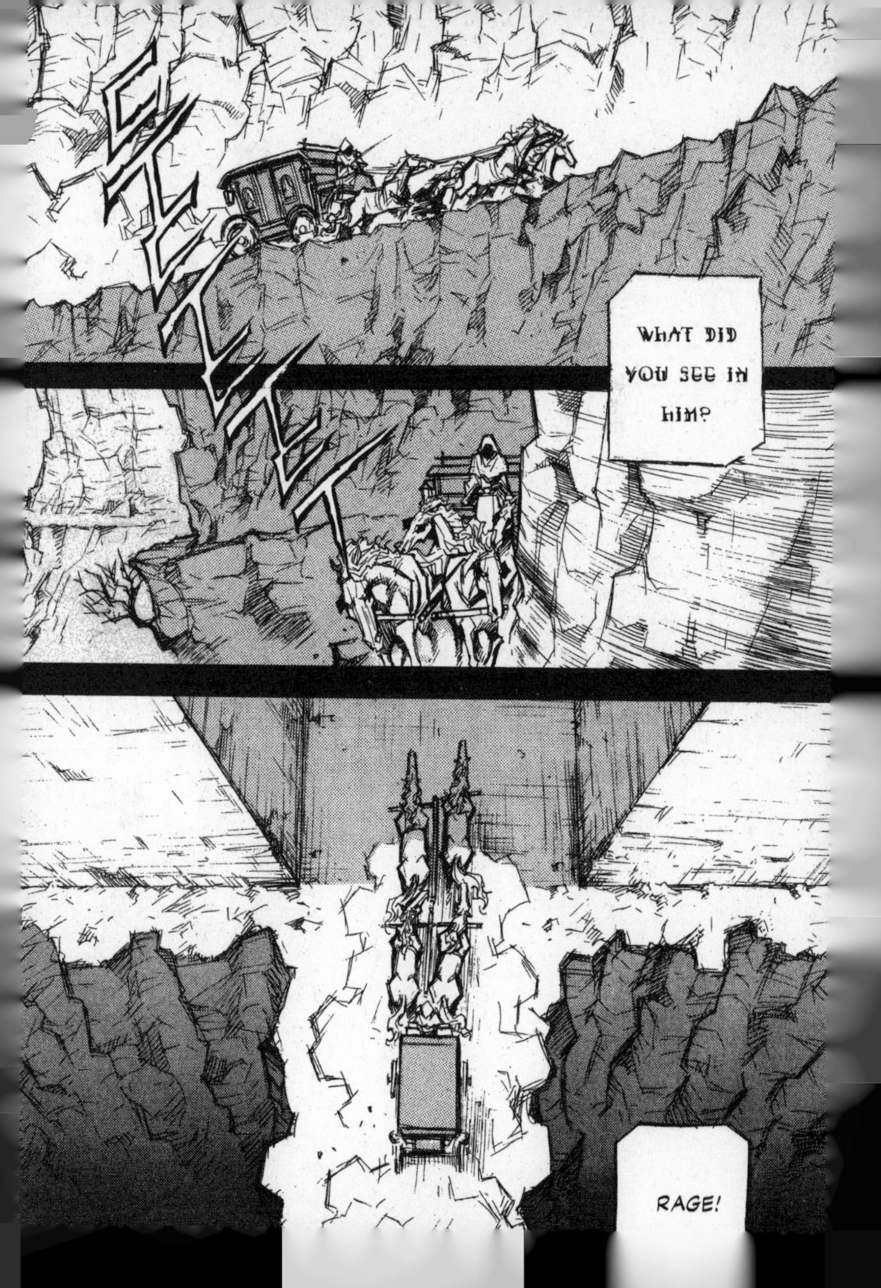
WHAT DID YOU SEE IN HIM?
RAGE!

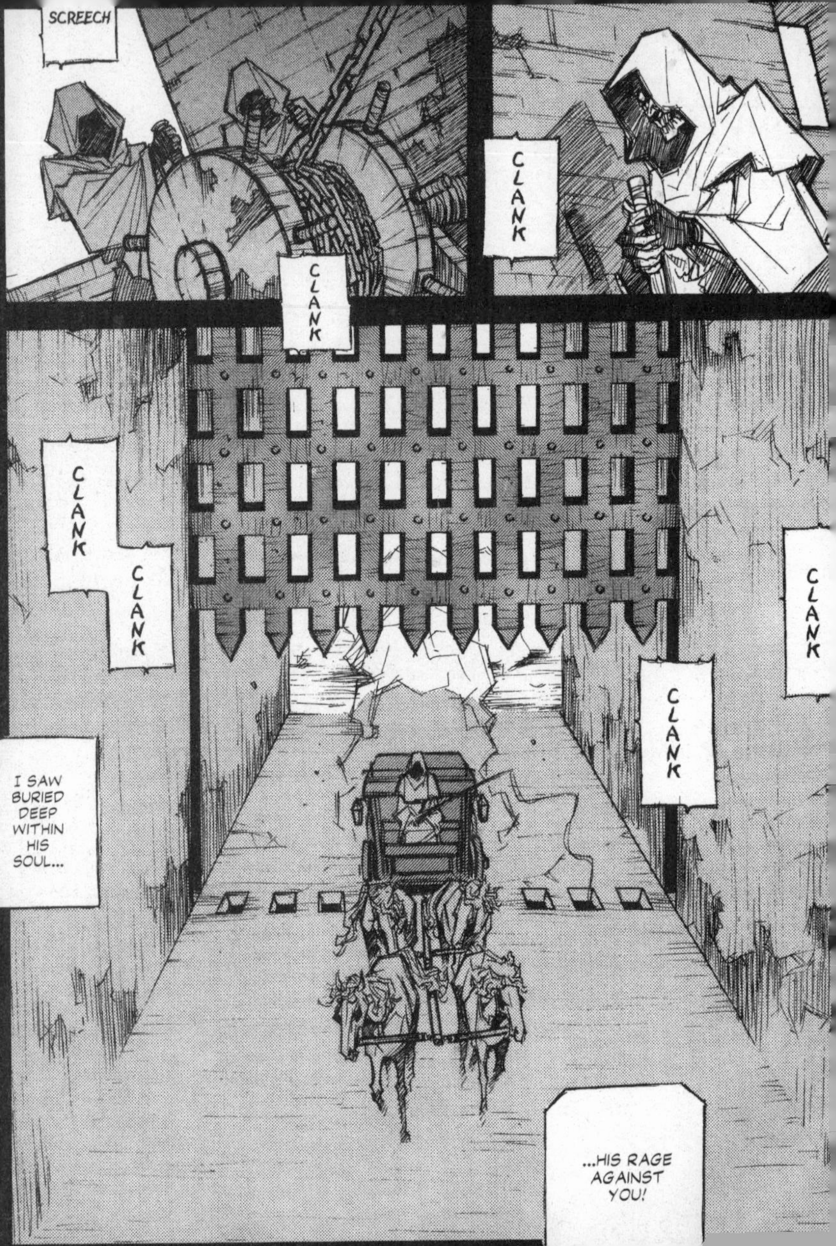
SCREECH
CLANK
CLANK
CLANK
CLANK
CLANK
CLANK
I SAW BURIED DEEP WITHIN HIS SOUL...
...HIS RAGE AGAINST YOU!

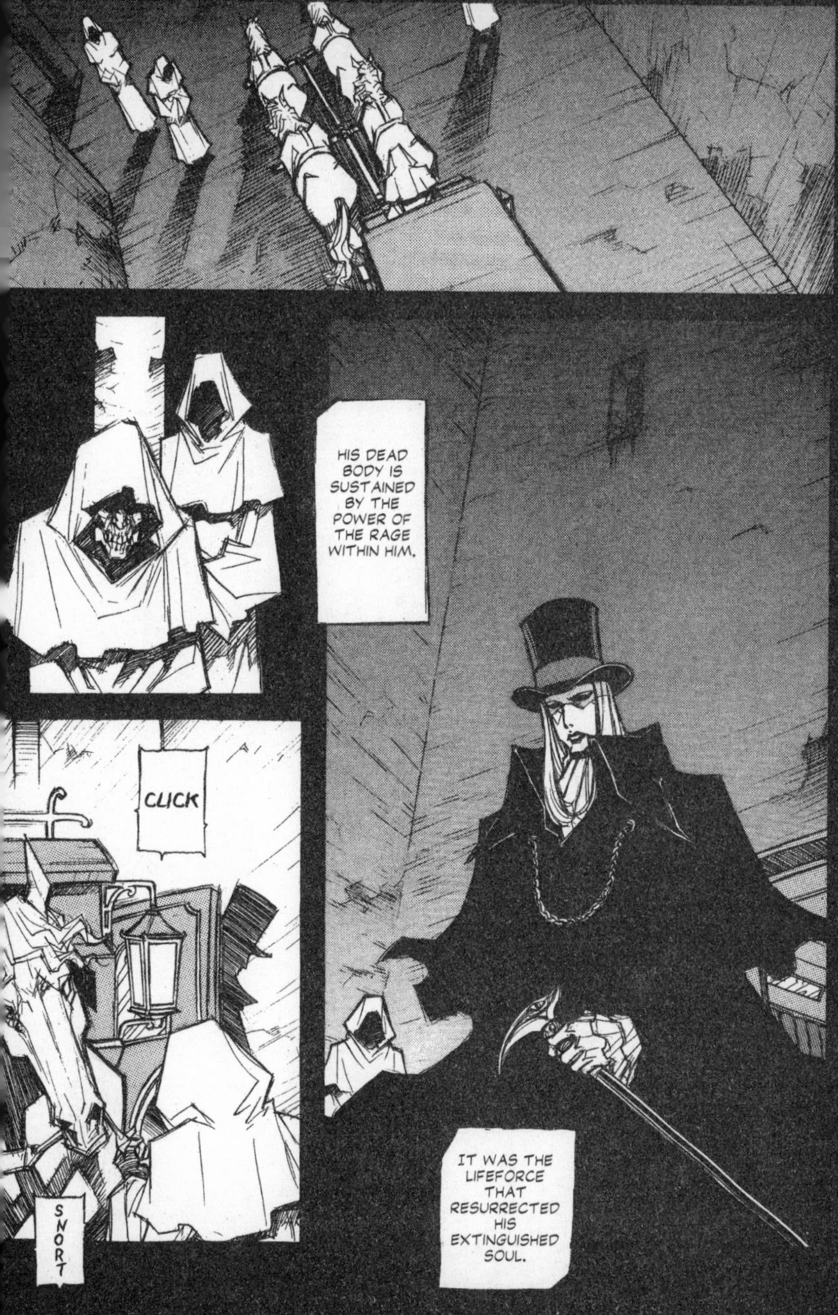
HIS DEAD BODY IS SUSTAINED BY THE POWER OF THE RAGE WITHIN HIM.
CLICK
SNORT
IT WAS THE LIFEFORCE THAT RESURRECTED HIS EXTINGUISHED SOUL.

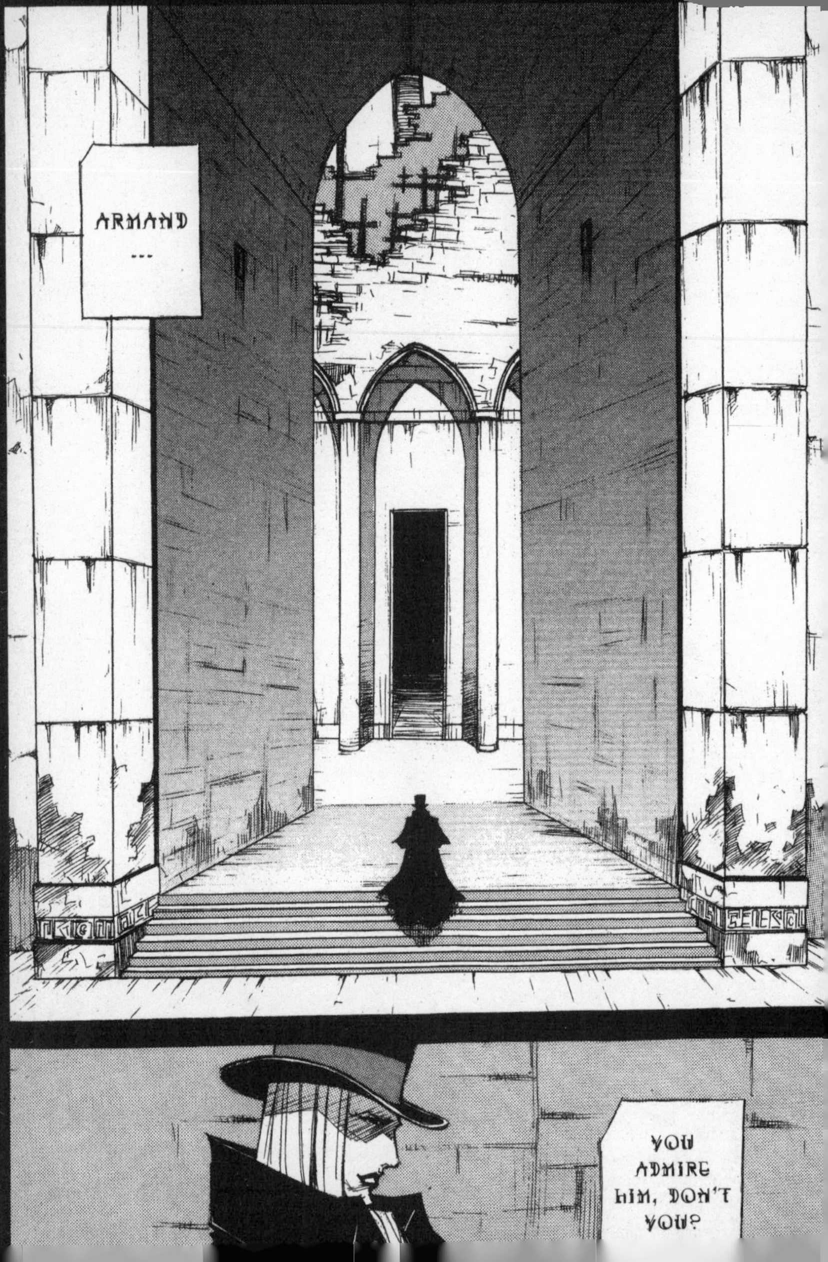
ARMAND ...
YOU ADMIRE HIM, DON'T YOU?

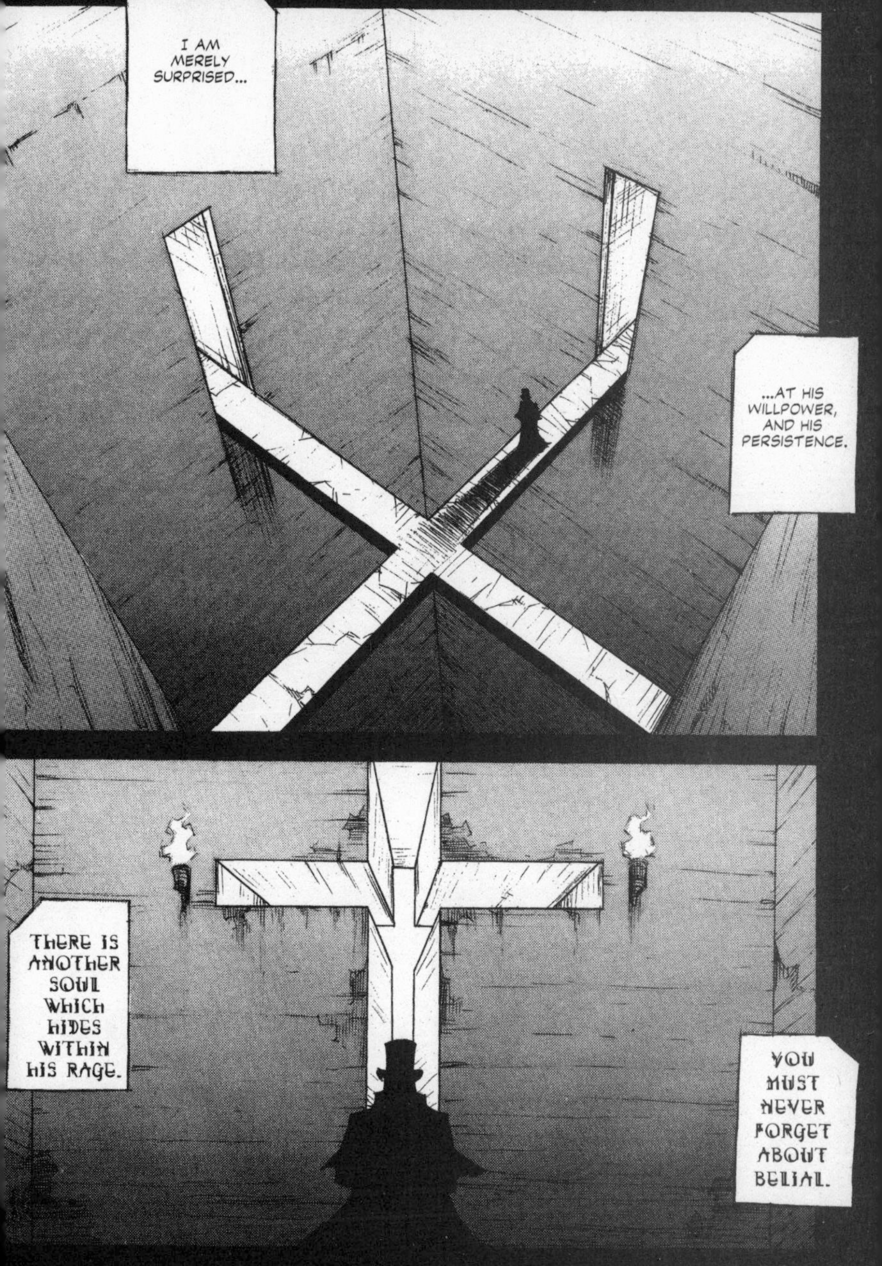

I AM MERELY SURPRISED...
...AT HIS WILLPOWER, AND HIS PERSISTENCE.
THERE IS ANOTHER SOUL WHICH HIDES WITHIN HIS RAGE.
YOU MUST NEVER FORGET ABOUT BELIAL.

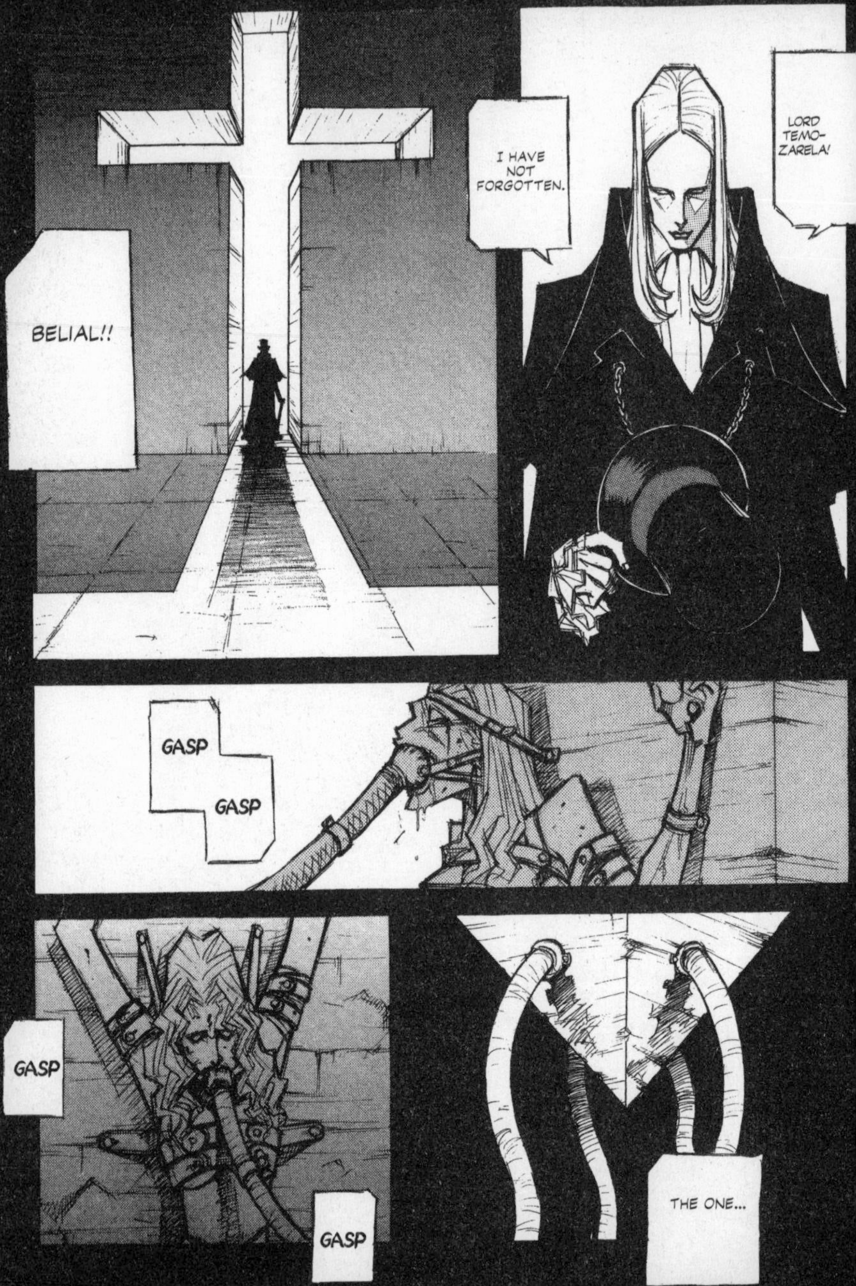
BELIAL!!
I HAVE NOT FORGOTTEN.
LORD TEMO-ZARELA!
GASP
GASP
GASP
GASP
THE ONE...

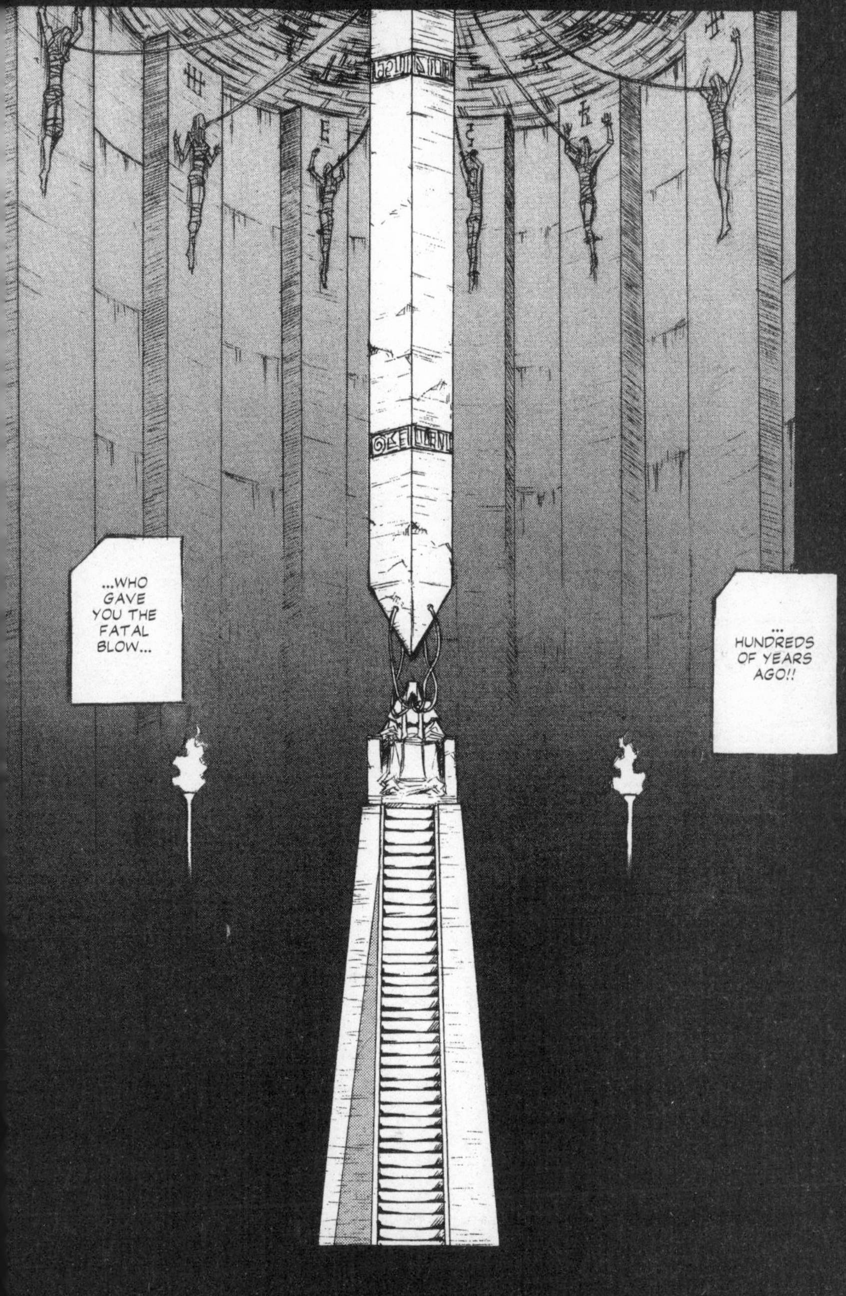
...WHO GAVE YOU THE FATAL BLOW...
...HUNDREDS OF YEARS AGO!!

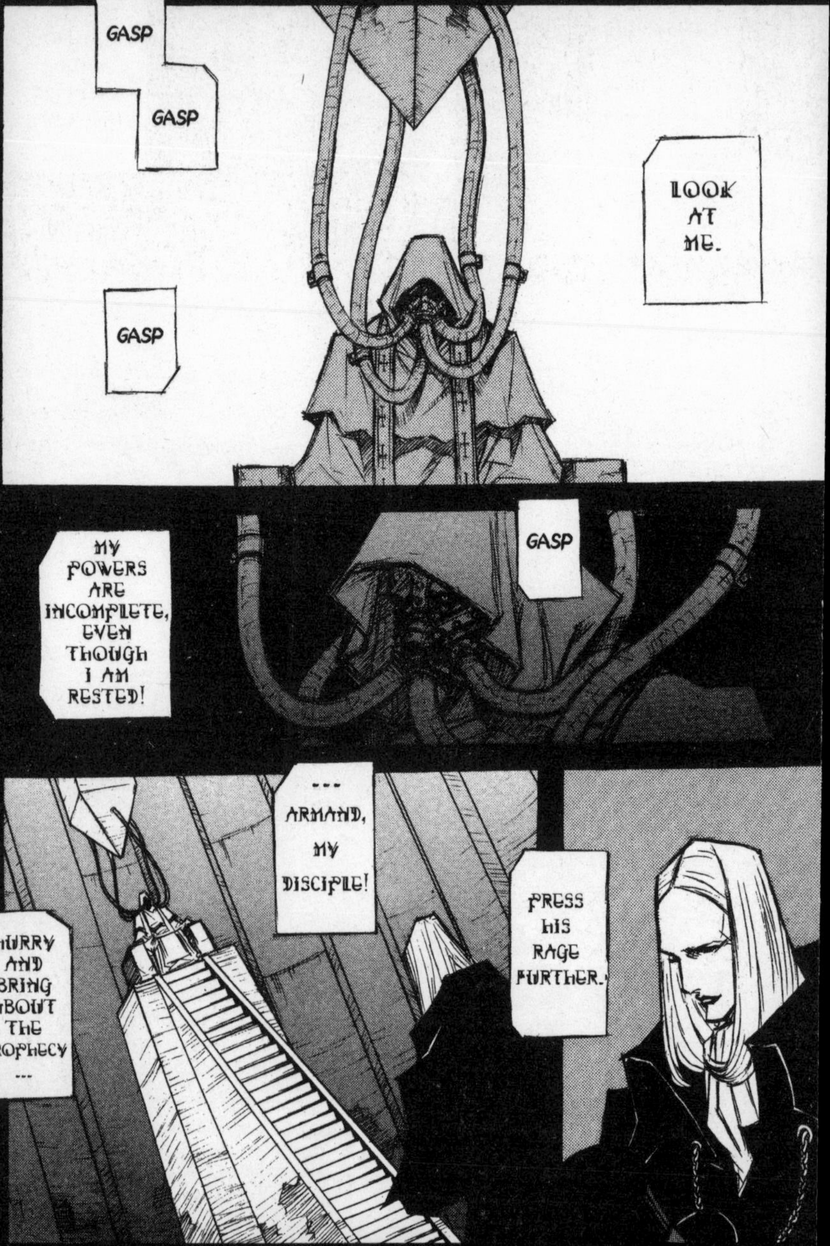
GASP
GASP
LOOK AT ME.
GASP
MY POWERS ARE INCOMPLETE, EVEN THOUGH I AM RESTED!
GASP
... ARMAND, MY DISCIPLE!
HURRY AND BRING ABOUT THE PROPHECY ...
PRESS HIS RAGE FURTHER.

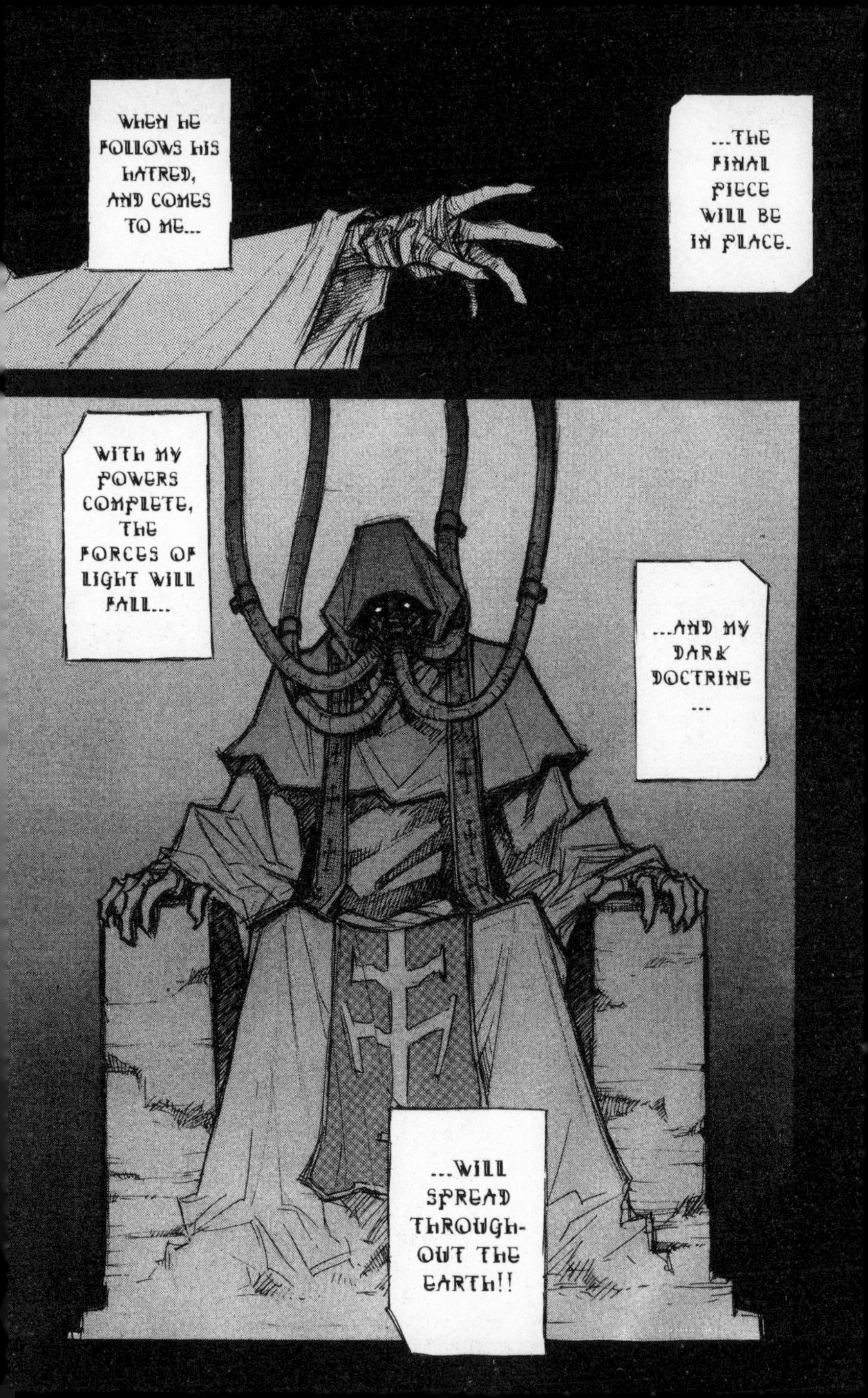
WHEN HE FOLLOWS HIS HATRED, AND COMES TO ME...
...THE FINAL PIECE WILL BE IN PLACE.
WITH MY POWERS COMPLETE, THE FORCES OF LIGHT WILL FALL...
...AND MY DARK DOCTRINE ...
...WILL SPREAD THROUGH-OUT THE EARTH!!

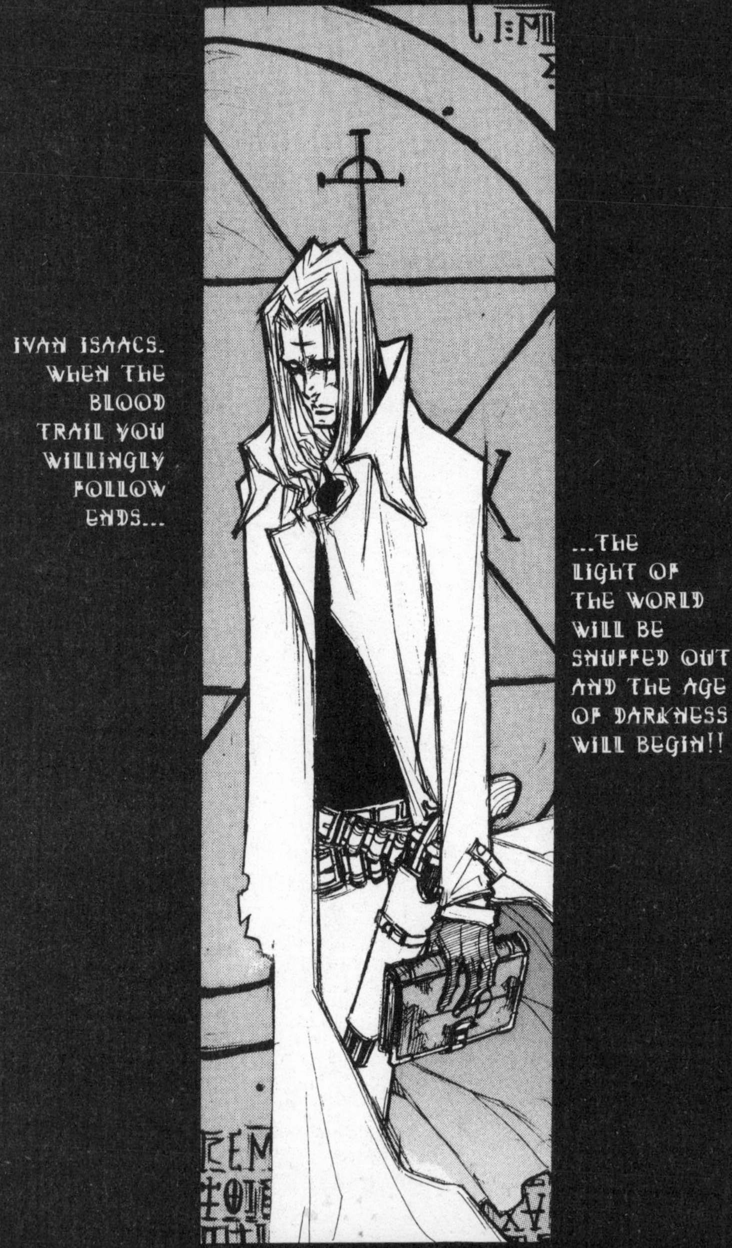
IVAN ISAACS. WHEN THE BLOOD TRAIL YOU WILLINGLY FOLLOW ENDS...
...THE LIGHT OF THE WORLD WILL BE SNUFFED OUT, AND THE AGE OF DARKNESS WILL BEGIN!!

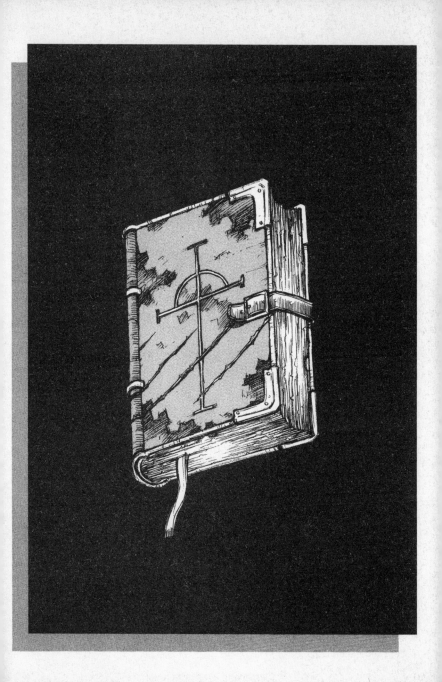

MANY BELIEVERS WANT NOTHING
MORE THAN TO WITNESS A MIRACLE
TO JUSTIFY THEIR FAITH IN GOD.

BUT THERE ARE OTHERS
WHO LOST THEIR FAITH AFTER
SEEING TOO MANY MIRACLES.

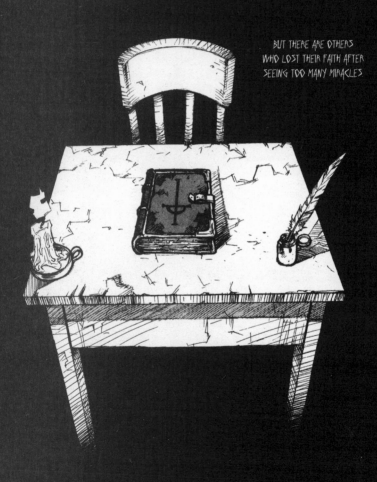

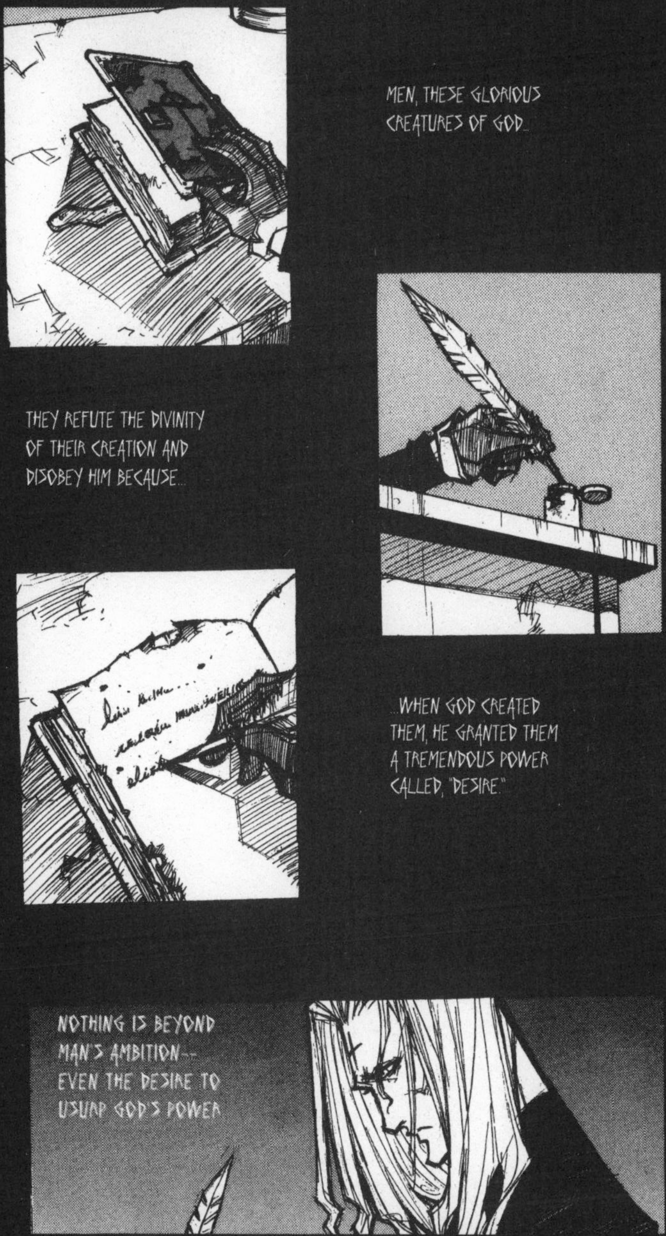
MEN, THESE GLORIOUS CREATURES OF GOD...
THEY REFUTE THE DIVINITY OF THEIR CREATION AND DISOBEY HIM BECAUSE...
...WHEN GOD CREATED THEM, HE GRANTED THEM A TREMENDOUS POWER CALLED, "DESIRE."
NOTHING IS BEYOND MAN'S AMBITION-- EVEN THE DESIRE TO USURP GOD'S POWER

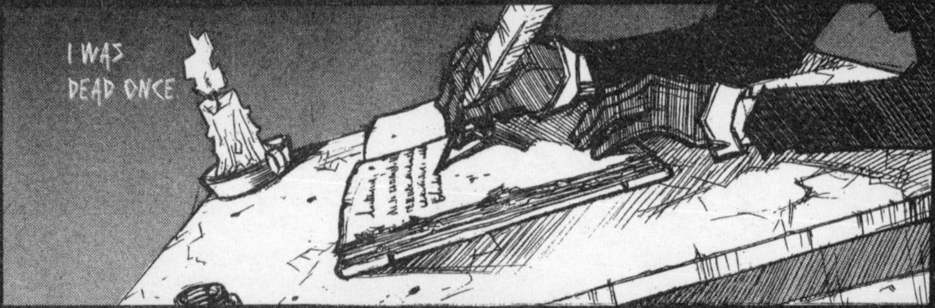
I WAS DEAD ONCE.

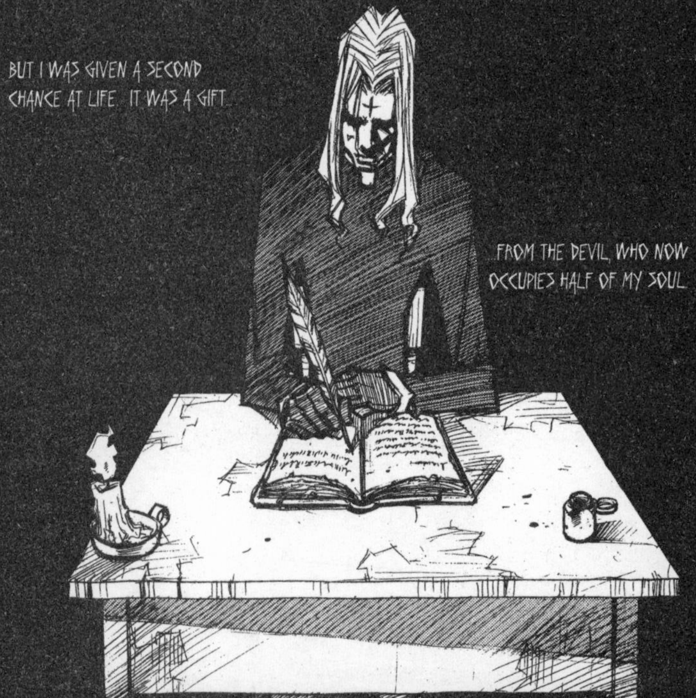
BUT I WAS GIVEN A SECOND CHANCE AT LIFE. IT WAS A GIFT...
...FROM THE DEVIL, WHO NOW OCCUPIES HALF OF MY SOUL.

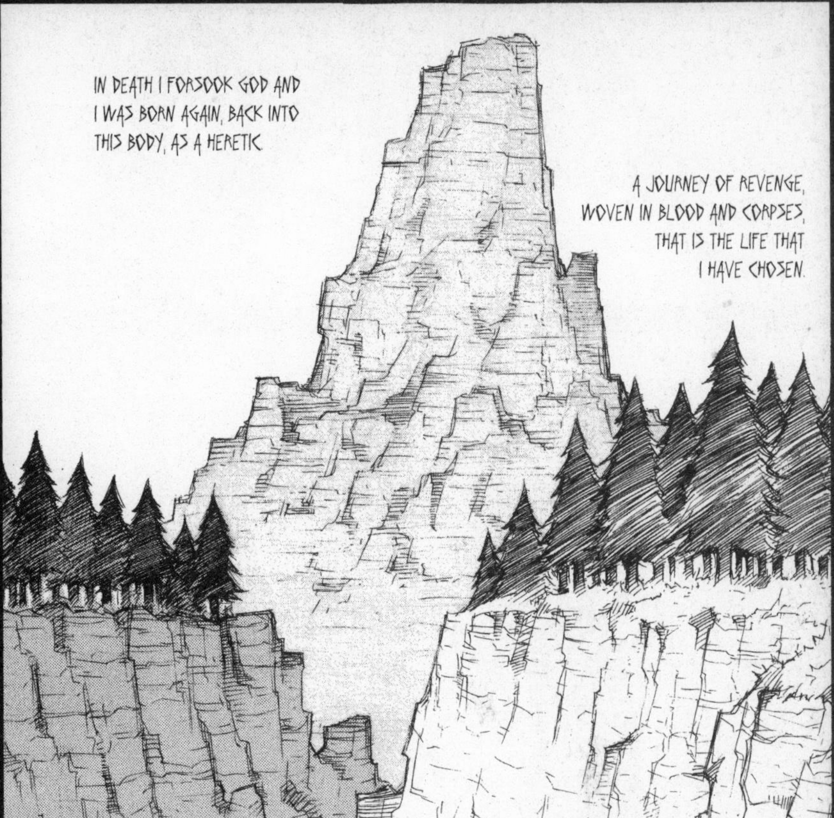
IN DEATH I FORSOOK GOD AND I WAS BORN AGAIN, BACK INTO THIS BODY, AS A HERETIC.
A JOURNEY OF REVENGE, WOVEN IN BLOOD AND CORPSES, THAT IS THE LIFE THAT I HAVE CHOSEN.
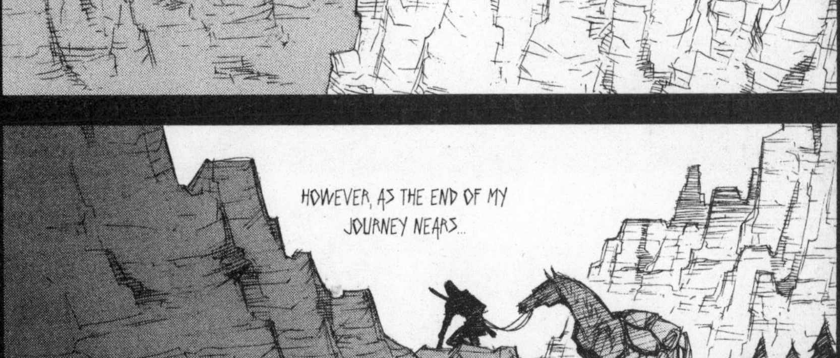
HOWEVER, AS THE END OF MY JOURNEY NEARS...

...EVEN MY TAINTED SOUL WILL BE UTTERLY DESTROYED.

THAT IS WHY, I AM LEAVING THESE WORDS.

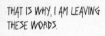

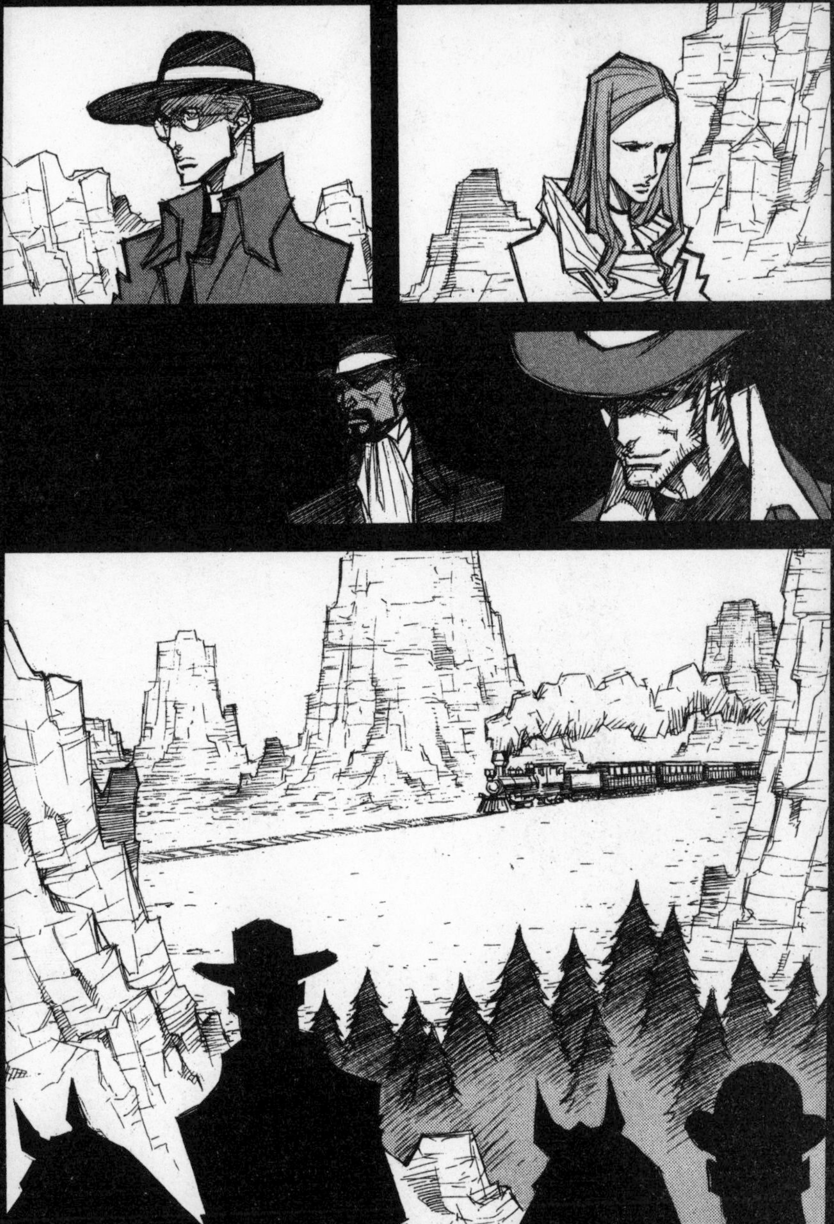

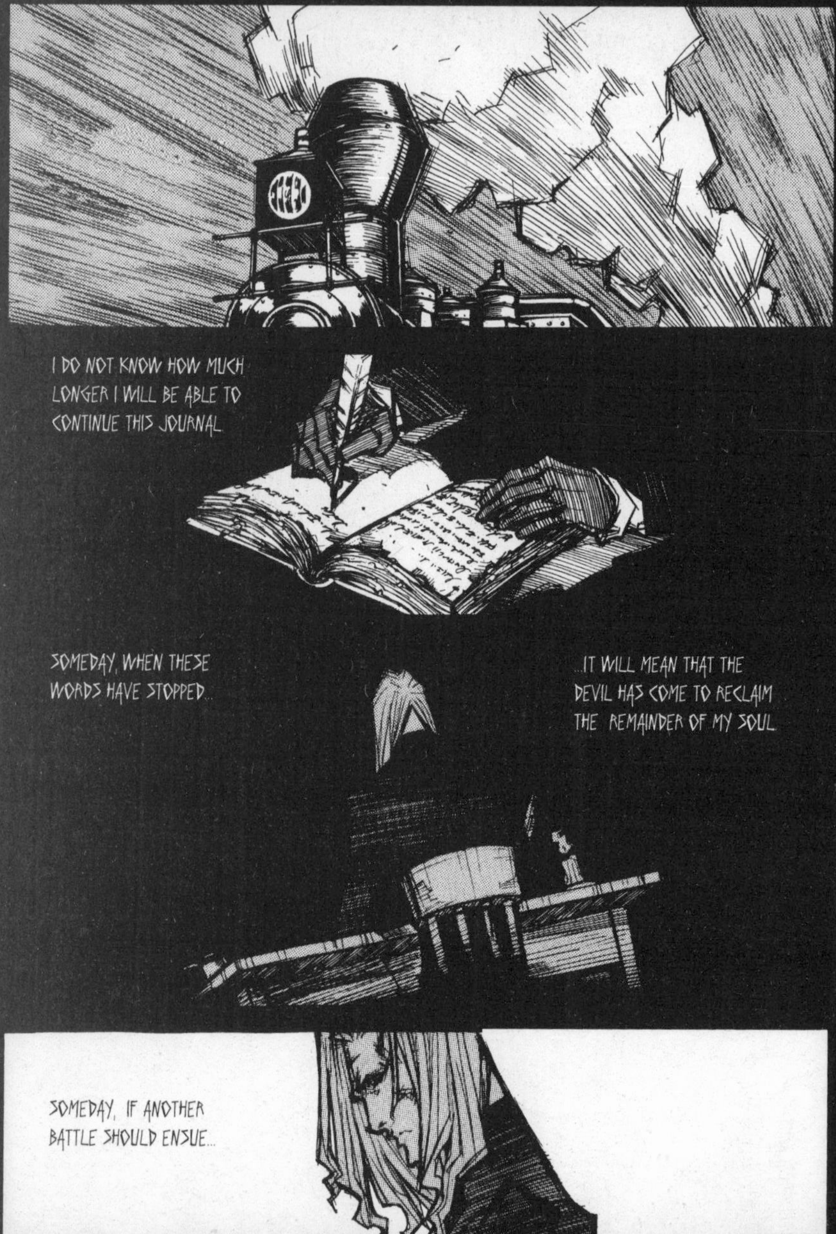
I DO NOT KNOW HOW MUCH LONGER I WILL BE ABLE TO CONTINUE THIS JOURNAL.
SOMEDAY, WHEN THESE WORDS HAVE STOPPED...
...IT WILL MEAN THAT THE DEVIL HAS COME TO RECLAIM THE REMAINDER OF MY SOUL.
SOMEDAY, IF ANOTHER BATTLE SHOULD ENSUE...

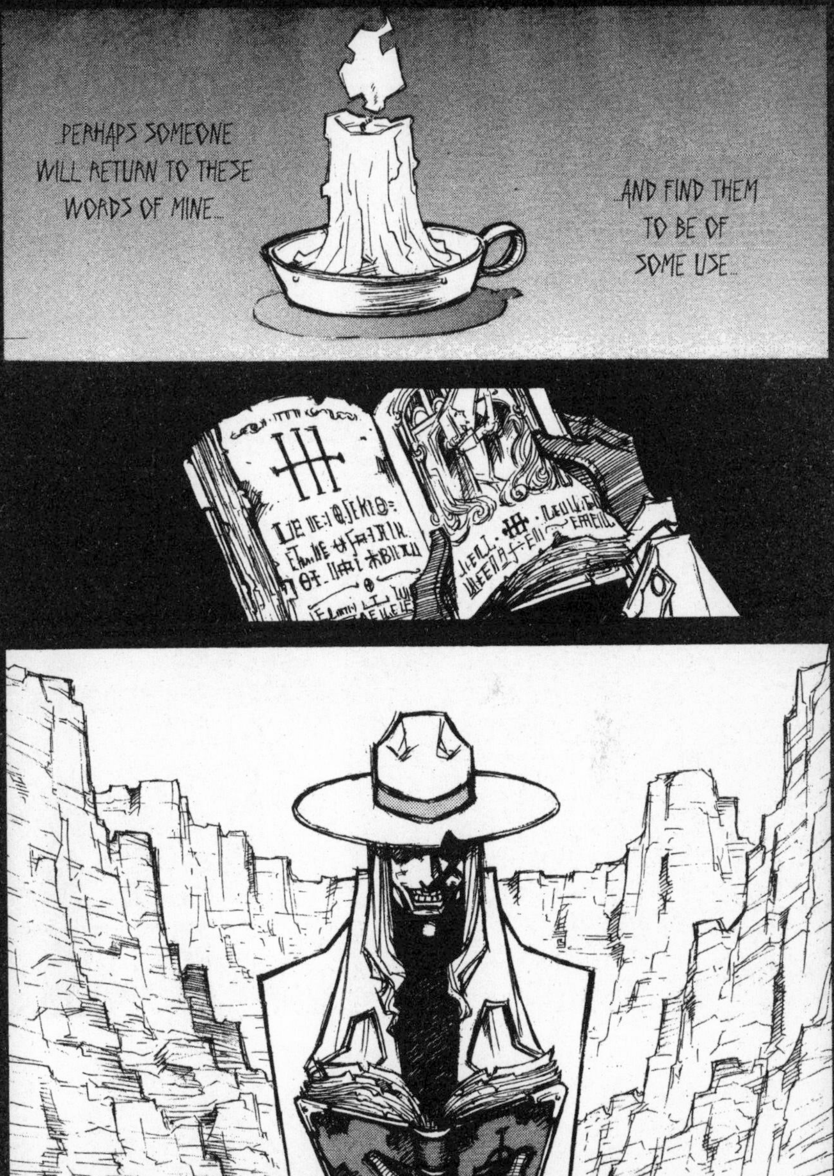
...PERHAPS SOMEONE WILL RETURN TO THESE WORDS OF MINE...
...AND FIND THEM TO BE OF SOME USE...

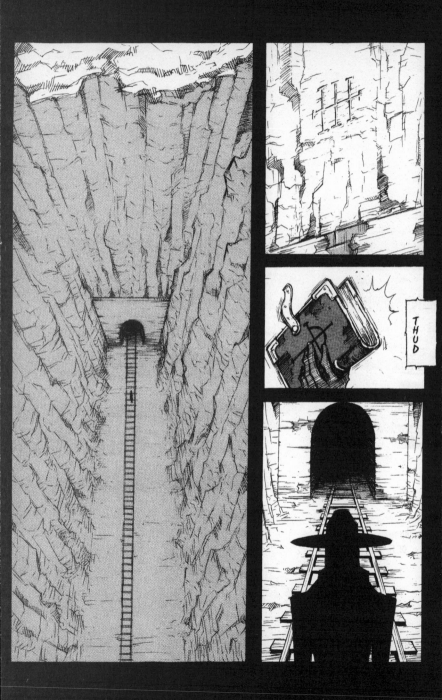

THUD

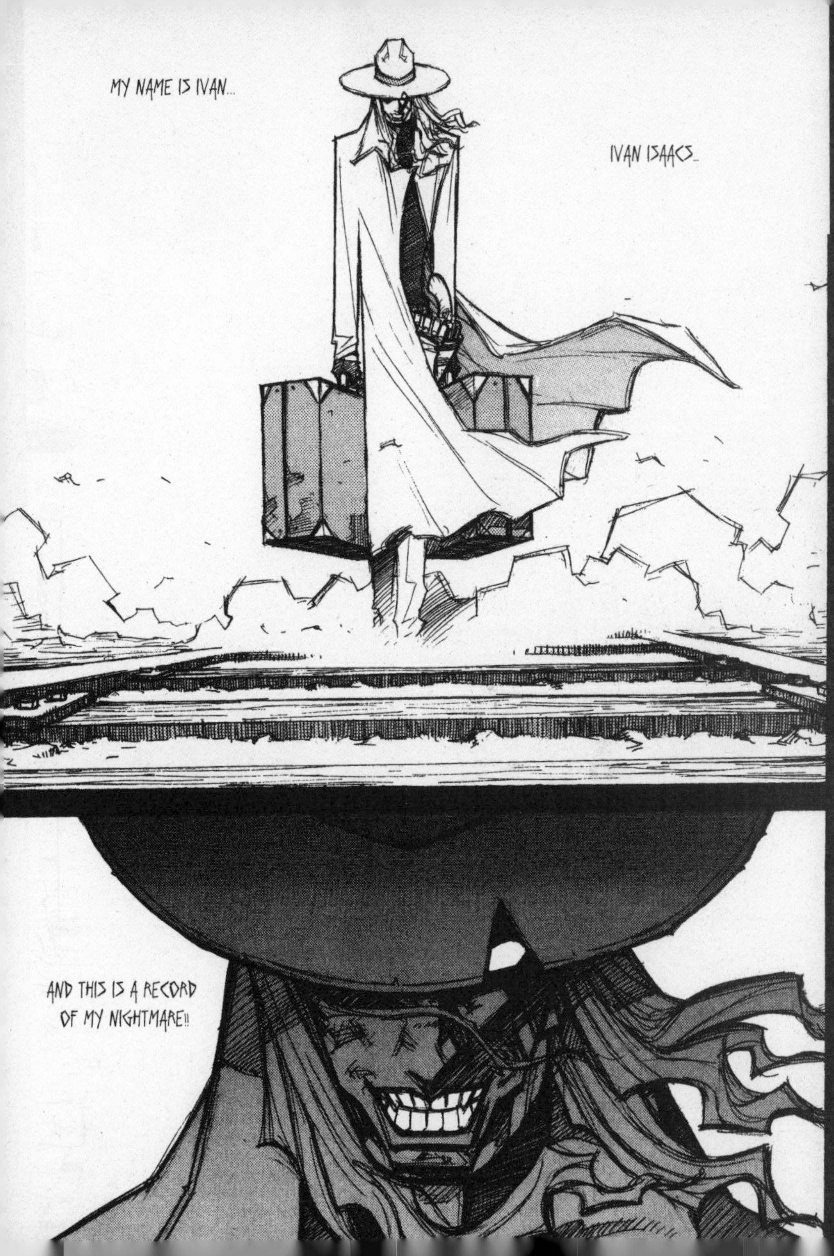
MY NAME IS IVAN...
IVAN ISAACS...
AND THIS IS A RECORD OF MY NIGHTMARE!!

✝ REQUIEM FOR THE DAMNED ✝

-END-

AND 300 YEARS LATER...

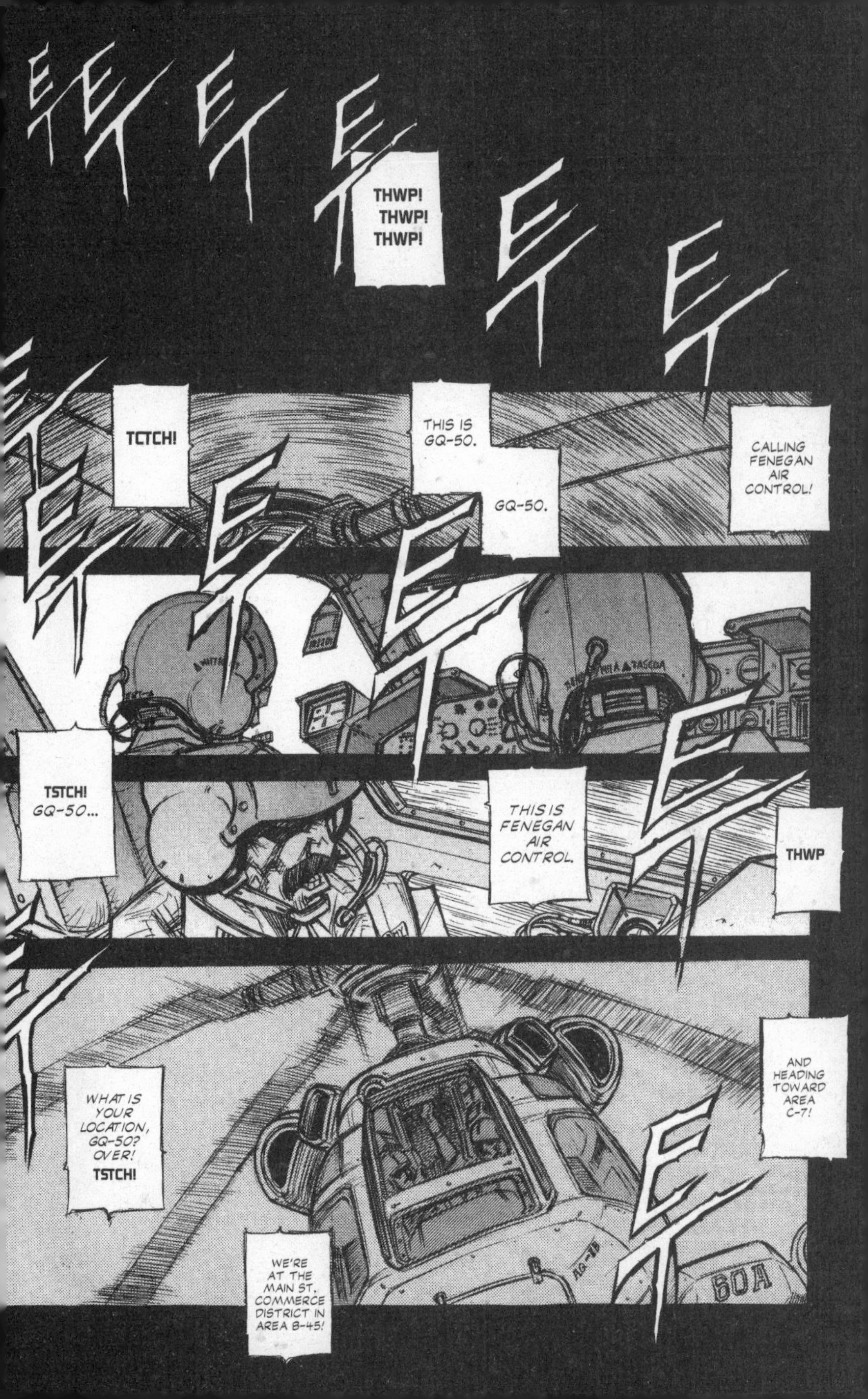
THWP! THWP! THWP!
TCTCH!
THIS IS GQ-50.
GQ-50.
CALLING FENEGAN AIR CONTROL!
TSTCH! GQ-50...
THIS IS FENEGAN AIR CONTROL.
THWP
WHAT IS YOUR LOCATION, GQ-50? OVER!
TSTCH!
WE'RE AT THE MAIN ST. COMMERCE DISTRICT IN AREA B-45!
AND HEADING TOWARD AREA C-7!

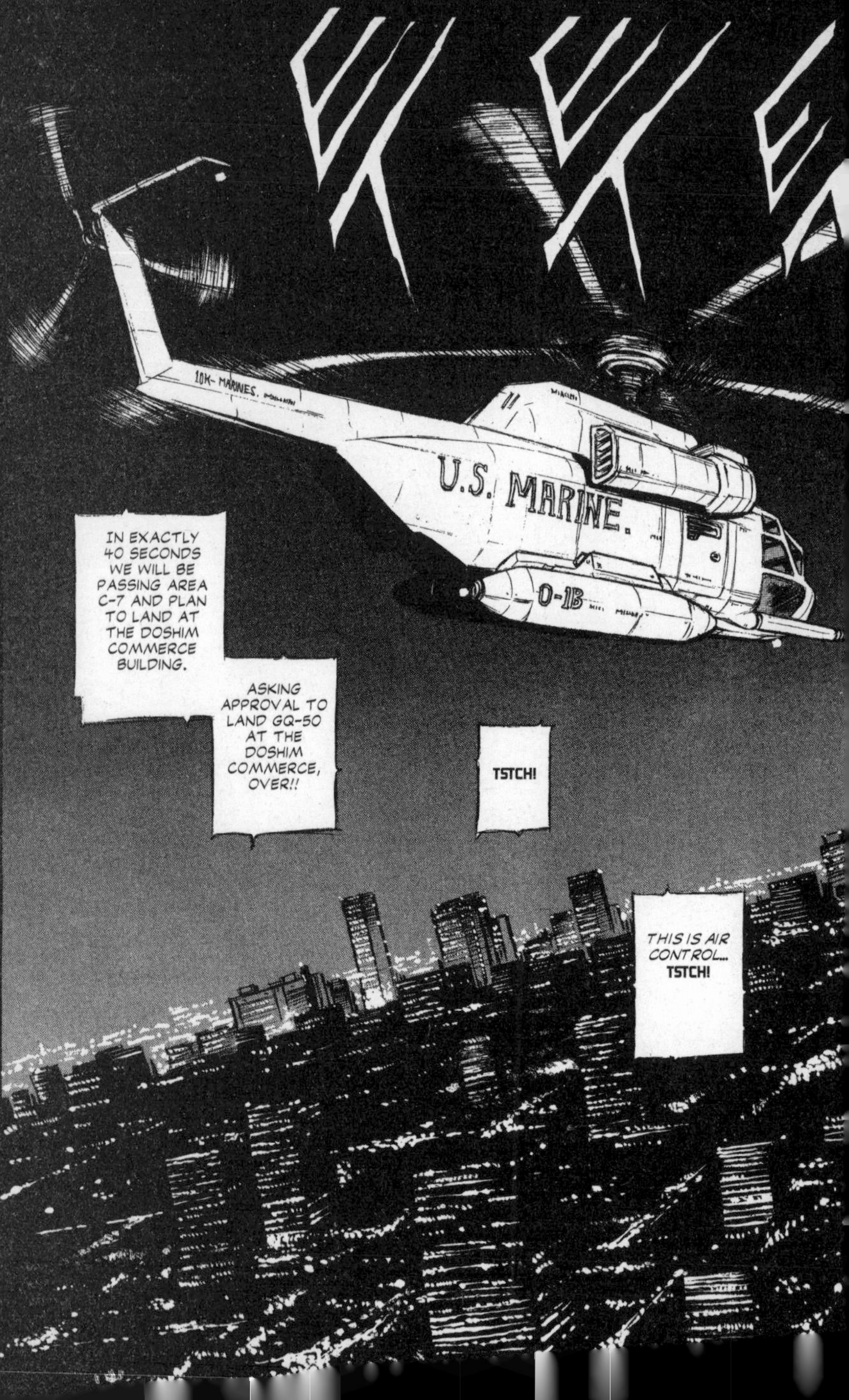
U.S. MARINE.
0-1B
IN EXACTLY 40 SECONDS WE WILL BE PASSING AREA C-7 AND PLAN TO LAND AT THE DOSHIM COMMERCE BUILDING.
ASKING APPROVAL TO LAND GQ-50 AT THE DOSHIM COMMERCE, OVER!!
TSTCH!
THIS IS AIR CONTROL... TSTCH!

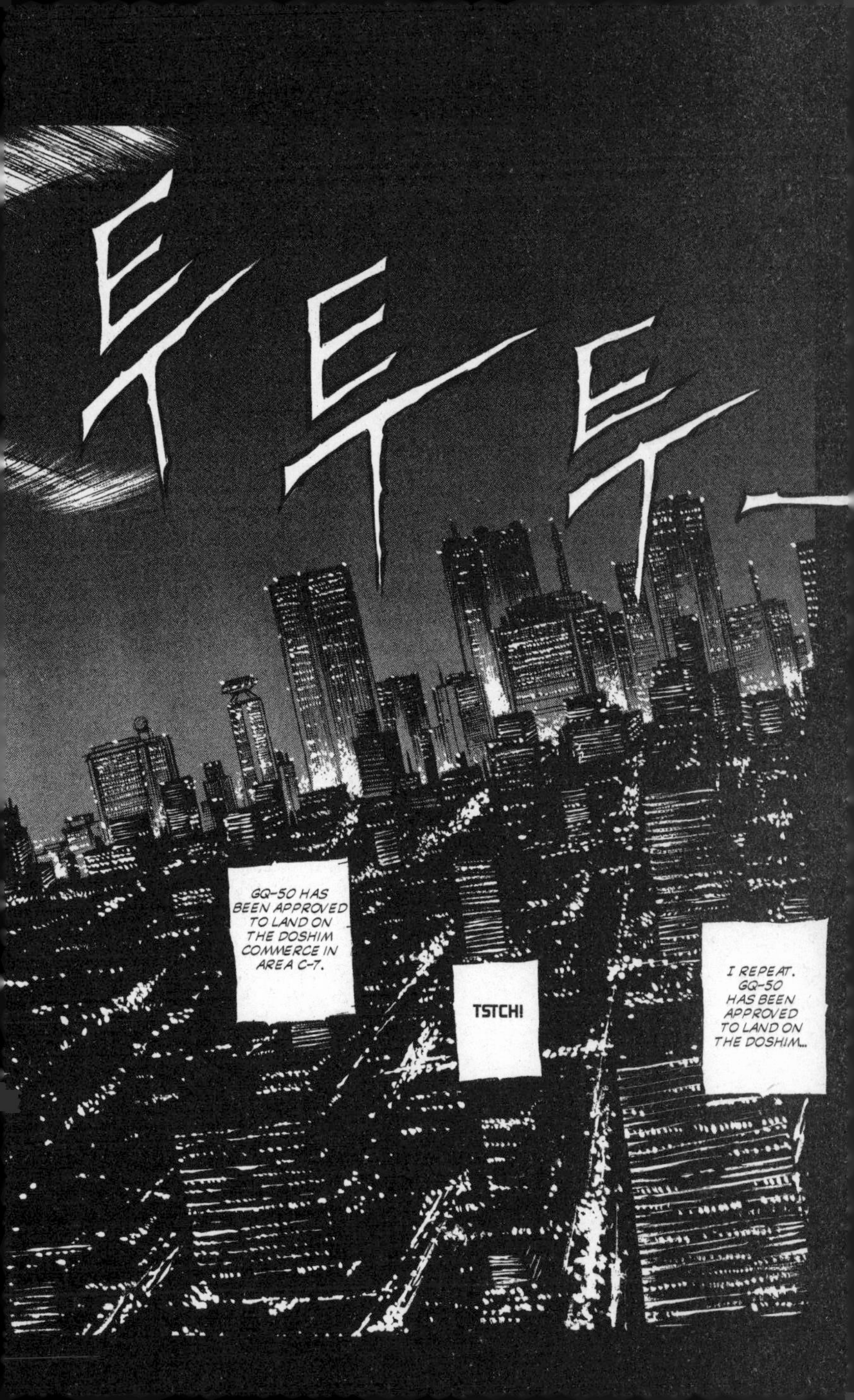
EEE
GQ-50 HAS BEEN APPROVED TO LAND ON THE DOSHIM COMMERCE IN AREA C-7.
TSTCH!
I REPEAT. GQ-50 HAS BEEN APPROVED TO LAND ON THE DOSHIM...

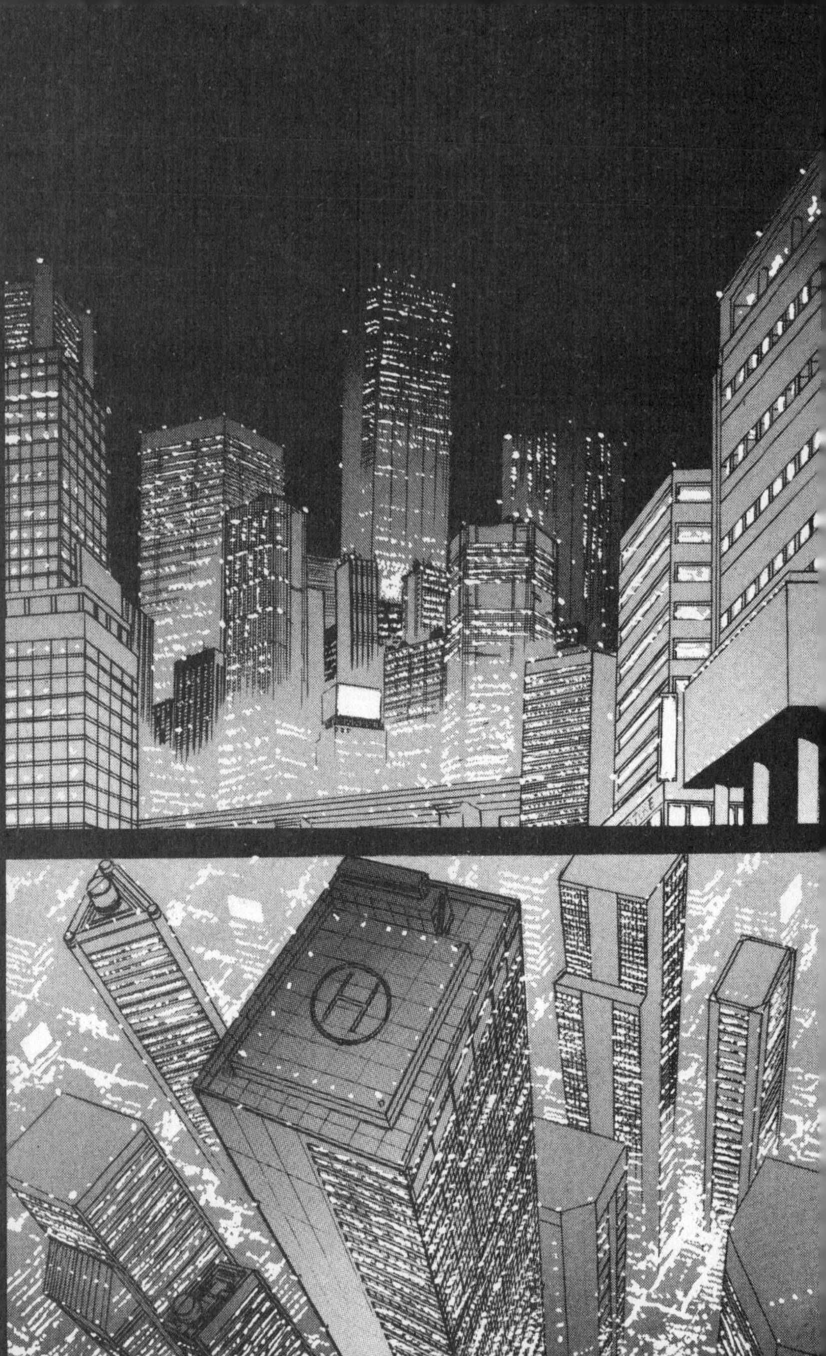

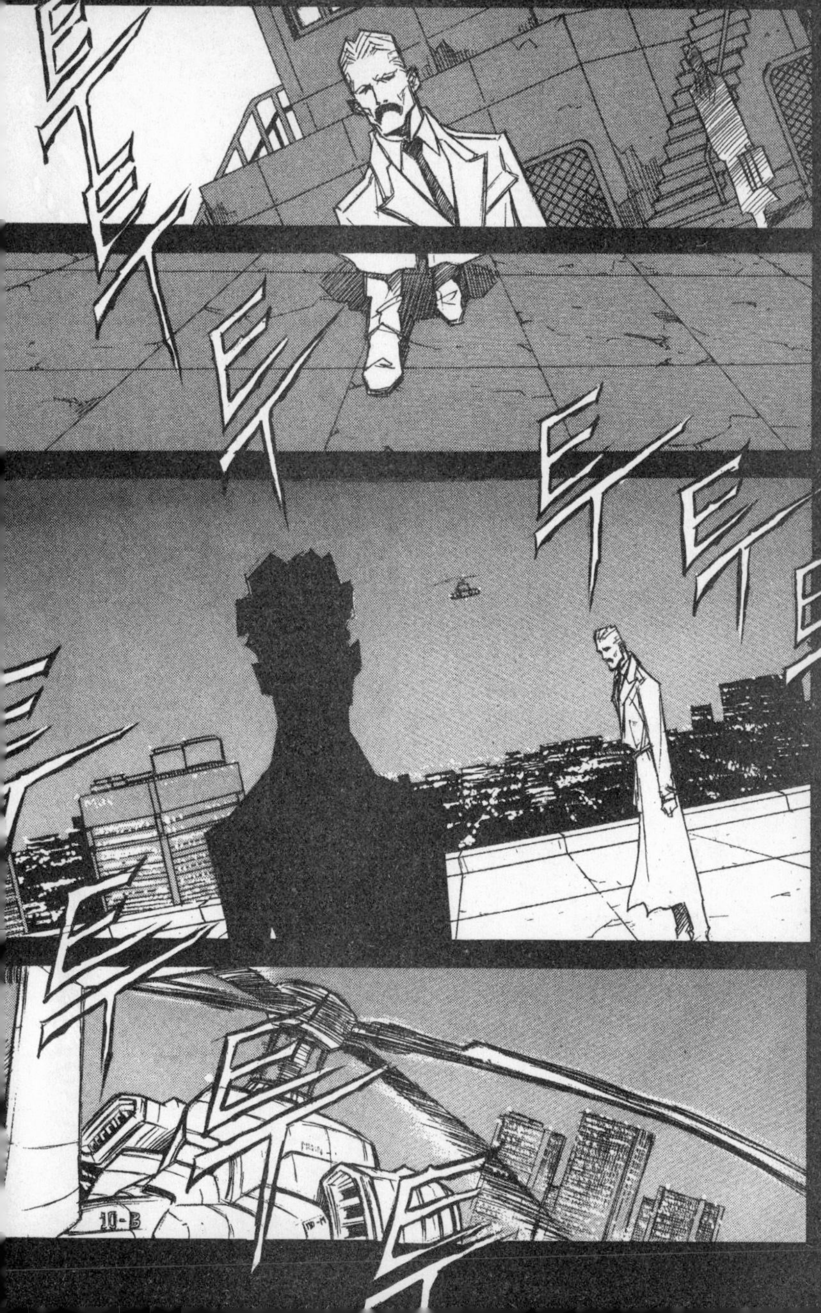
10-B

...IN RECENT YEARS HAVE BEEN CONSIDERED SENSATIONALIST. BUT IN THEIR DEFENSE...

...OUR UNDERSTANDING OF HELL IS IN A CONSTANT STATE OF REVISION THROUGHOUT HISTORY, REFLECTING THE SENTIMENTS OF THE TIME.

THAT IS TO SAY THAT THE CHURCH ITSELF DEFINED HELL IN SUCH A WAY AS TO BEST SERVE THE CHURCH'S INTERESTS.

PERHAPS THE BEST EXAMPLE OF HELL'S CHANGING NATURE CAN BE SEEN IN THE MIDDLE AGES.

IT'S WELL DOCUMENTED THAT TRIALS OF CULTS WERE RAMPANT IN EUROPE, SHOWING THE CHURCH'S FEAR OF A TANGIBLE EVIL.

AT THIS TIME, THE DESCRIPTION OF HELL BECAME MORE VISCERAL AND EXPLICIT IN NATURE...

SHOWING A PROPENSITY FOR CRUELTY AND INDECENCY.

SAINT SEBASTIAN ROYAL CATHOLIC THEOLOGICAL

IRONICALLY, THESE DEPICTIONS OF HELL WERE MIRRORED BY THE VERY CHURCH ITSELF DURING THE INQUISITION.

HELL WAS NO LONGER AN ABSTRACT BUT A PHYSICAL FORCE THAT COULD ATTACK US HERE ON EARTH...

...AND THE CHURCH FELT COMPELLED TO RESPOND IN KIND.

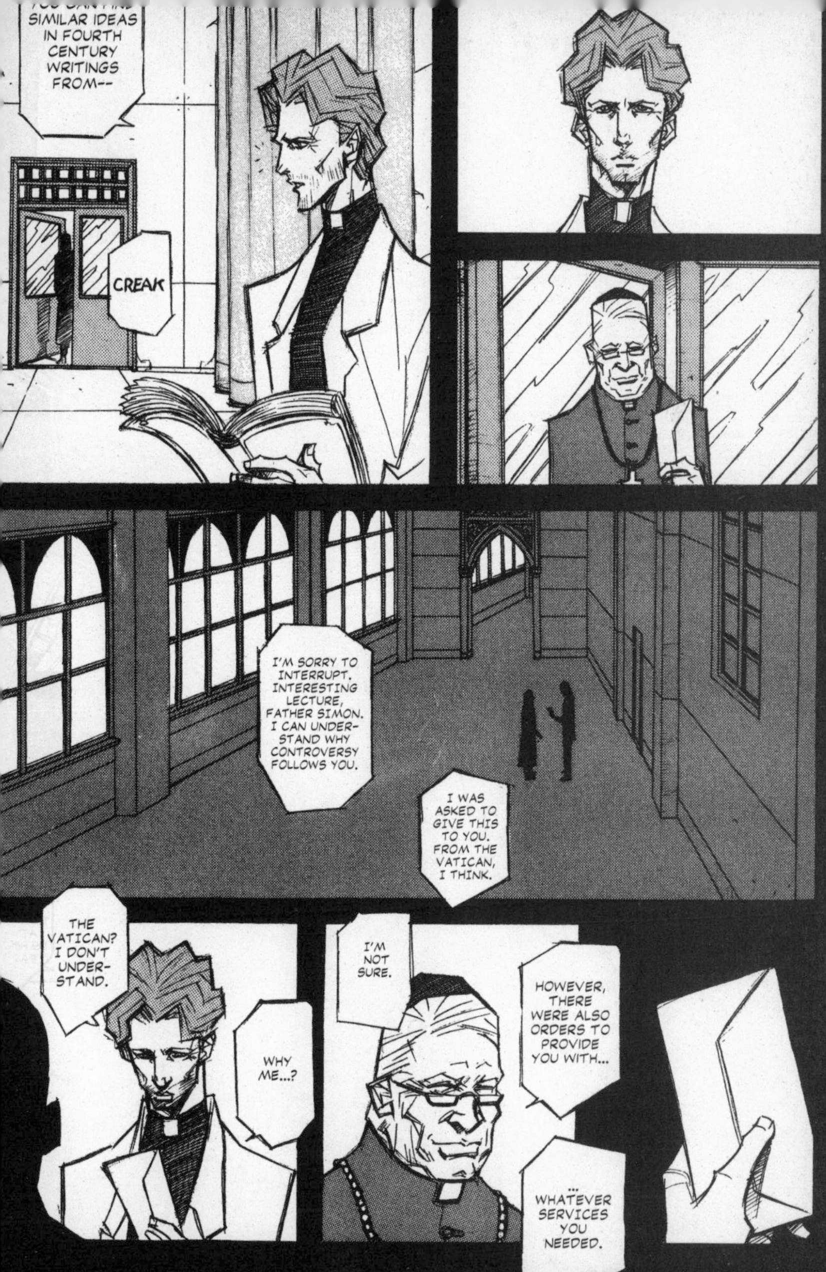
SIMILAR IDEAS IN FOURTH CENTURY WRITINGS FROM--
CREAK
I'M SORRY TO INTERRUPT. INTERESTING LECTURE, FATHER SIMON. I CAN UNDERSTAND WHY CONTROVERSY FOLLOWS YOU.
I WAS ASKED TO GIVE THIS TO YOU. FROM THE VATICAN, I THINK.
THE VATICAN? I DON'T UNDERSTAND.
WHY ME...?
I'M NOT SURE.
HOWEVER, THERE WERE ALSO ORDERS TO PROVIDE YOU WITH...
...WHATEVER SERVICES YOU NEEDED.

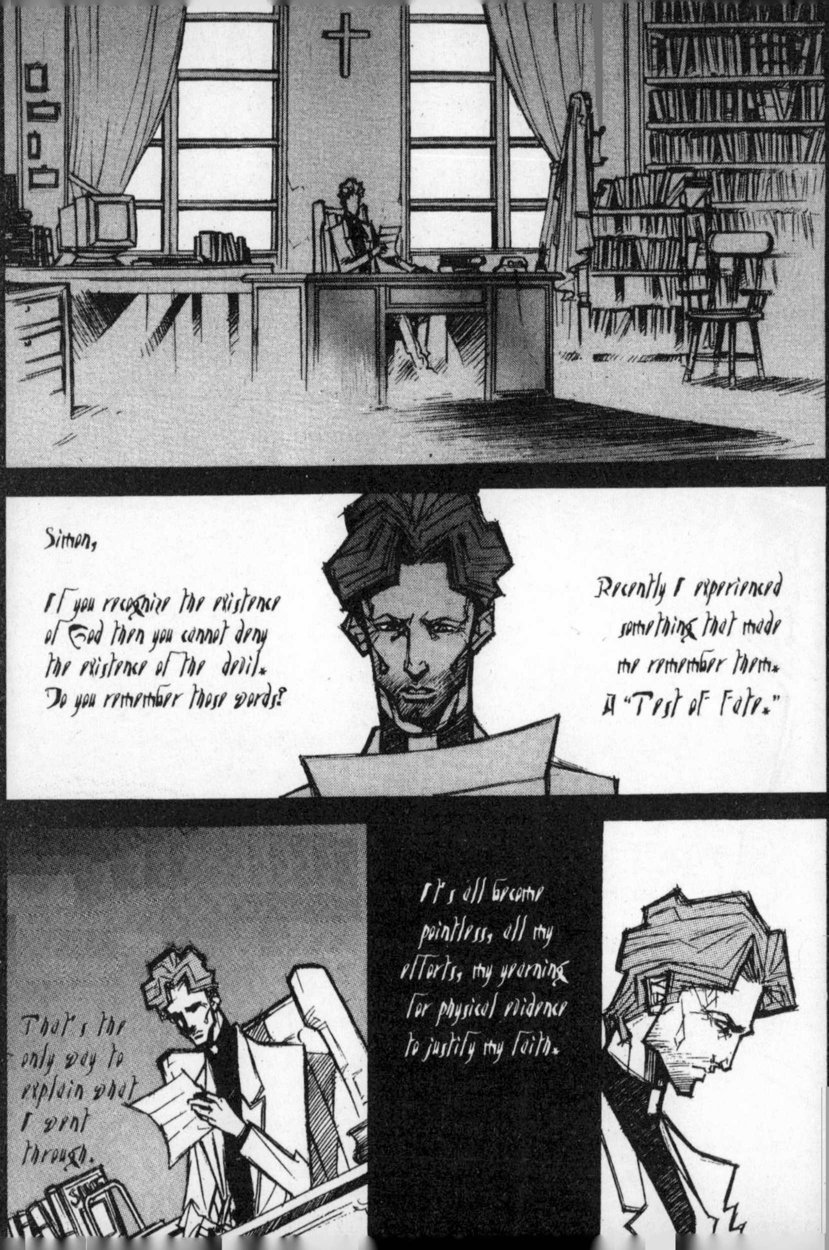
Simon,
If you recognize the existence of God then you cannot deny the existence of the devil. Do you remember those words?
Recently I experienced something that made me remember them. A "Test of Fate."
That's the only way to explain what I went through.
It's all become pointless, all my efforts, my yearning for physical evidence to justify my faith.

Please come, Simon. Your belief in faith is urgently needed, more than ever. Your Friend,

-Graham Albin-

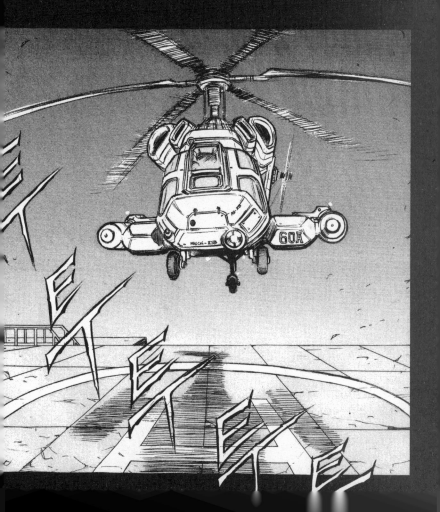

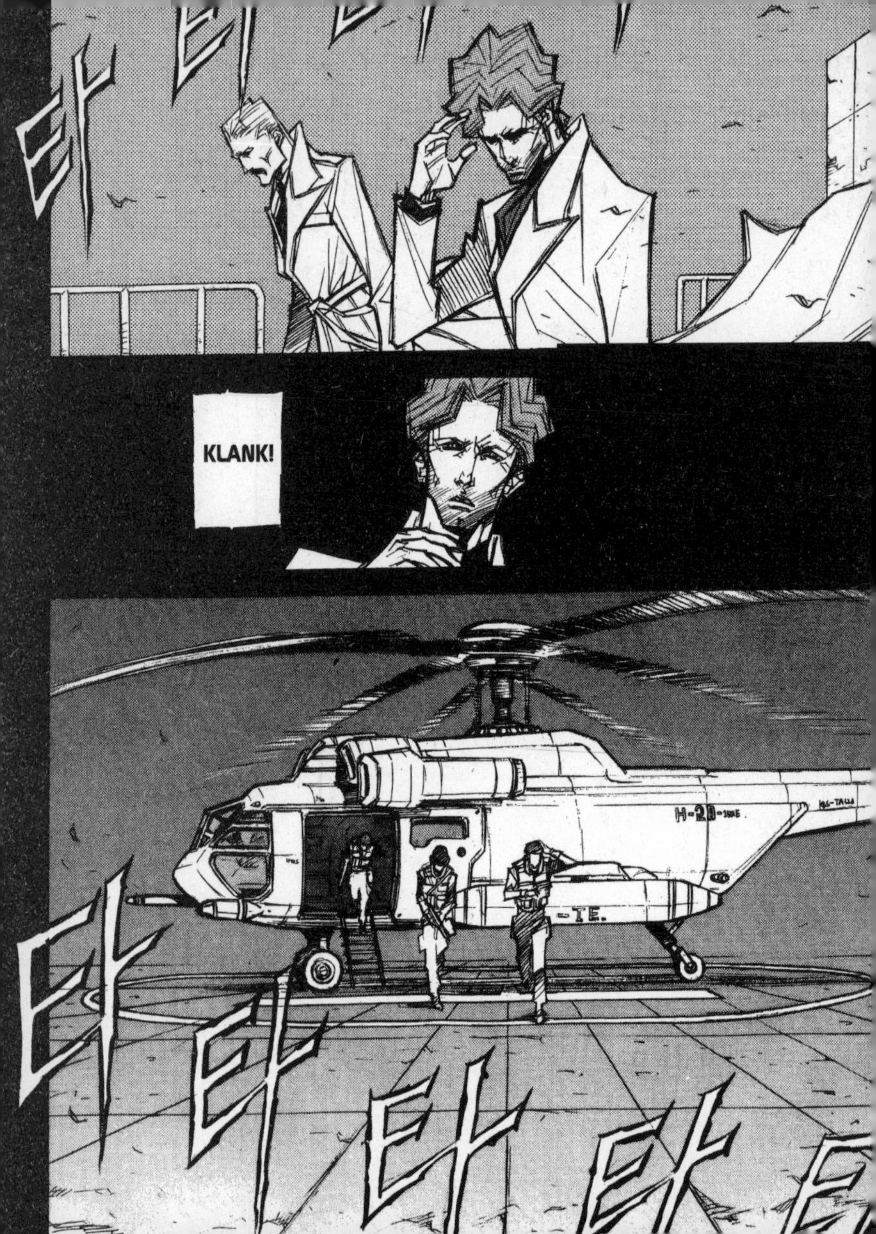
KLANK!

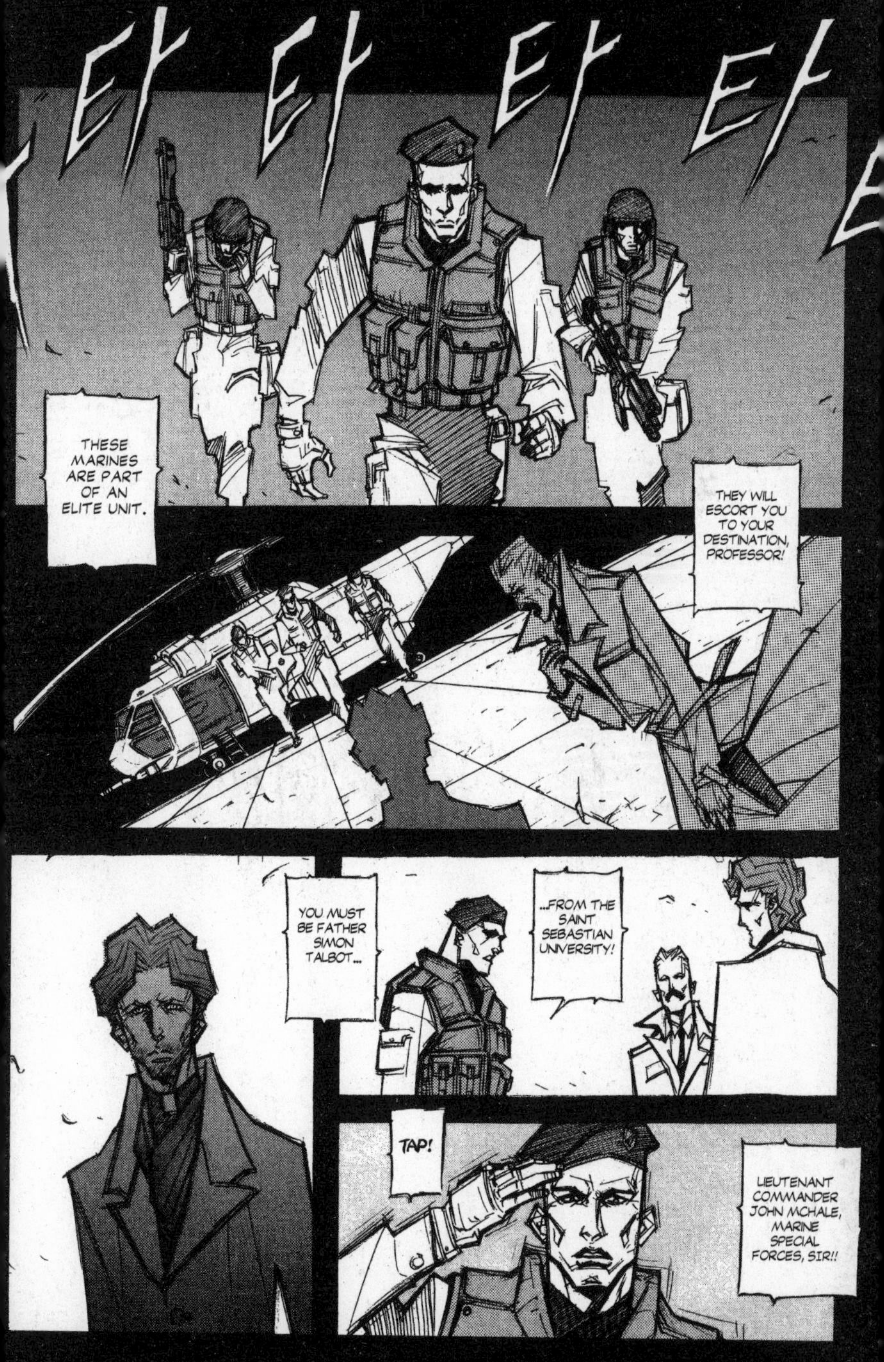
THESE MARINES ARE PART OF AN ELITE UNIT.
THEY WILL ESCORT YOU TO YOUR DESTINATION, PROFESSOR!
YOU MUST BE FATHER SIMON TALBOT...
...FROM THE SAINT SEBASTIAN UNIVERSITY!
TAP!
LIEUTENANT COMMANDER JOHN MCHALE, MARINE SPECIAL FORCES, SIR!!

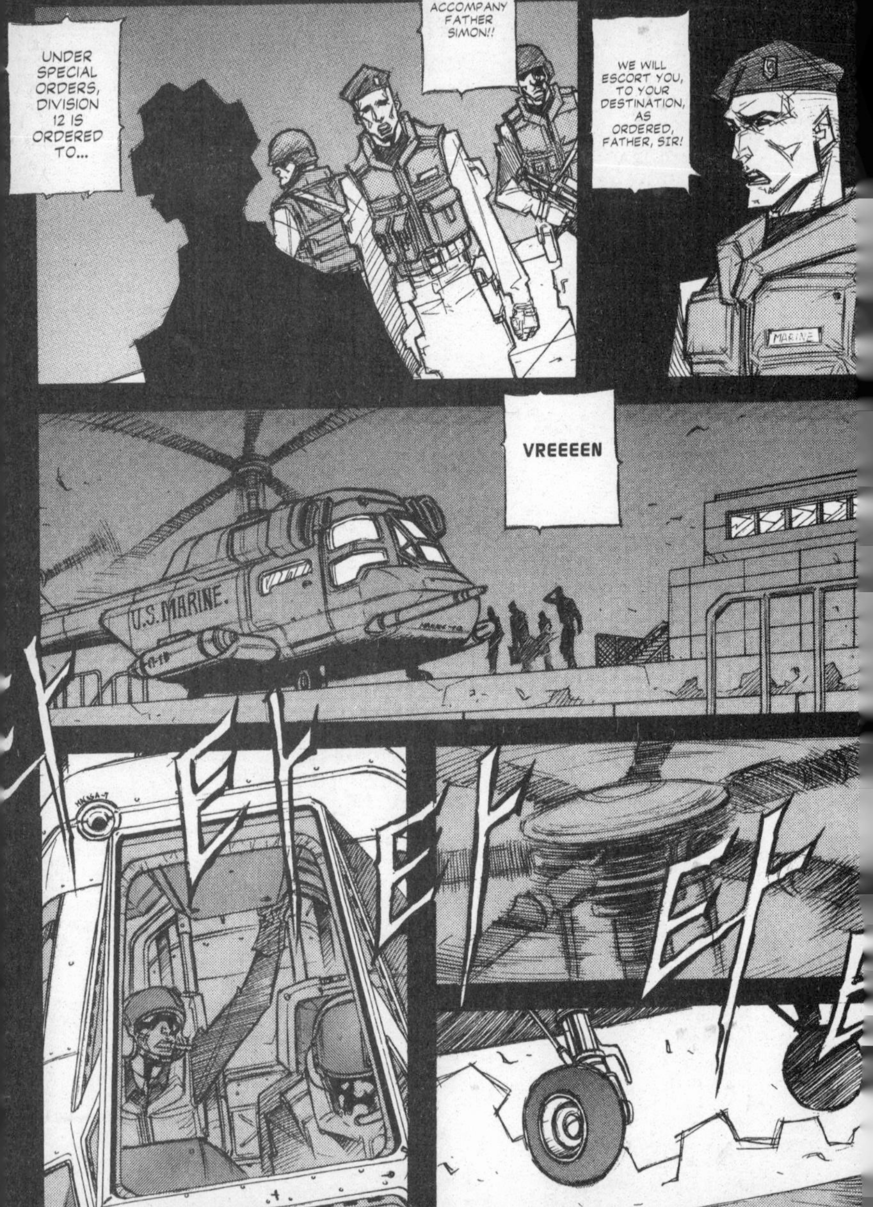
UNDER SPECIAL ORDERS, DIVISION 12 IS ORDERED TO...
...ACCOMPANY FATHER SIMON!!
WE WILL ESCORT YOU, TO YOUR DESTINATION, AS ORDERED, FATHER, SIR!
MARINE
VREEEEN
U.S. MARINE.

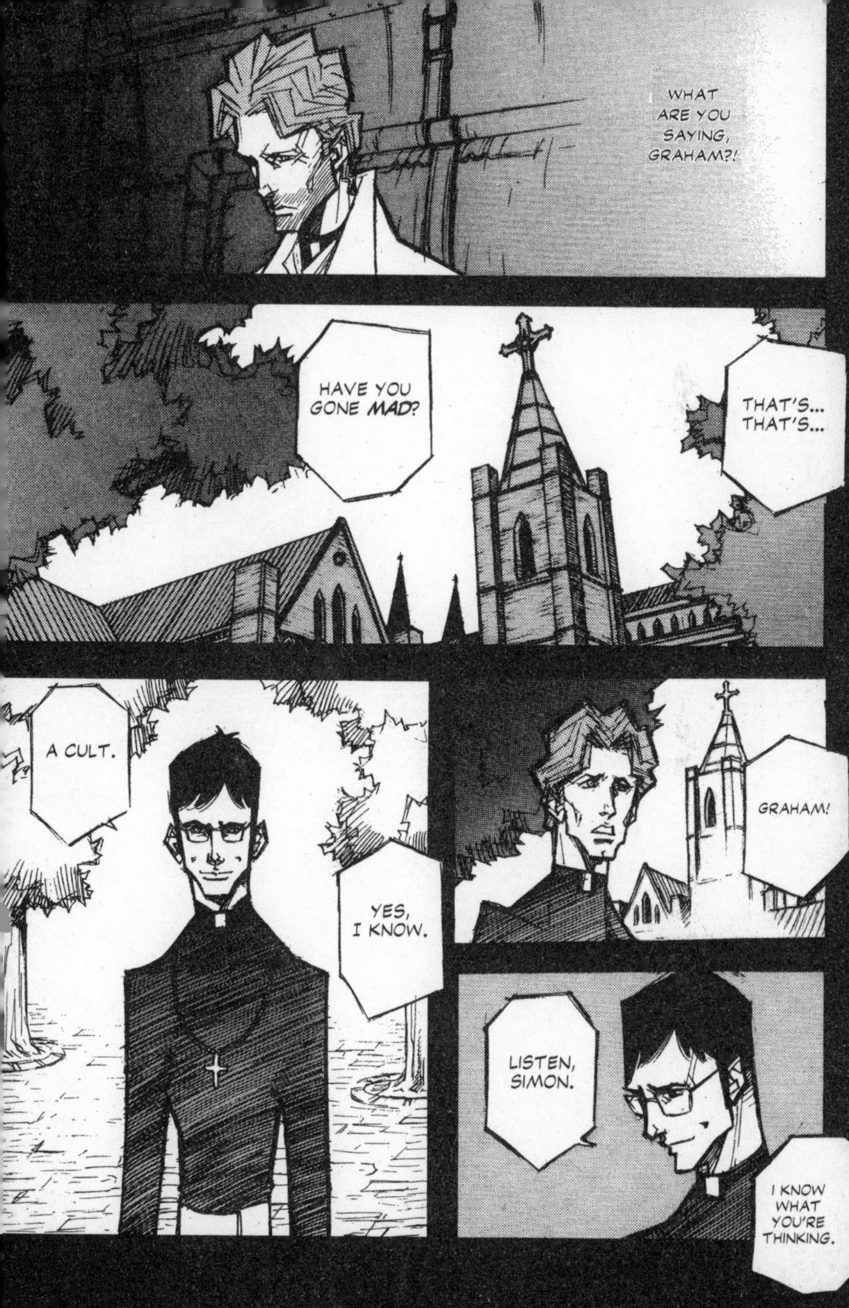
WHAT ARE YOU SAYING, GRAHAM?!
HAVE YOU GONE *MAD*?
THAT'S... THAT'S...
A CULT.
YES, I KNOW.
GRAHAM!
LISTEN, SIMON.
I KNOW WHAT YOU'RE THINKING.

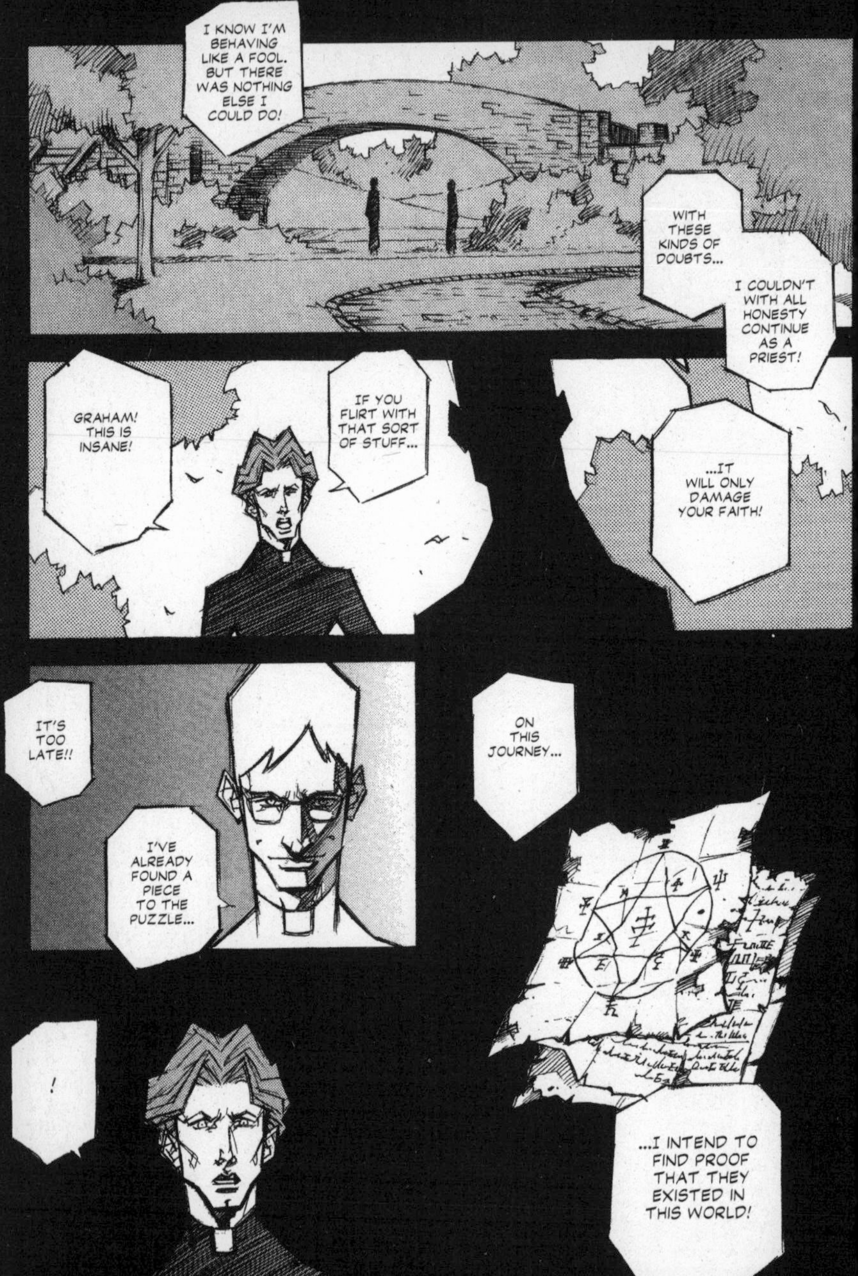
I KNOW I'M BEHAVING LIKE A FOOL. BUT THERE WAS NOTHING ELSE I COULD DO!
WITH THESE KINDS OF DOUBTS...
I COULDN'T WITH ALL HONESTY CONTINUE AS A PRIEST!
GRAHAM! THIS IS INSANE!
IF YOU FLIRT WITH THAT SORT OF STUFF...
...IT WILL ONLY DAMAGE YOUR FAITH!
IT'S TOO LATE!!
I'VE ALREADY FOUND A PIECE TO THE PUZZLE...
!
ON THIS JOURNEY...
...I INTEND TO FIND PROOF THAT THEY EXISTED IN THIS WORLD!

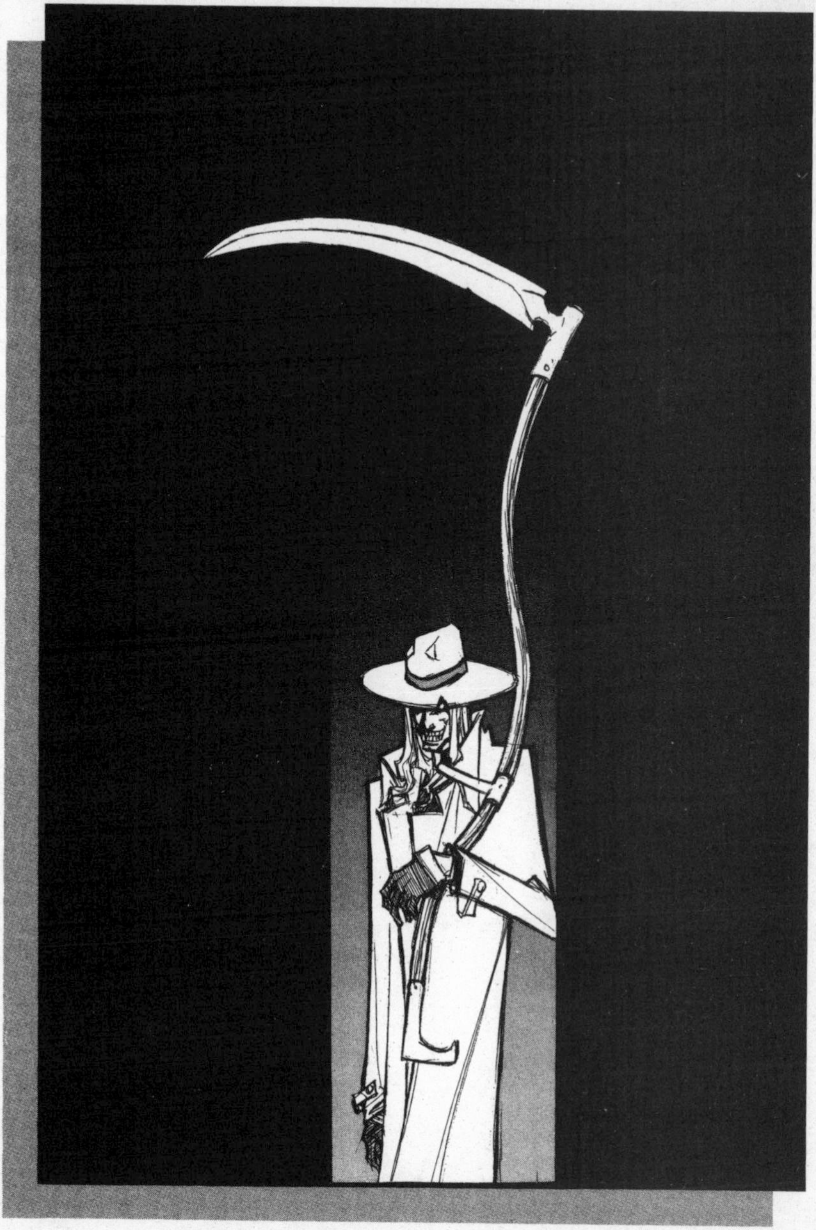

MORE THAN ANYONE ELSE I KNEW, HE WAS DEEPLY FAITHFUL AND TRULY BLESSED WITH GRACE...

...AND HE LOVED DEDICATING HIS LIFE TO THE PRIESTHOOD.

BUT IN A SINGLE DAY, HE LOST ALL HIS DEEP DESIRE TO BECOME A PRIEST BECAUSE OF ONE BOOK...

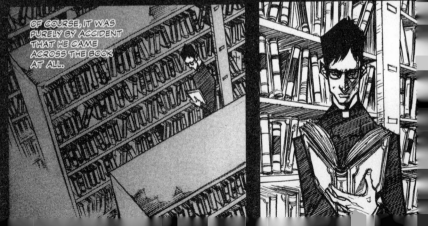

OF COURSE, IT WAS PURELY BY ACCIDENT THAT HE CAME ACROSS THE BOOK AT ALL.

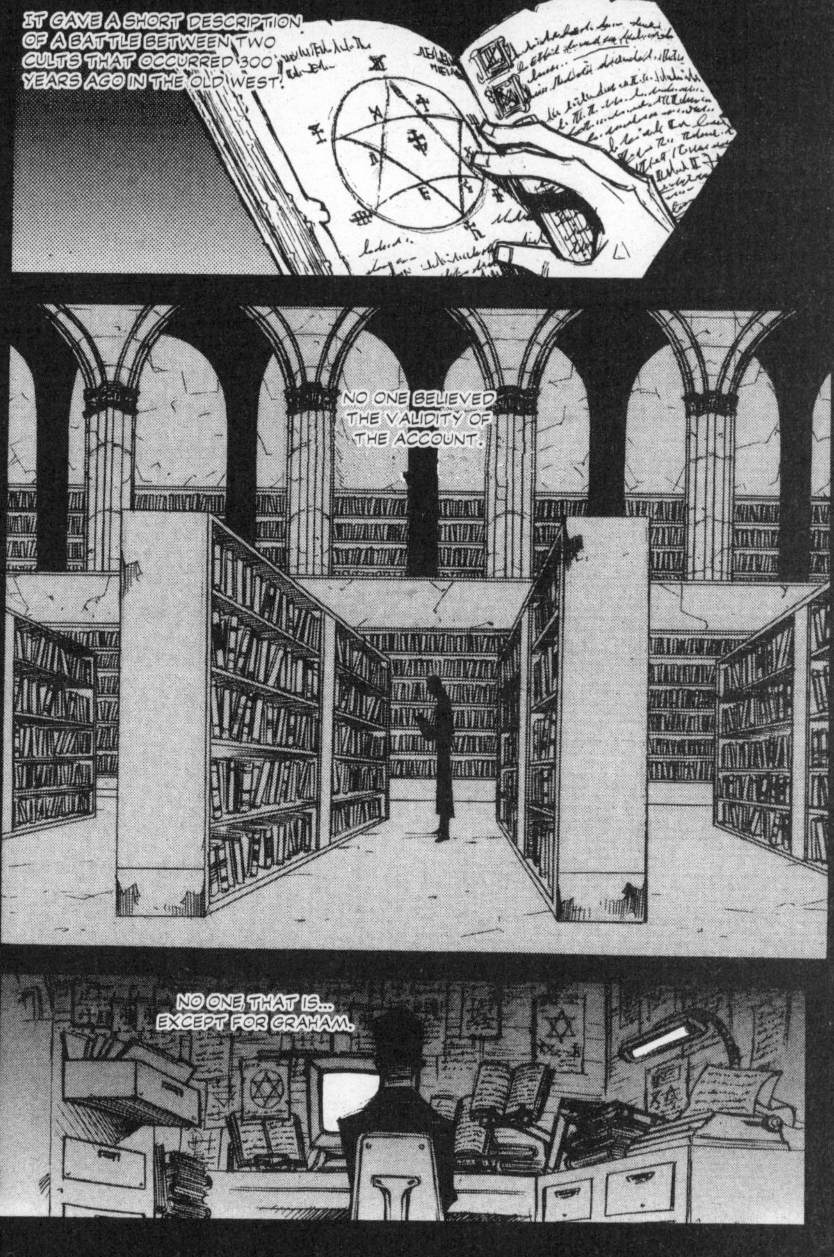
IT GAVE A SHORT DESCRIPTION OF A BATTLE BETWEEN TWO CULTS THAT OCCURRED 300 YEARS AGO IN THE OLD WEST.
NO ONE BELIEVED THE VALIDITY OF THE ACCOUNT.
NO ONE THAT IS... EXCEPT FOR GRAHAM.

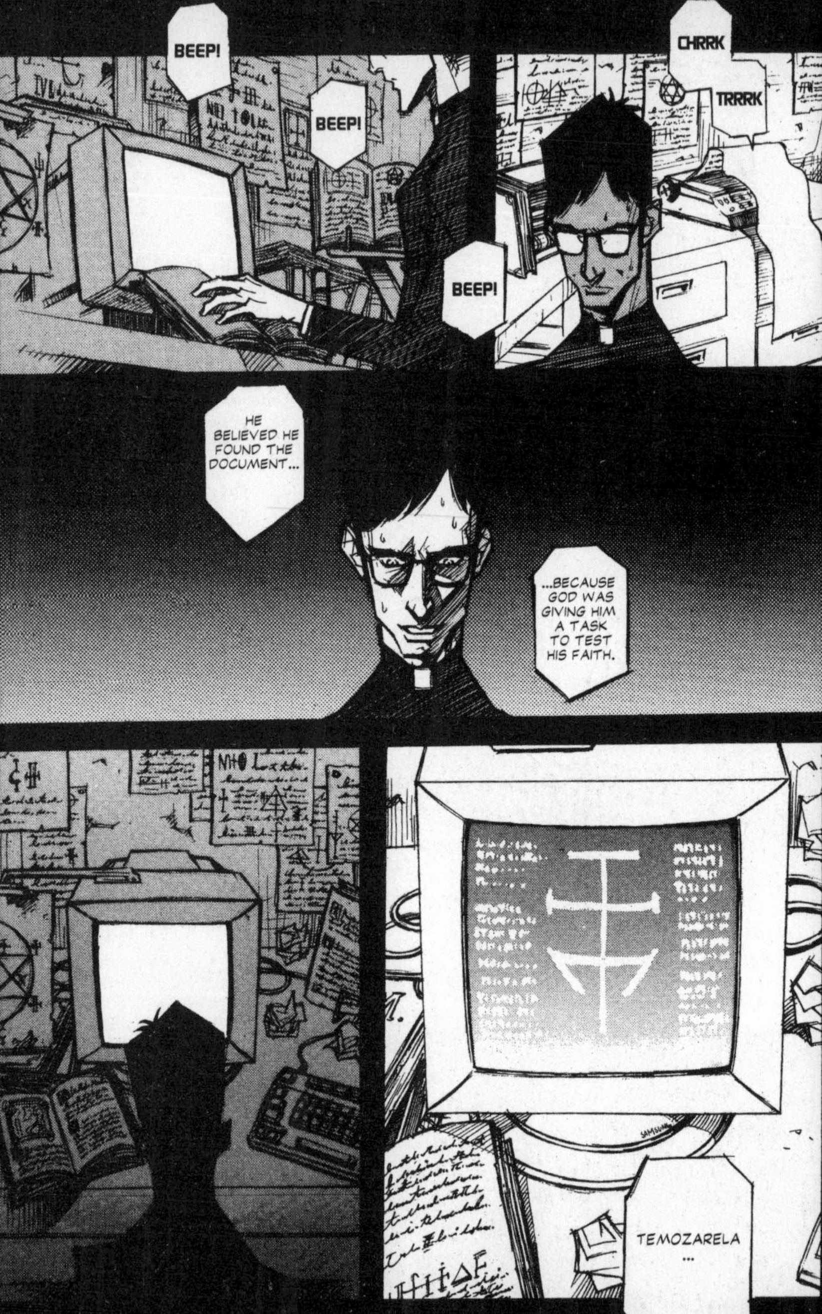
BEEP!
BEEP!
CHRRK
TRRRK
BEEP!
HE BELIEVED HE FOUND THE DOCUMENT...
...BECAUSE GOD WAS GIVING HIM A TASK TO TEST HIS FAITH.
TEMOZARELA ...

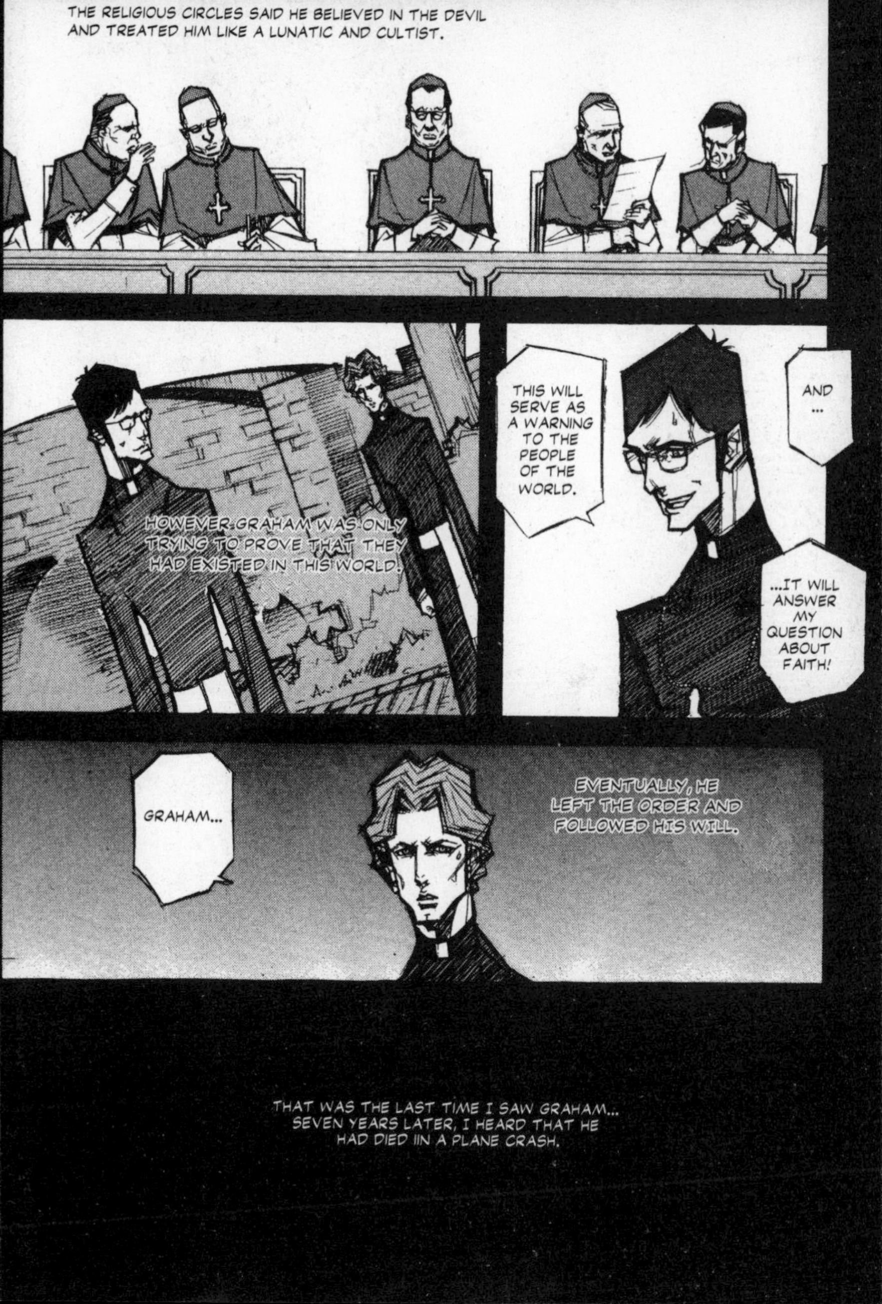
THE RELIGIOUS CIRCLES SAID HE BELIEVED IN THE DEVIL AND TREATED HIM LIKE A LUNATIC AND CULTIST.
HOWEVER GRAHAM WAS ONLY TRYING TO PROVE THAT THEY HAD EXISTED IN THIS WORLD.
THIS WILL SERVE AS A WARNING TO THE PEOPLE OF THE WORLD.
AND ...
...IT WILL ANSWER MY QUESTION ABOUT FAITH!
GRAHAM...
EVENTUALLY, HE LEFT THE ORDER AND FOLLOWED HIS WILL.
THAT WAS THE LAST TIME I SAW GRAHAM... SEVEN YEARS LATER, I HEARD THAT HE HAD DIED IIN A PLANE CRASH.

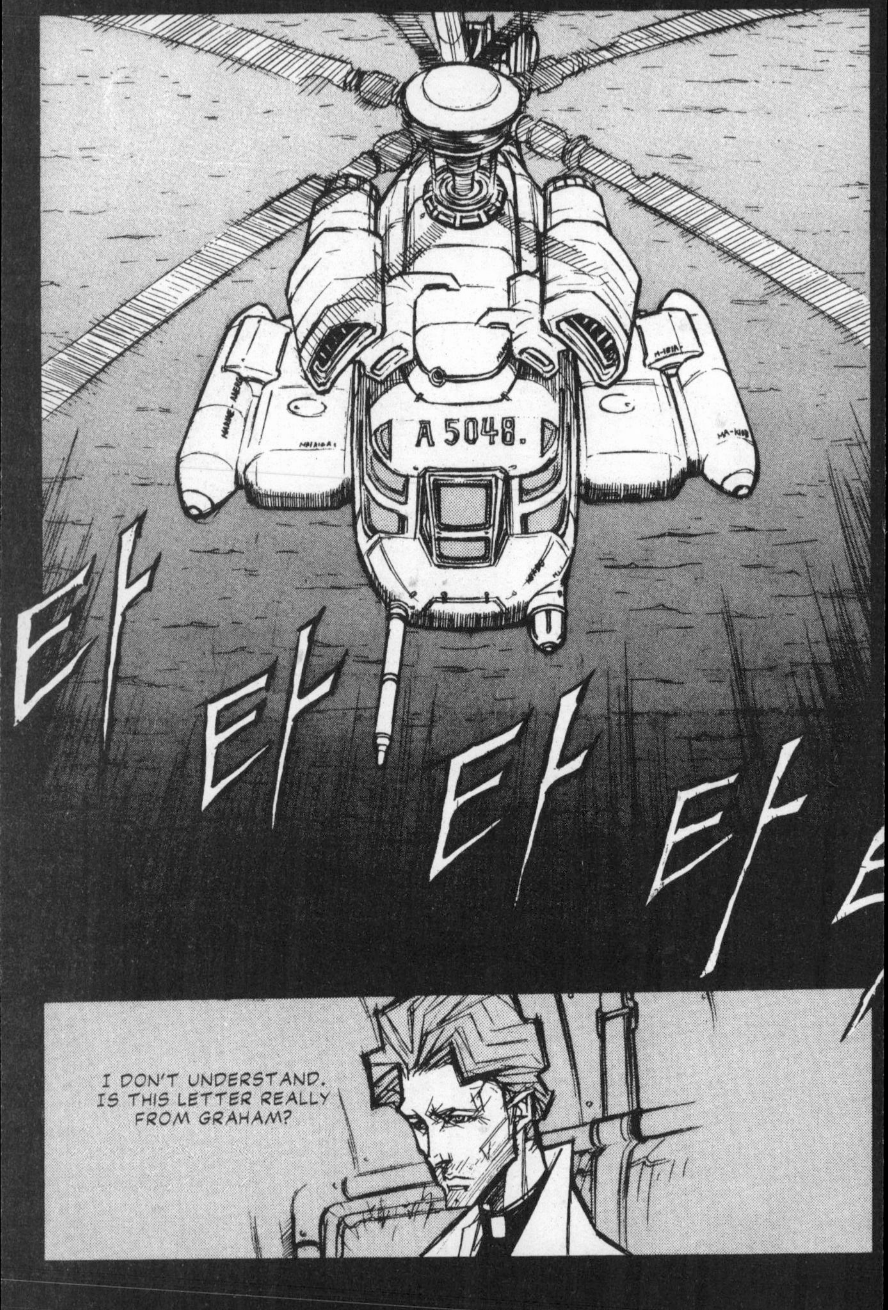
A 5048.
타 타 타 타
I DON'T UNDERSTAND. IS THIS LETTER REALLY FROM GRAHAM?

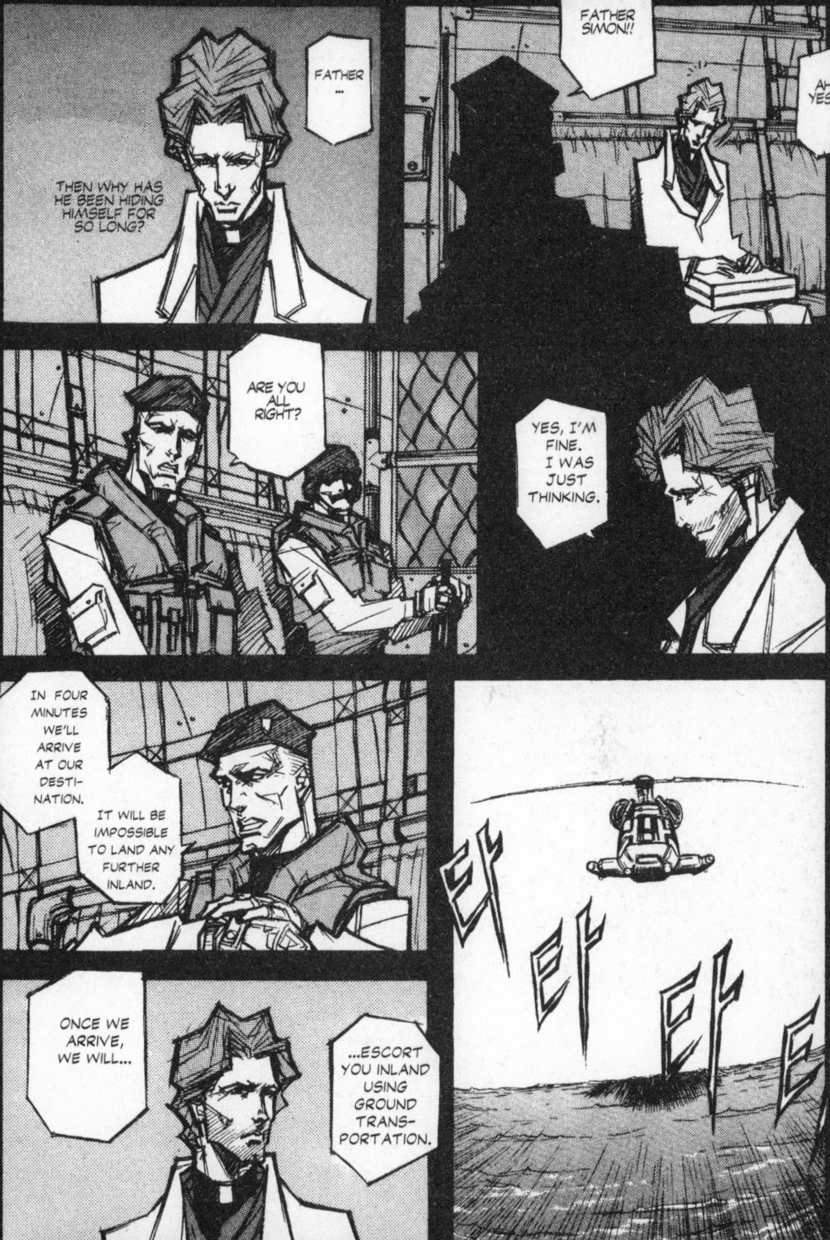
FATHER ...
THEN WHY HAS HE BEEN HIDING HIMSELF FOR SO LONG?
FATHER SIMON!!
AH! YES...
ARE YOU ALL RIGHT?
YES, I'M FINE. I WAS JUST THINKING.
IN FOUR MINUTES WE'LL ARRIVE AT OUR DESTI-NATION.
IT WILL BE IMPOSSIBLE TO LAND ANY FURTHER INLAND.
ONCE WE ARRIVE, WE WILL...
...ESCORT YOU INLAND USING GROUND TRANS-PORTATION.

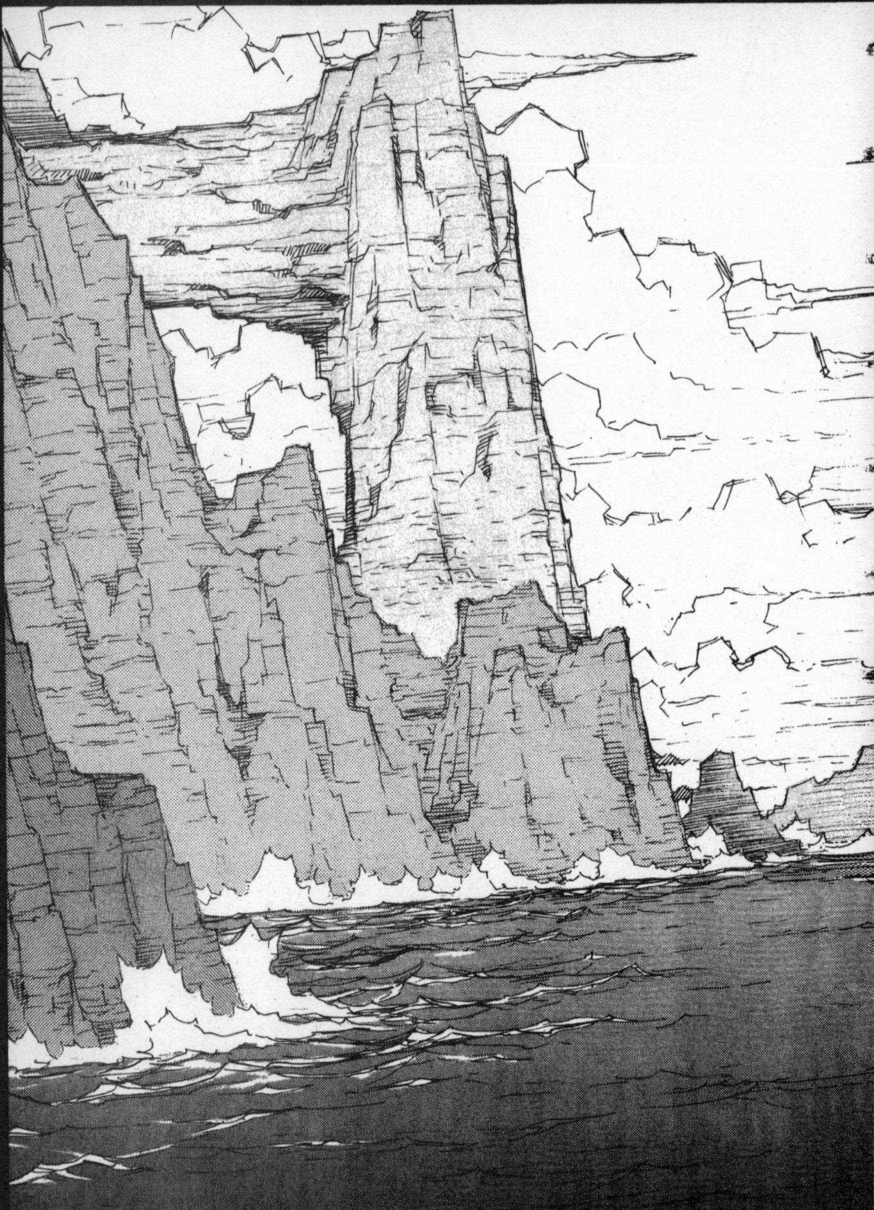

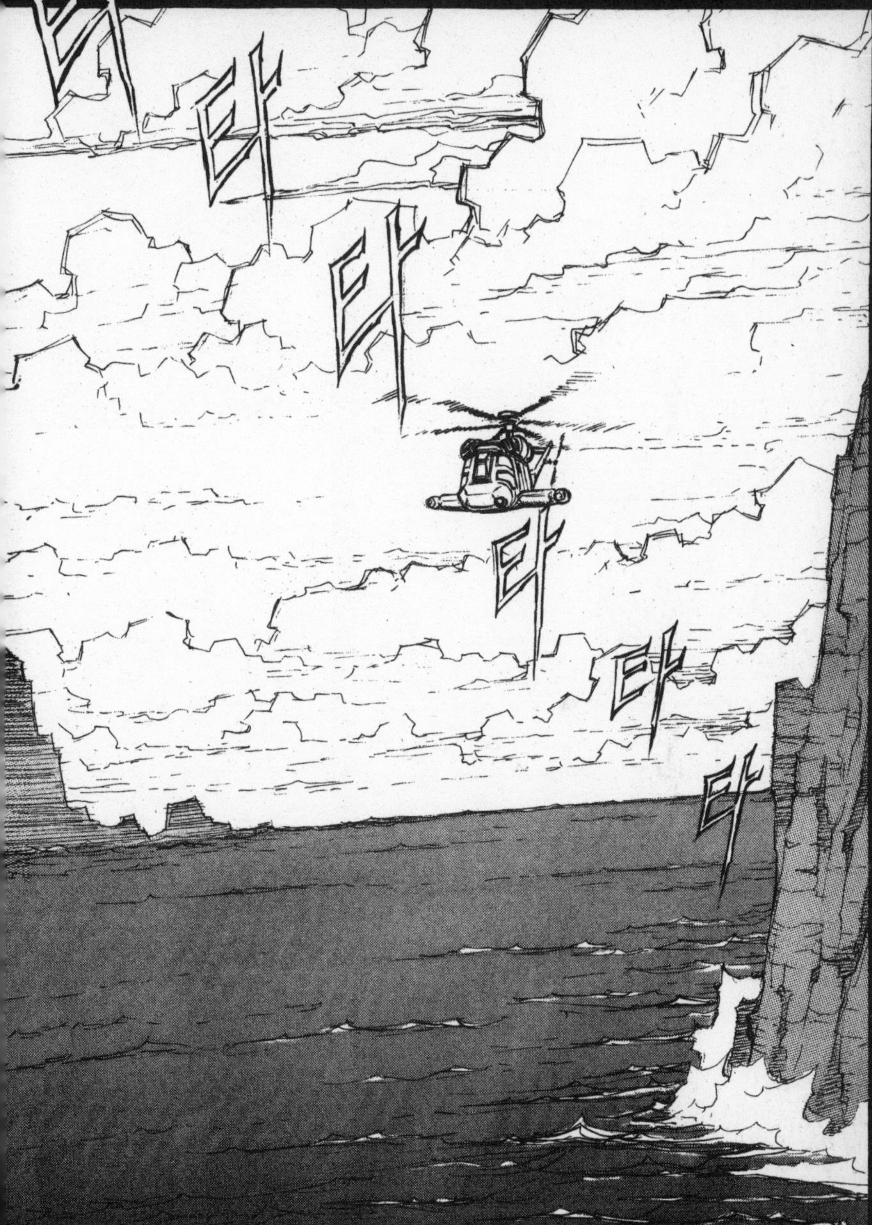
타
타
타
타
타
타

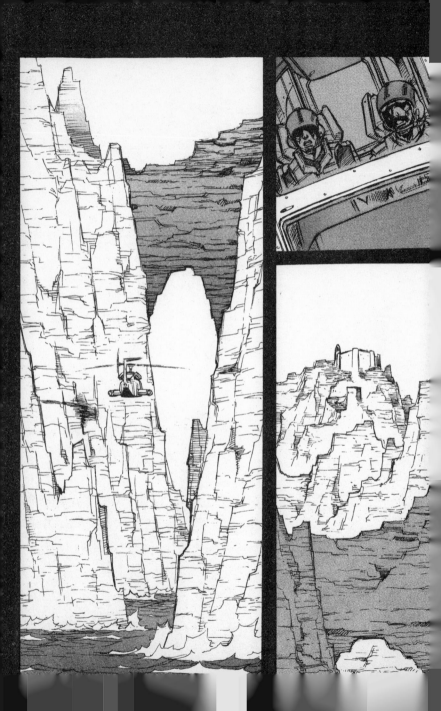

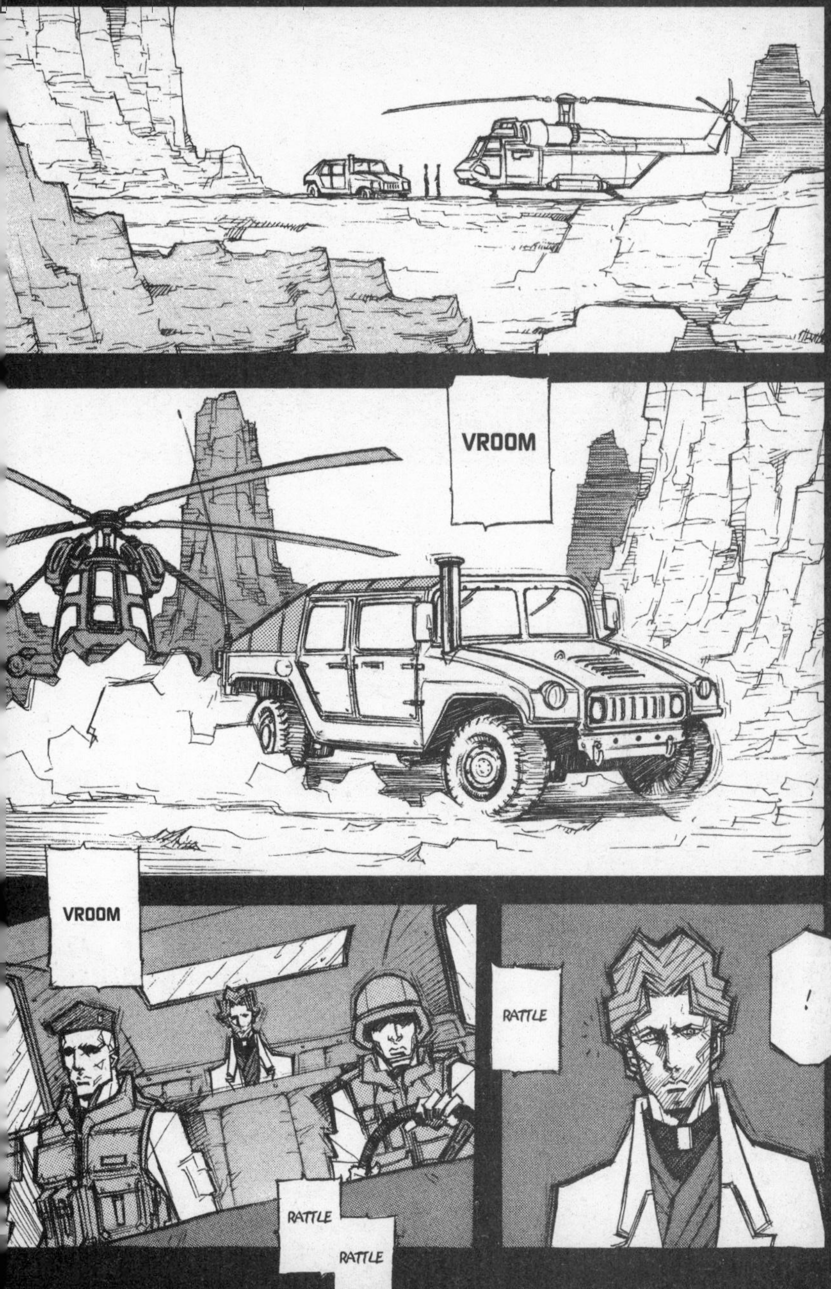
VROOM
VROOM
RATTLE
RATTLE
RATTLE
!

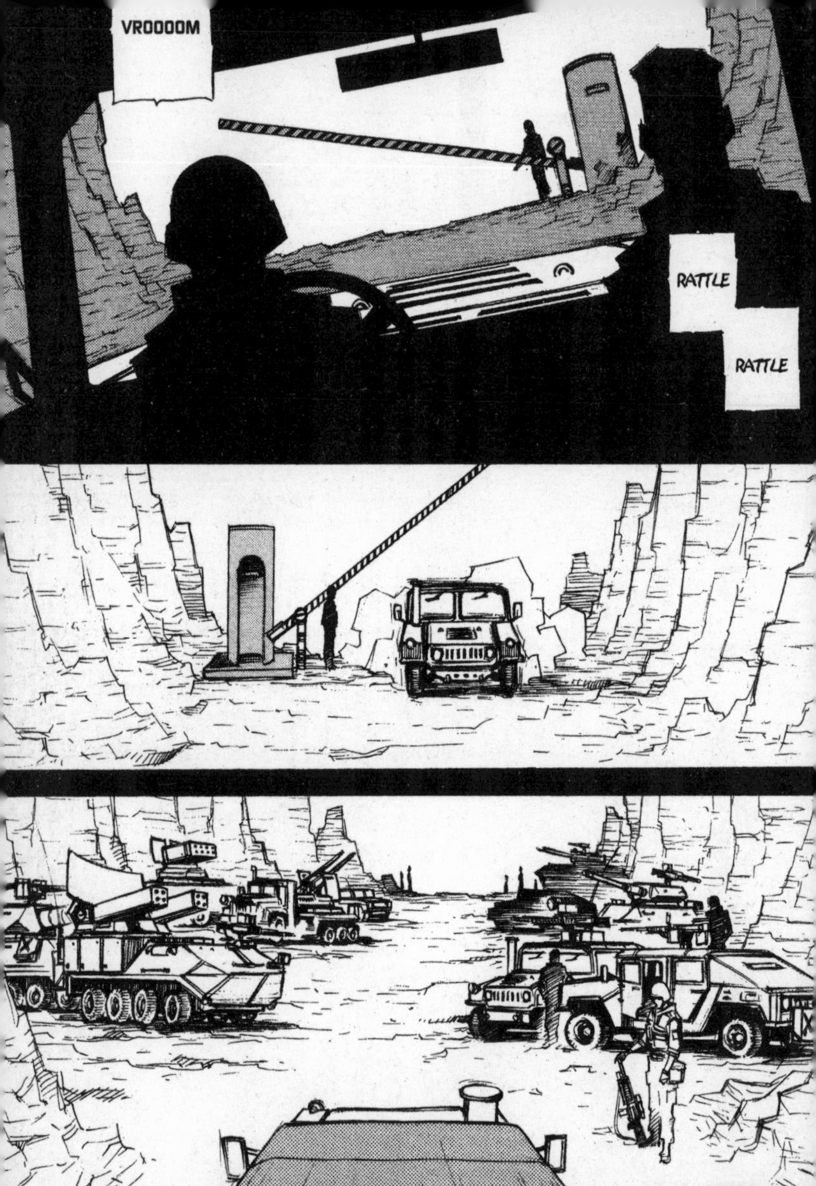
VROOOOM
RATTLE
RATTLE

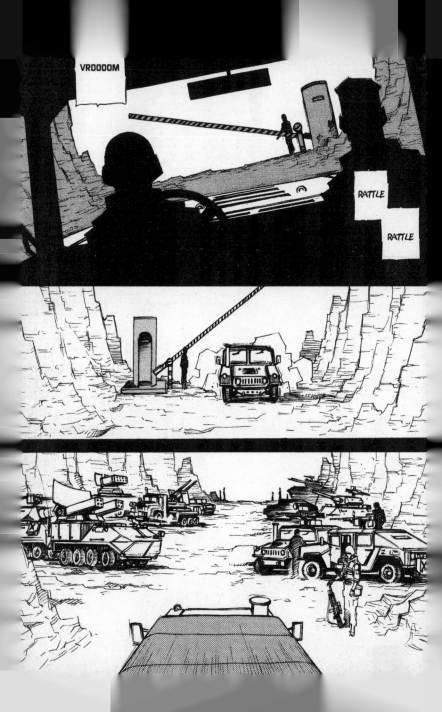

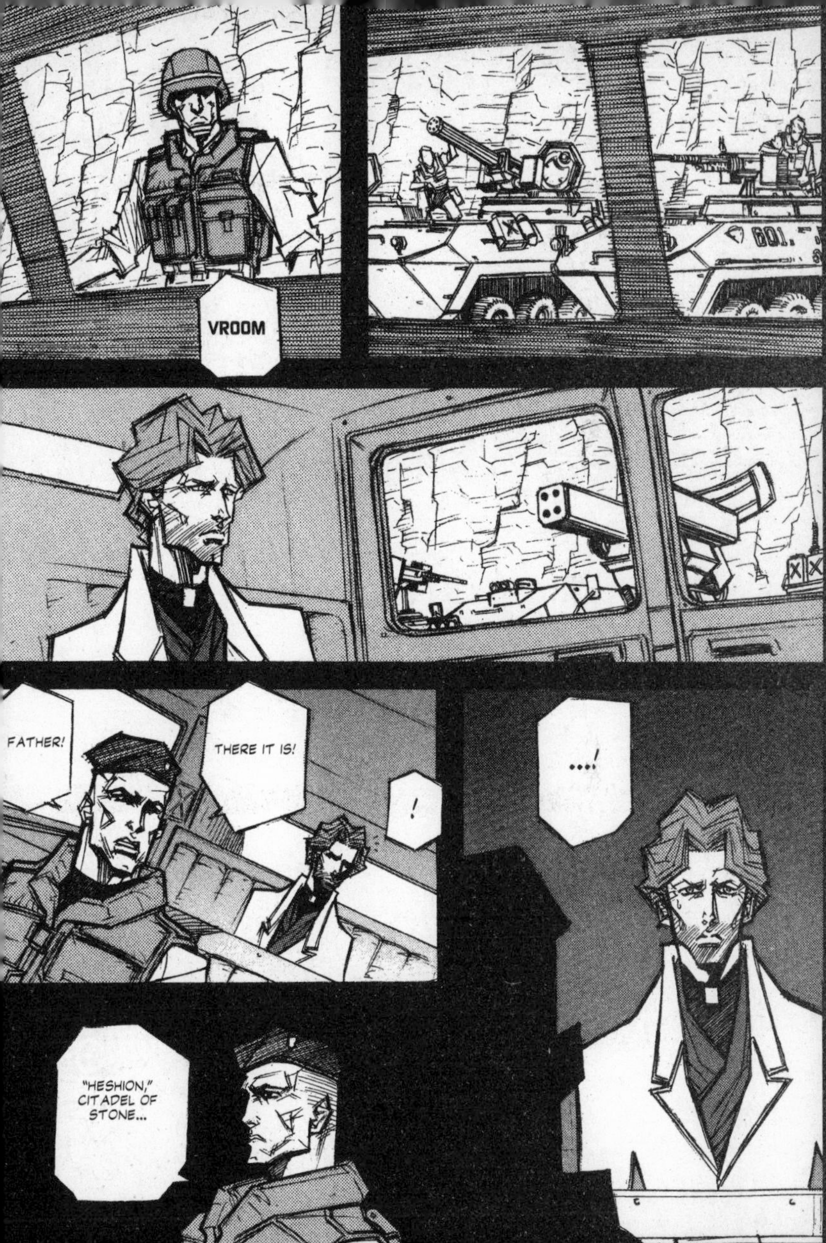
VROOM
601.
FATHER!
THERE IT IS!
!
...!
"HESHION," CITADEL OF STONE...

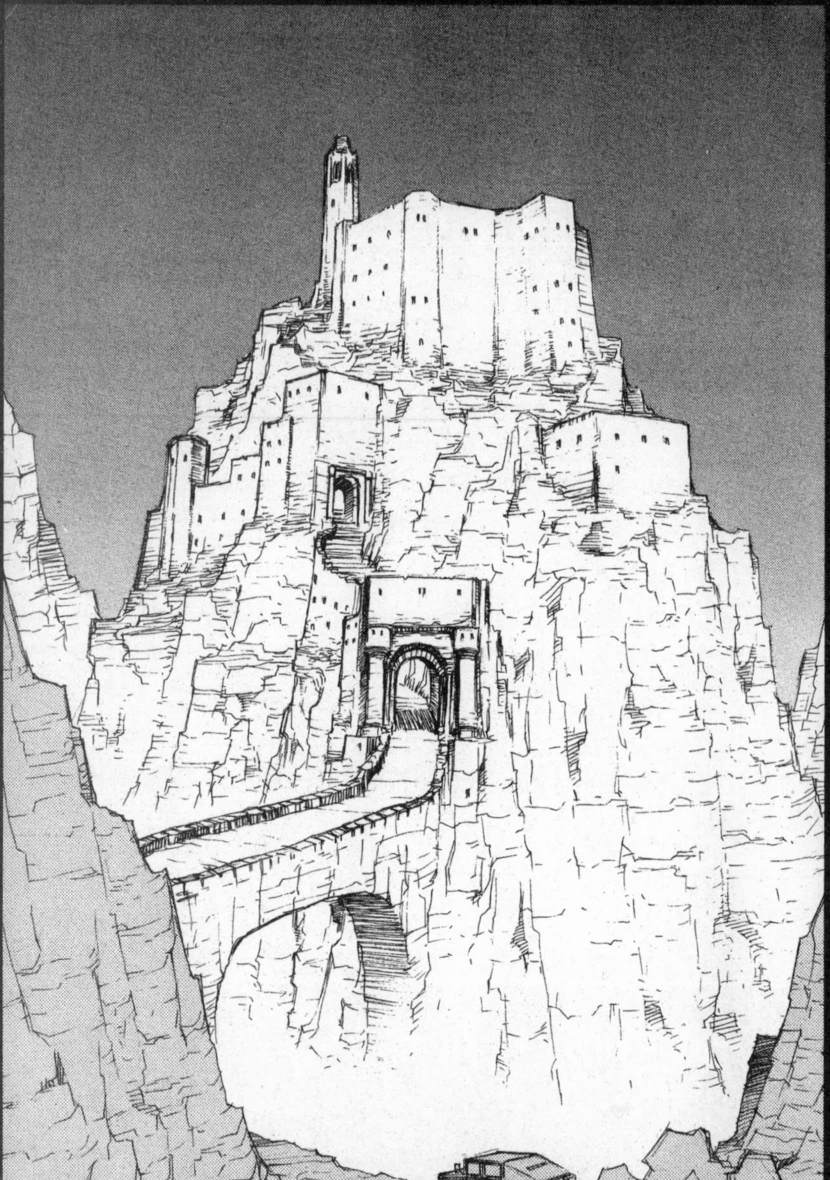

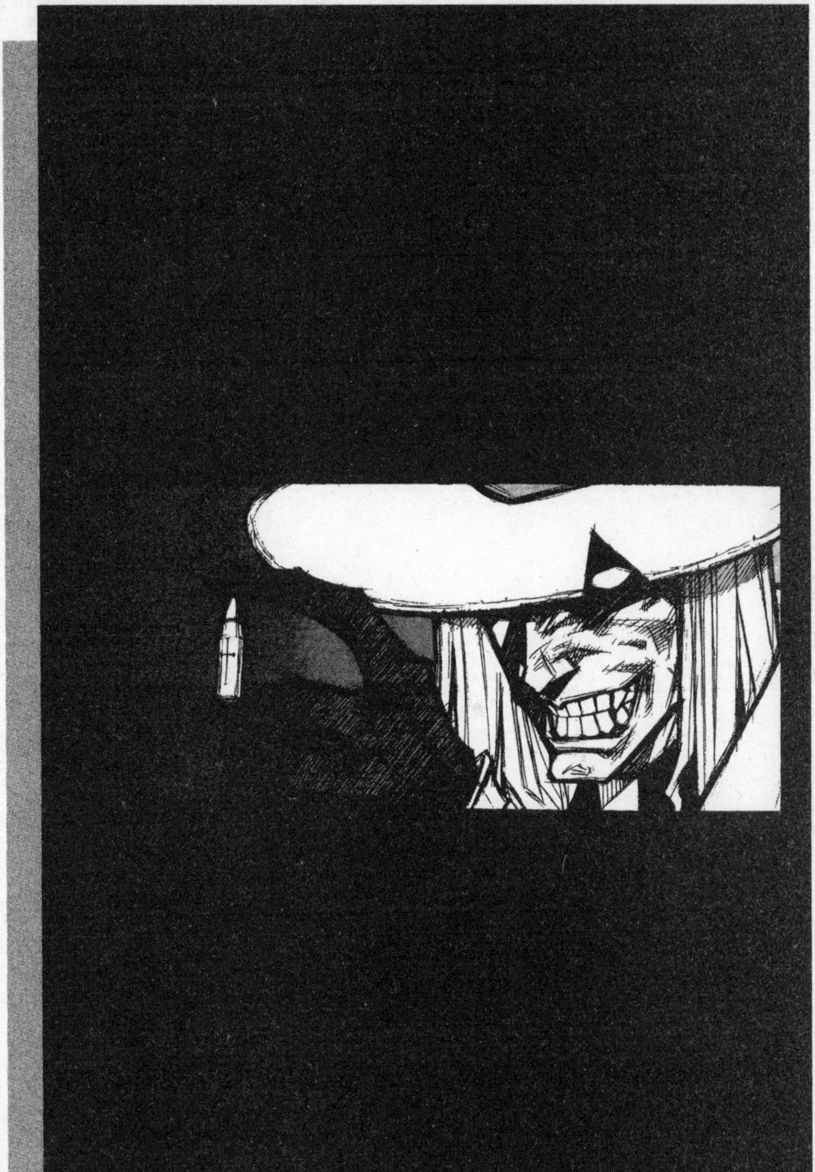

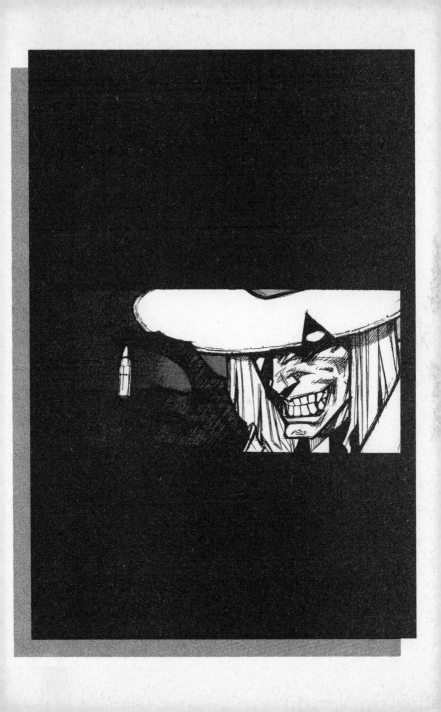

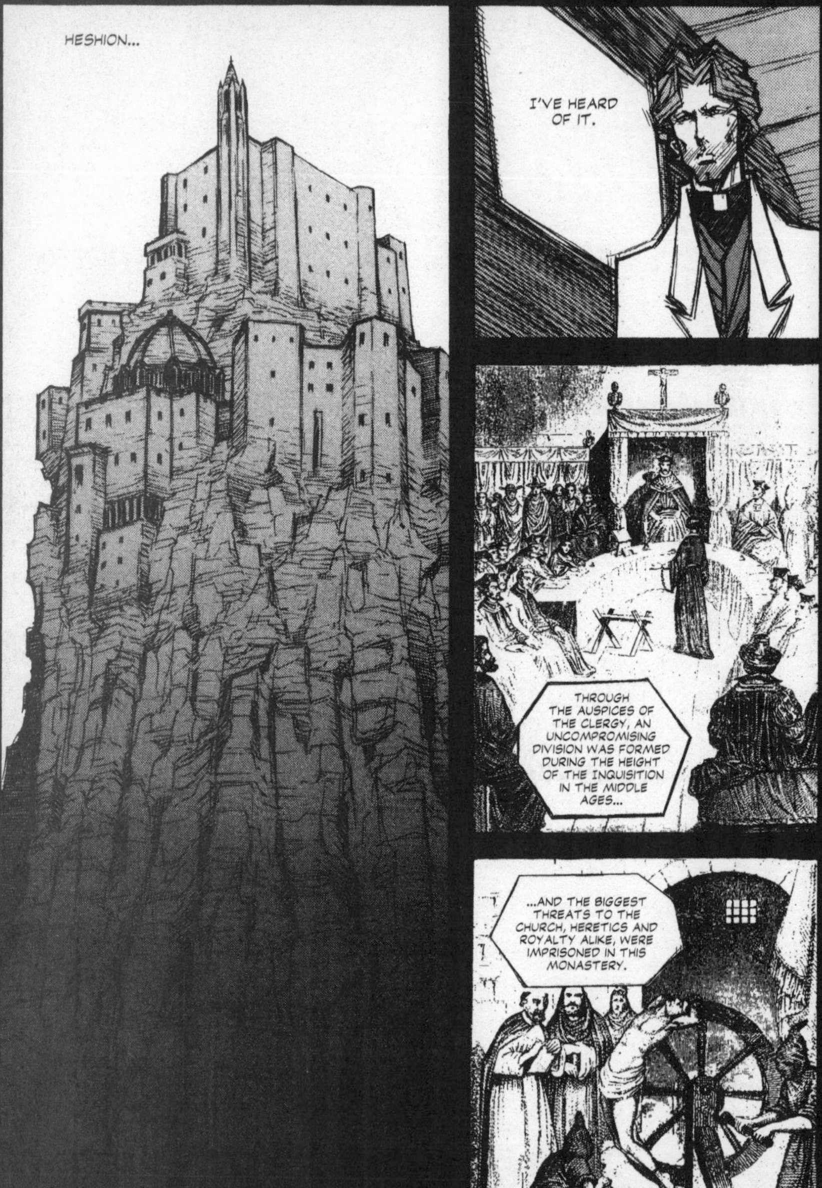
HESHION...
I'VE HEARD OF IT.
THROUGH THE AUSPICES OF THE CLERGY, AN UNCOMPROMISING DIVISION WAS FORMED DURING THE HEIGHT OF THE INQUISITION IN THE MIDDLE AGES...
...AND THE BIGGEST THREATS TO THE CHURCH, HERETICS AND ROYALTY ALIKE, WERE IMPRISONED IN THIS MONASTERY.

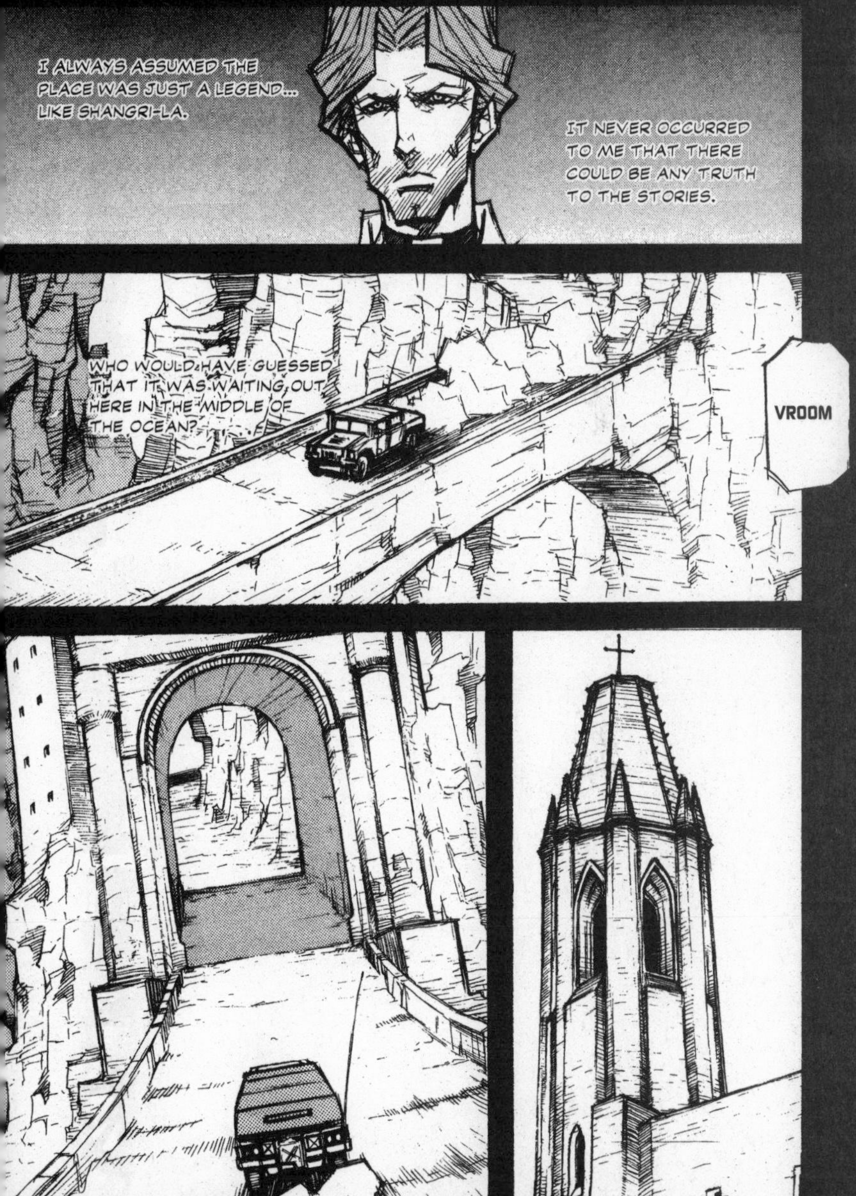
I ALWAYS ASSUMED THE PLACE WAS JUST A LEGEND... LIKE SHANGRI-LA.
IT NEVER OCCURRED TO ME THAT THERE COULD BE ANY TRUTH TO THE STORIES.
WHO WOULD HAVE GUESSED THAT IT WAS WAITING OUT HERE IN THE MIDDLE OF THE OCEAN?
VROOM

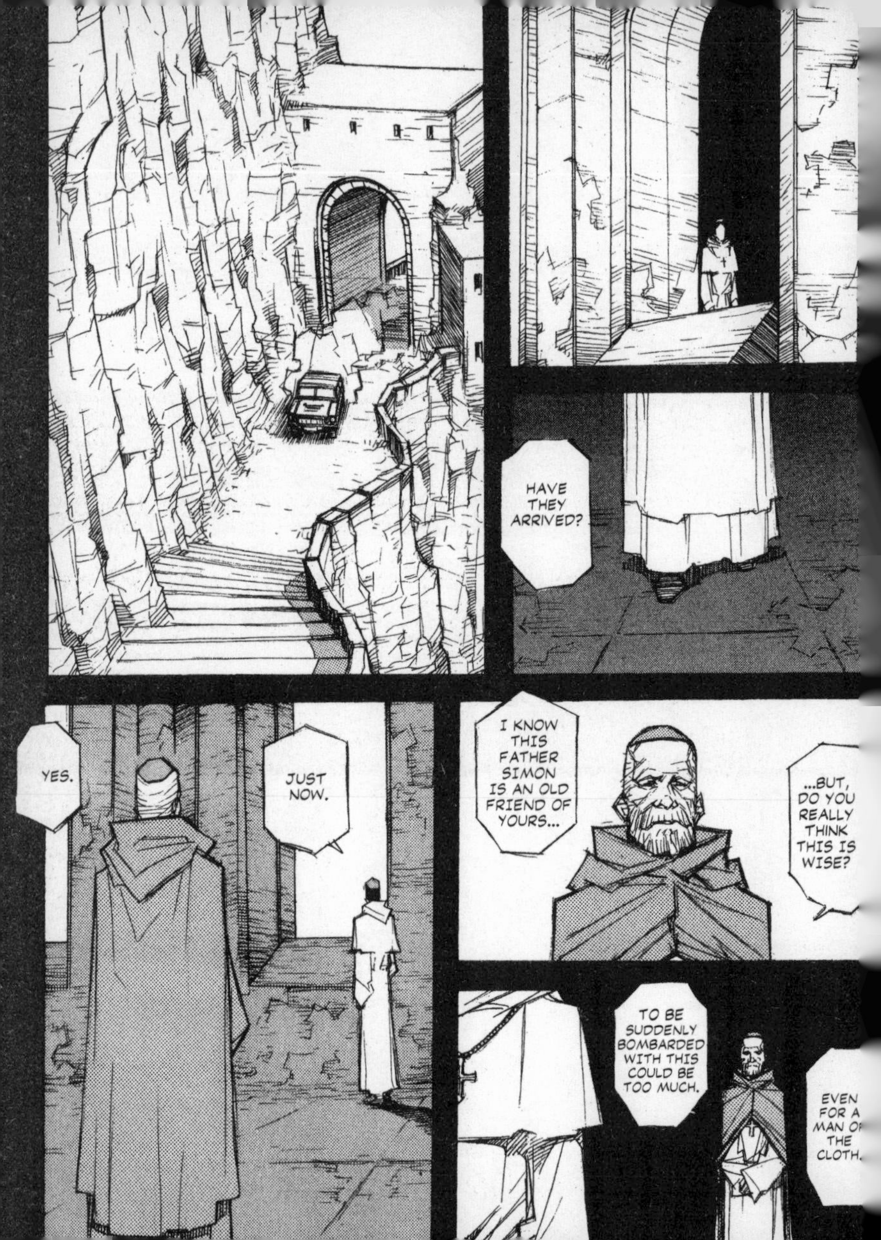
HAVE THEY ARRIVED?
YES.
JUST NOW.
I KNOW THIS FATHER SIMON IS AN OLD FRIEND OF YOURS...
...BUT, DO YOU REALLY THINK THIS IS WISE?
TO BE SUDDENLY BOMBARDED WITH THIS COULD BE TOO MUCH.
EVEN FOR A MAN OF THE CLOTH.

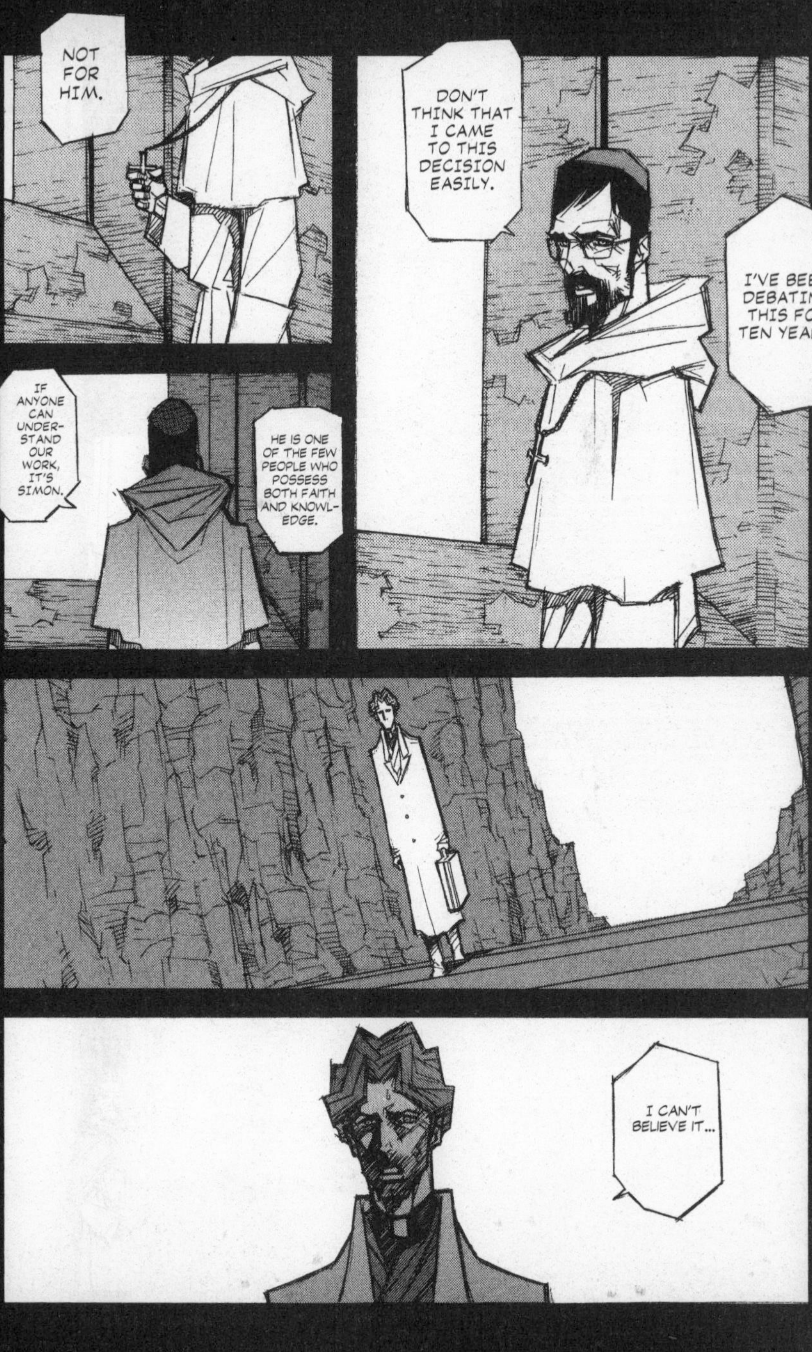
NOT FOR HIM.
IF ANYONE CAN UNDER-STAND OUR WORK, IT'S SIMON.
HE IS ONE OF THE FEW PEOPLE WHO POSSESS BOTH FAITH AND KNOWL-EDGE.
DON'T THINK THAT I CAME TO THIS DECISION EASILY.
I'VE BEEN DEBATING THIS FOR TEN YEARS.
I CAN'T BELIEVE IT...

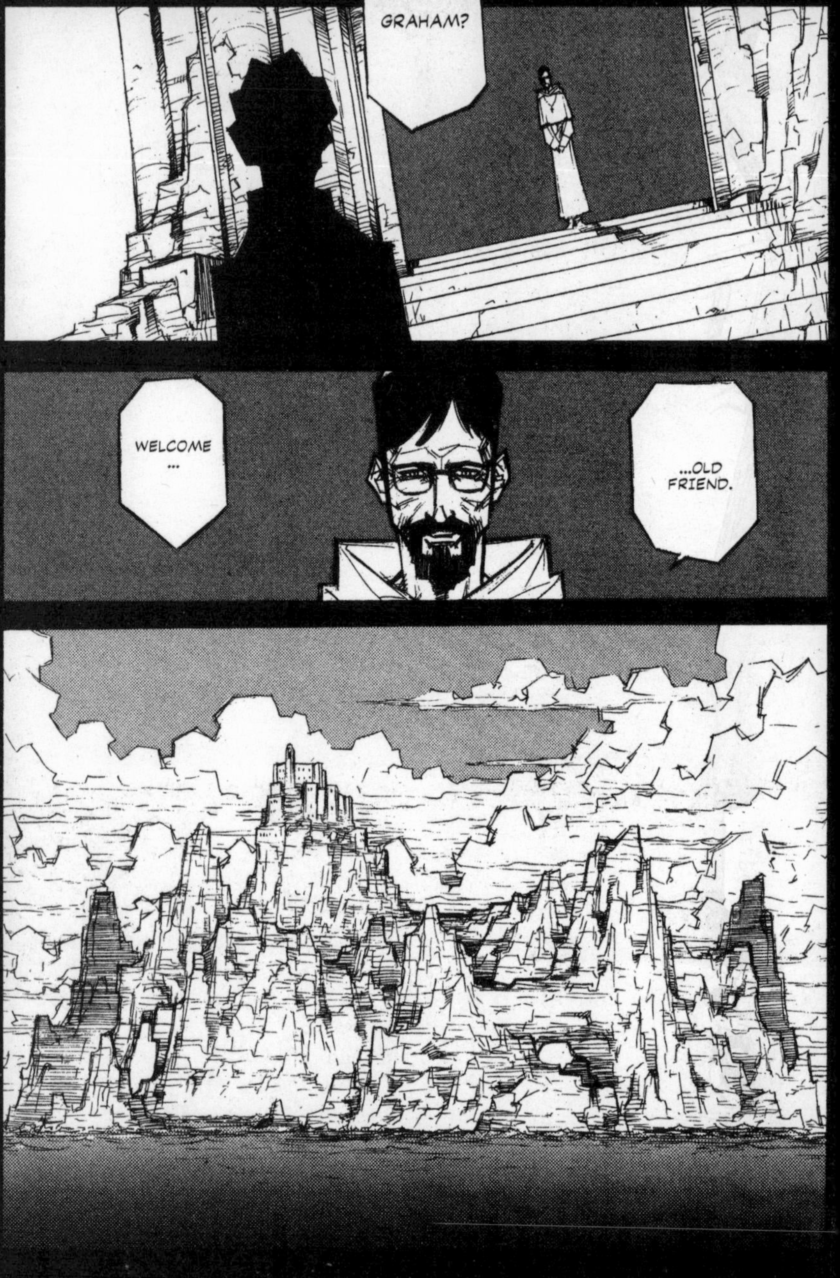
GRAHAM?
WELCOME ...
...OLD FRIEND.

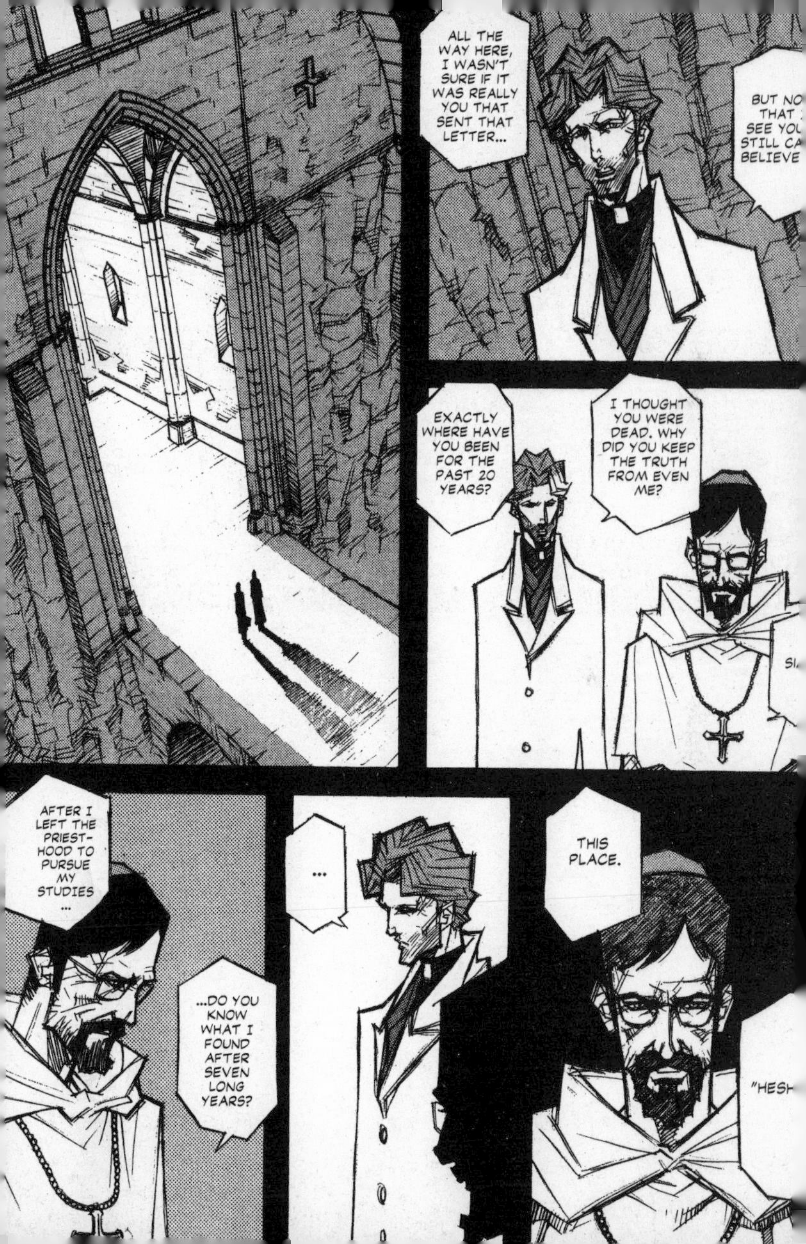
ALL THE WAY HERE, I WASN'T SURE IF IT WAS REALLY YOU THAT SENT THAT LETTER...
BUT NO THAT SEE YOU STILL CA BELIEVE
EXACTLY WHERE HAVE YOU BEEN FOR THE PAST 20 YEARS?
I THOUGHT YOU WERE DEAD. WHY DID YOU KEEP THE TRUTH FROM EVEN ME?
AFTER I LEFT THE PRIEST-HOOD TO PURSUE MY STUDIES ...
...DO YOU KNOW WHAT I FOUND AFTER SEVEN LONG YEARS?
...
THIS PLACE.

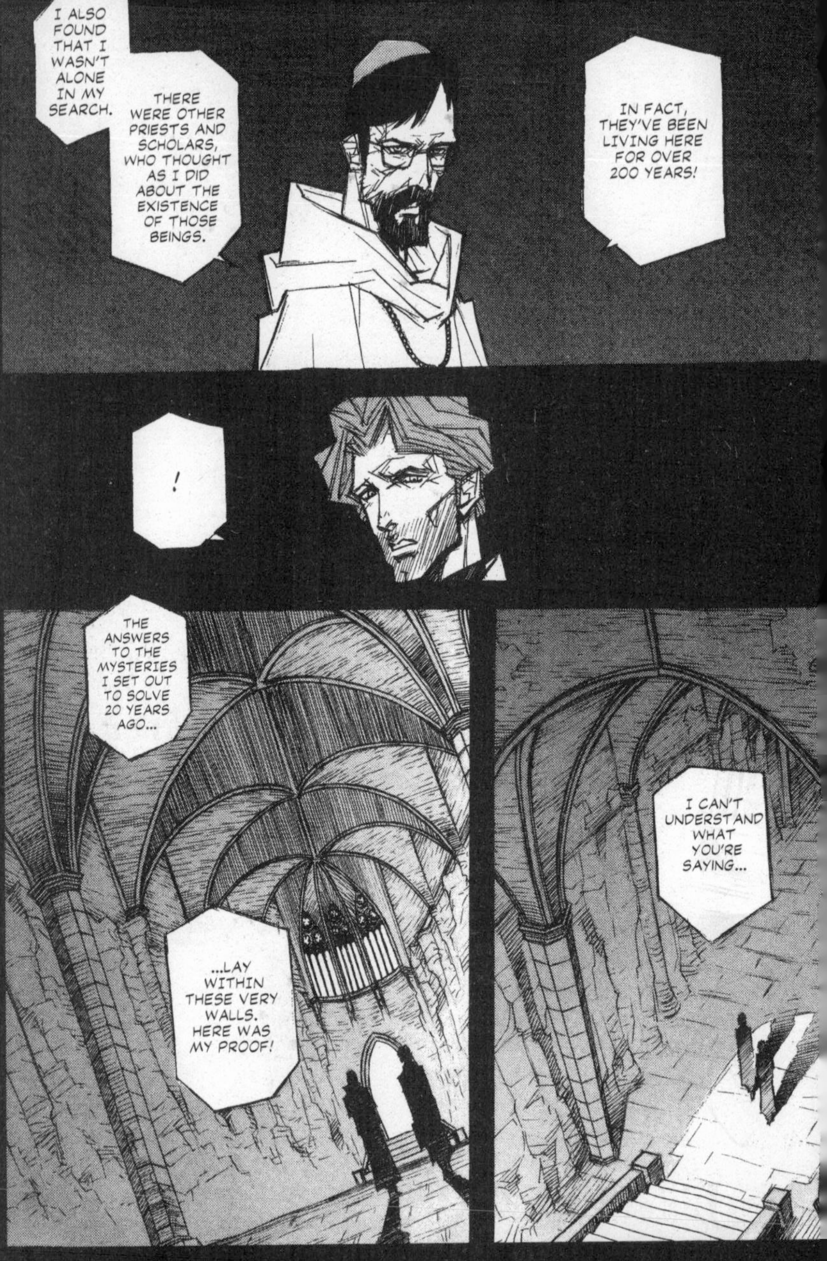
I ALSO FOUND THAT I WASN'T ALONE IN MY SEARCH.
THERE WERE OTHER PRIESTS AND SCHOLARS, WHO THOUGHT AS I DID ABOUT THE EXISTENCE OF THOSE BEINGS.
IN FACT, THEY'VE BEEN LIVING HERE FOR OVER 200 YEARS!
!
THE ANSWERS TO THE MYSTERIES I SET OUT TO SOLVE 20 YEARS AGO...
...LAY WITHIN THESE VERY WALLS. HERE WAS MY PROOF!
I CAN'T UNDERSTAND WHAT YOU'RE SAYING...

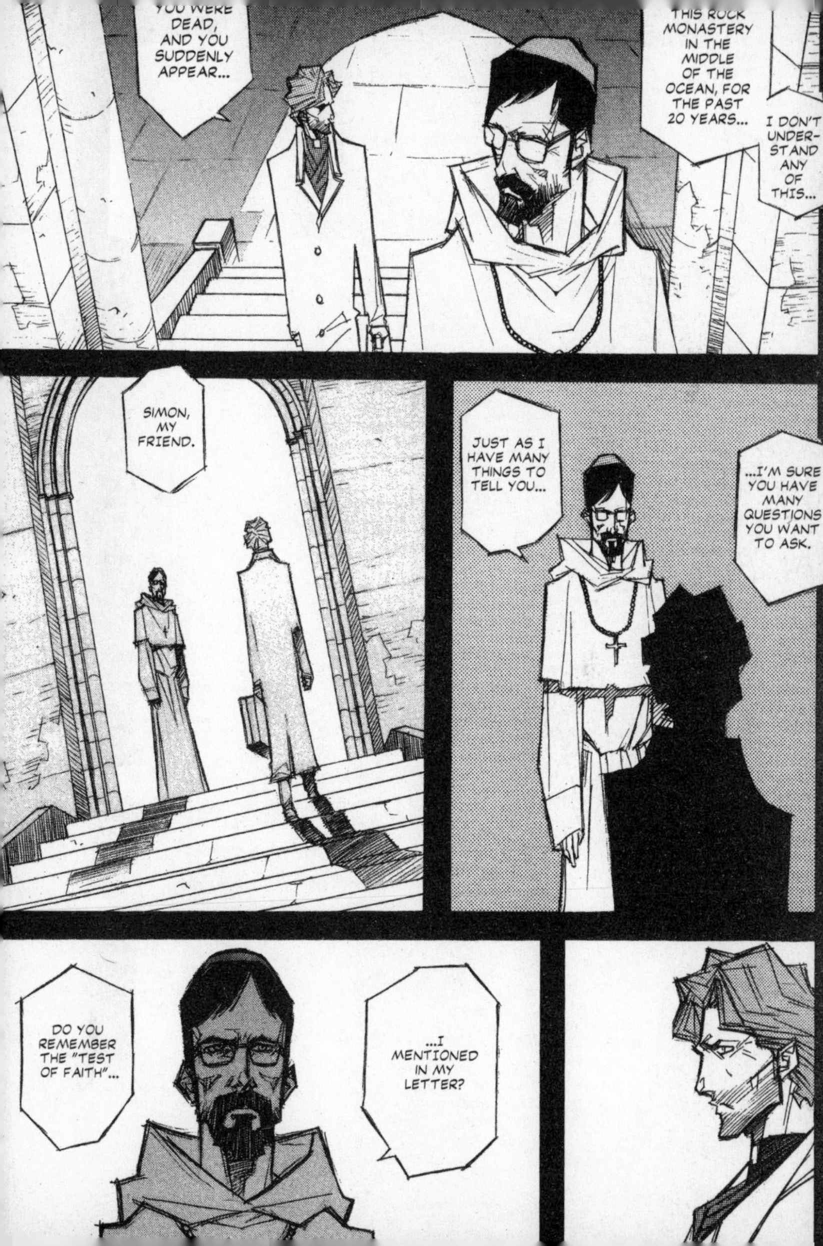
YOU WERE DEAD, AND YOU SUDDENLY APPEAR...
THIS ROCK MONASTERY IN THE MIDDLE OF THE OCEAN, FOR THE PAST 20 YEARS...
I DON'T UNDER-STAND ANY OF THIS...
SIMON, MY FRIEND.
JUST AS I HAVE MANY THINGS TO TELL YOU...
...I'M SURE YOU HAVE MANY QUESTIONS YOU WANT TO ASK.
DO YOU REMEMBER THE "TEST OF FAITH"...
...I MENTIONED IN MY LETTER?

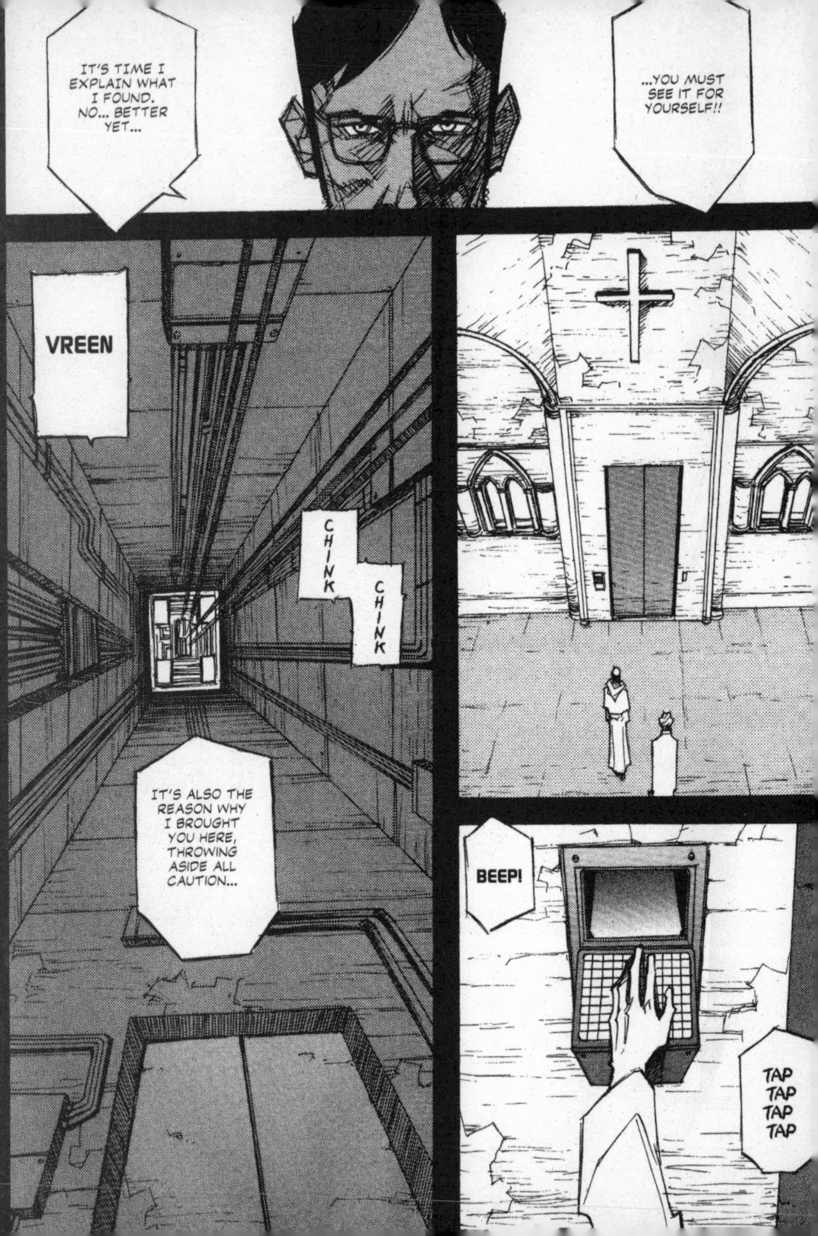
IT'S TIME I EXPLAIN WHAT I FOUND. NO... BETTER YET...
...YOU MUST SEE IT FOR YOURSELF!!
VREEN
CHINK
CHINK
IT'S ALSO THE REASON WHY I BROUGHT YOU HERE, THROWING ASIDE ALL CAUTION...
BEEP!
TAP TAP TAP TAP

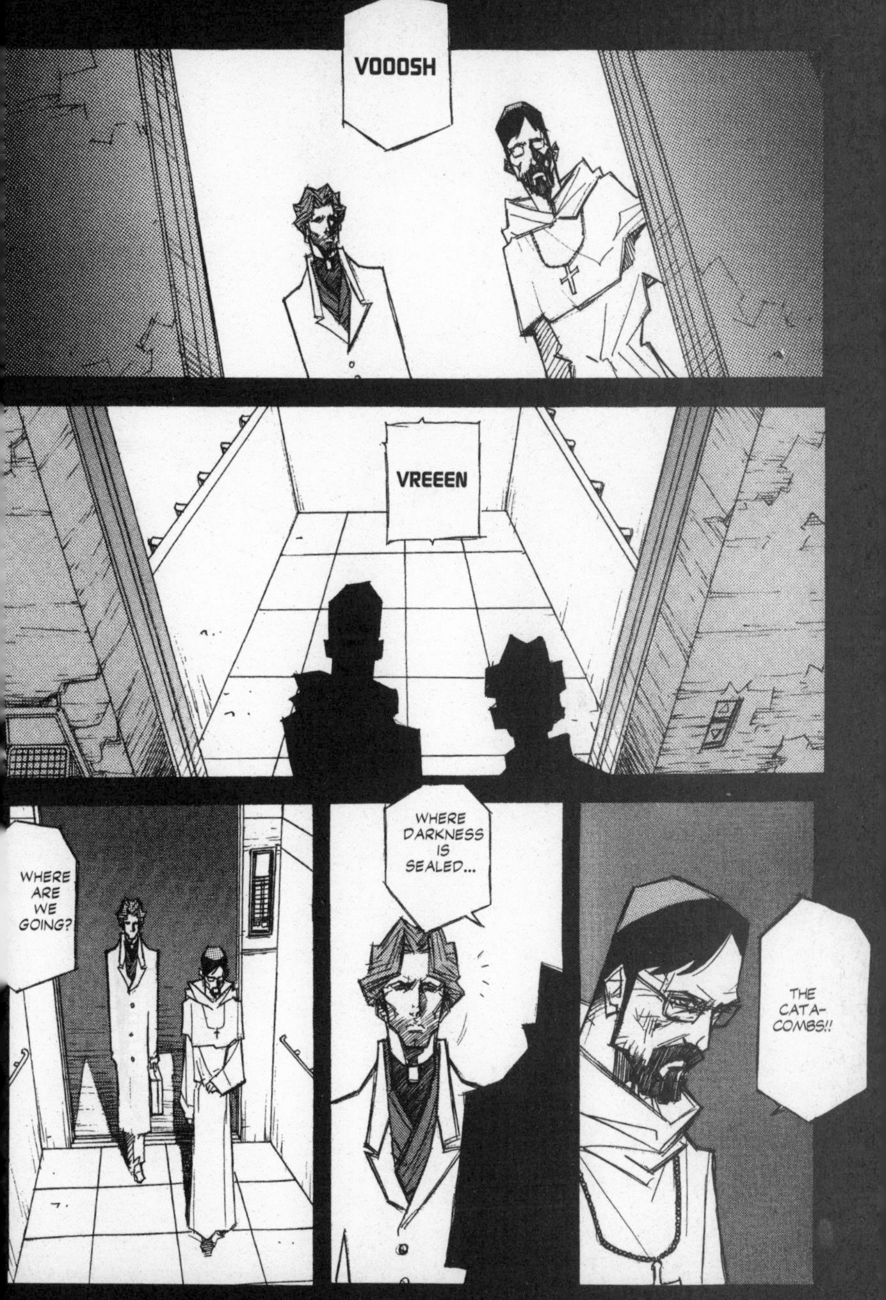
VOOOSH
VREEEN
WHERE ARE WE GOING?
WHERE DARKNESS IS SEALED...
THE CATA-COMBS!!

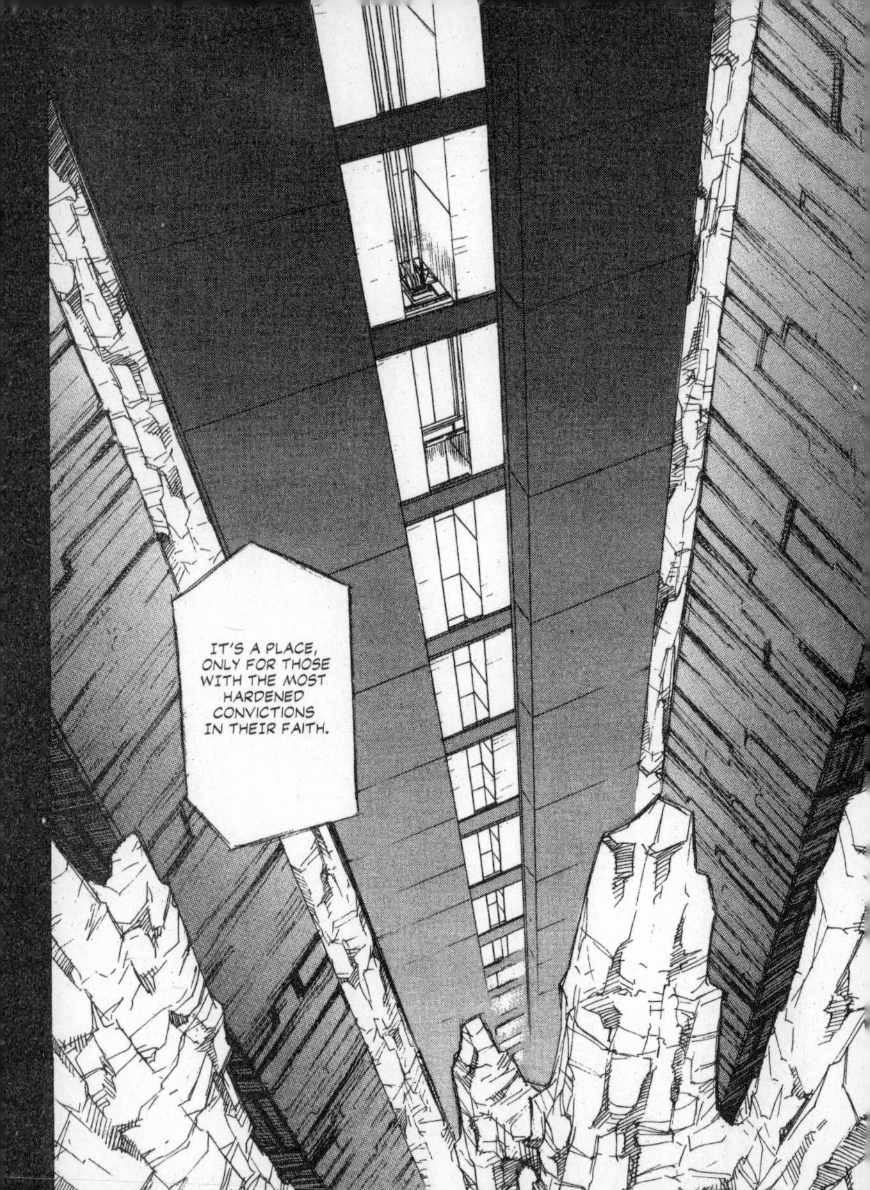
IT'S A PLACE, ONLY FOR THOSE WITH THE MOST HARDENED CONVICTIONS IN THEIR FAITH.

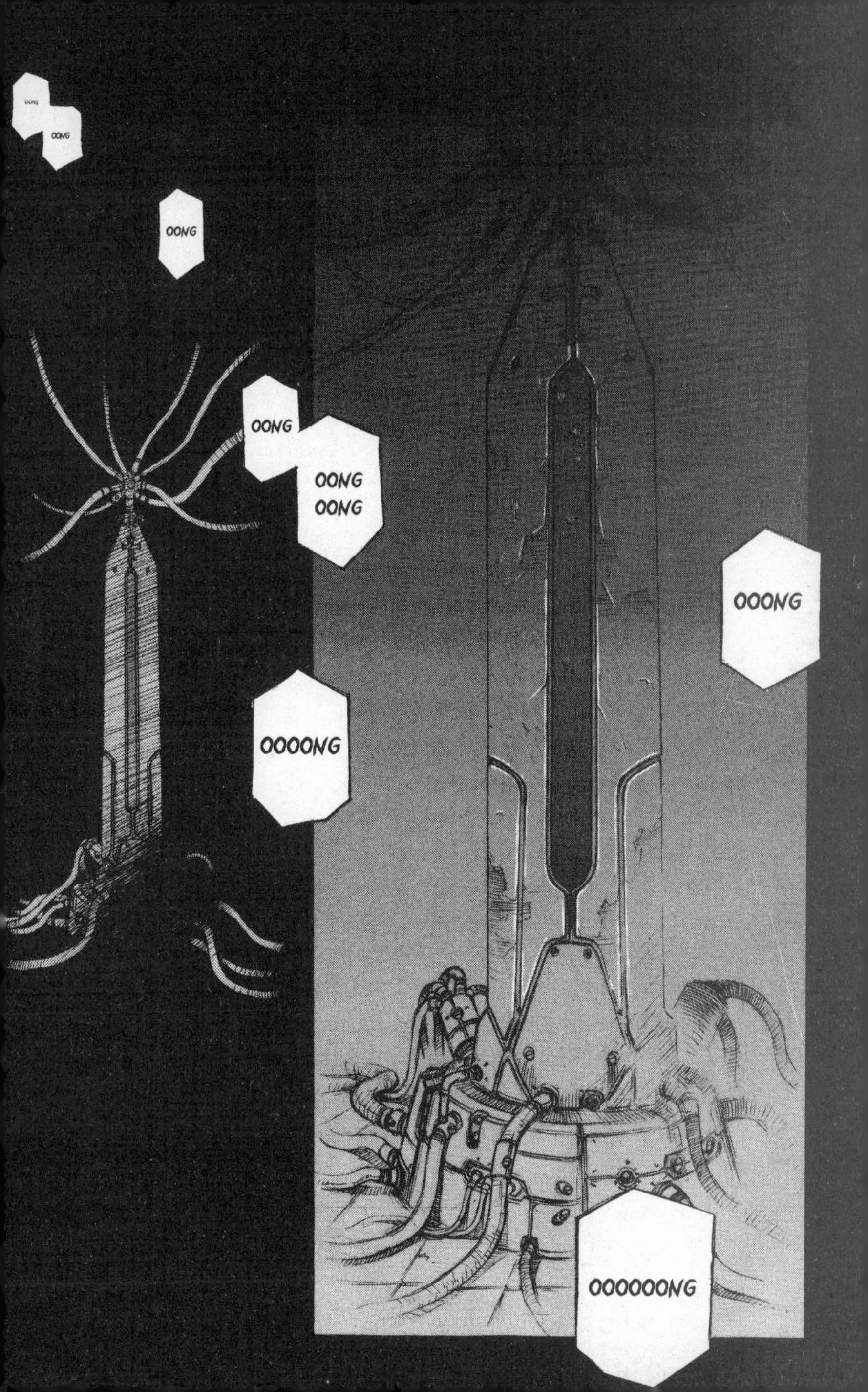
OONG
OONG
OONG
OONG
OONG
OONG
OOOONG
OOONG
OOOOOONG

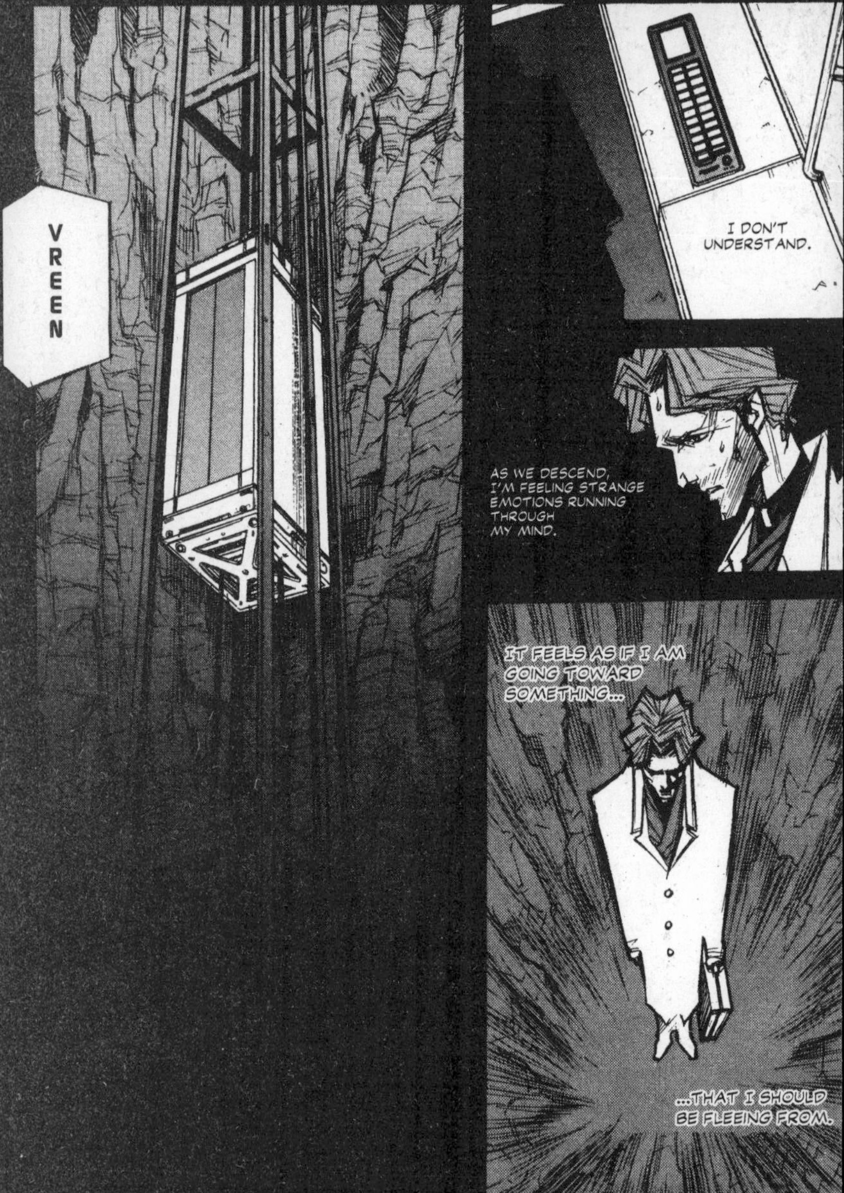
V R E E N
I DON'T UNDERSTAND.
AS WE DESCEND, I'M FEELING STRANGE EMOTIONS RUNNING THROUGH MY MIND.
IT FEELS AS IF I AM GOING TOWARD SOMETHING...
...THAT I SHOULD BE FLEEING FROM.

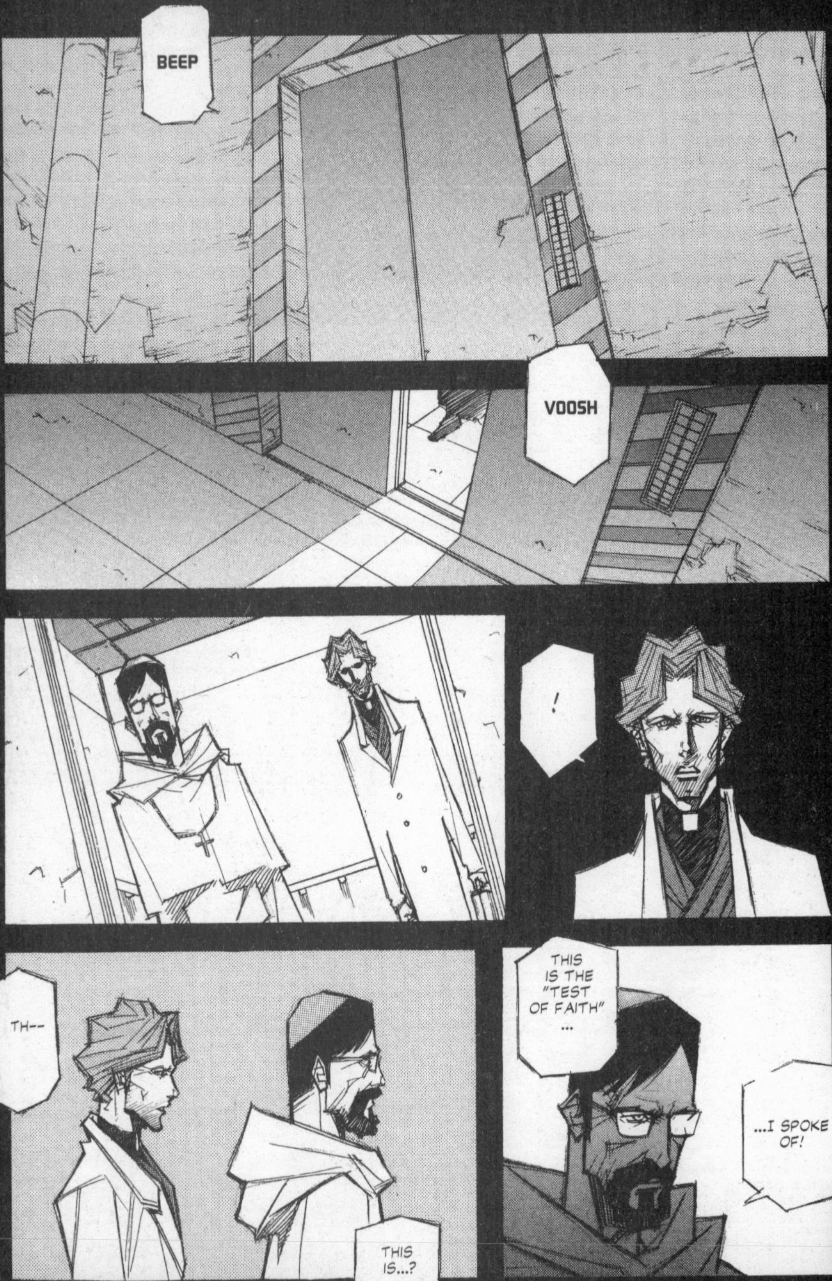
BEEP
VOOSH
!
TH--
THIS IS...?
THIS IS THE "TEST OF FAITH" ...
...I SPOKE OF!

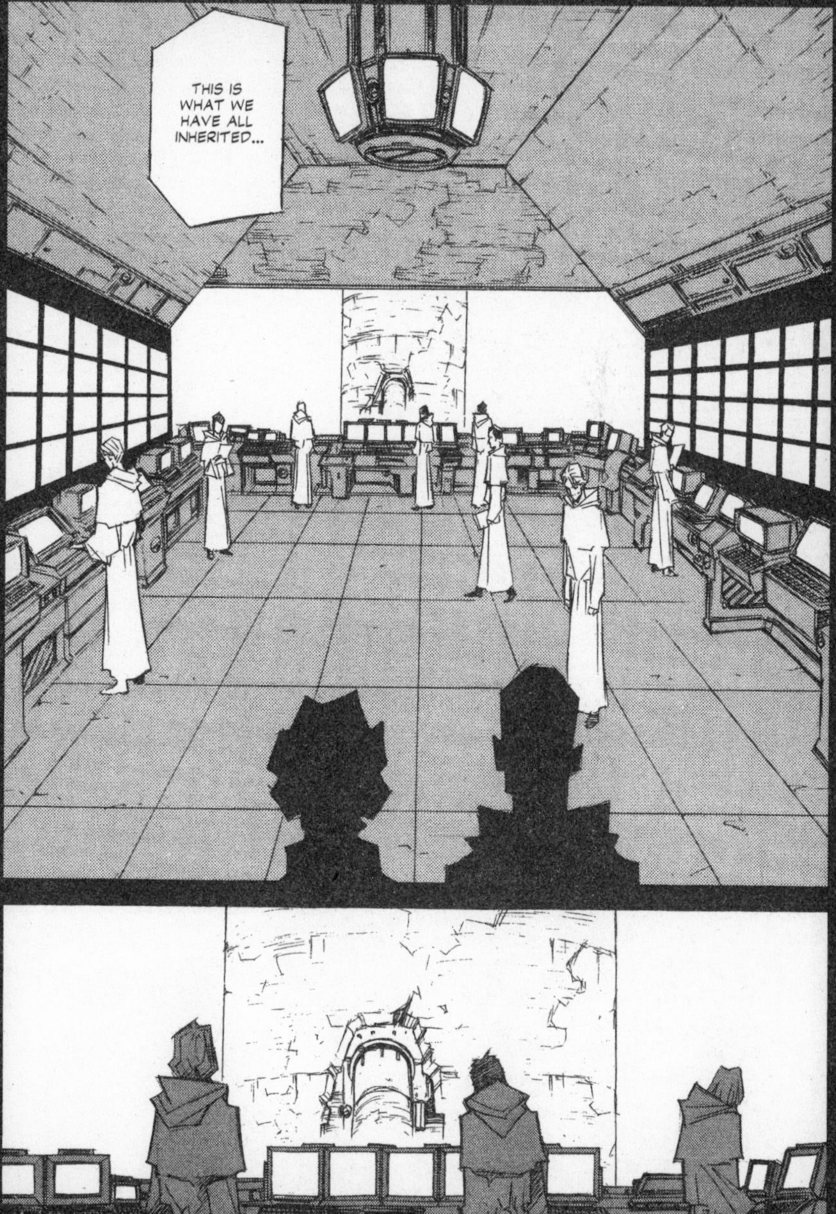
THIS IS WHAT WE HAVE ALL INHERITED...

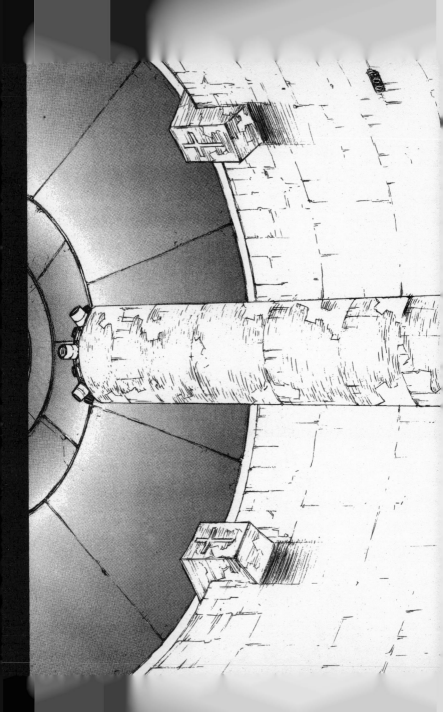

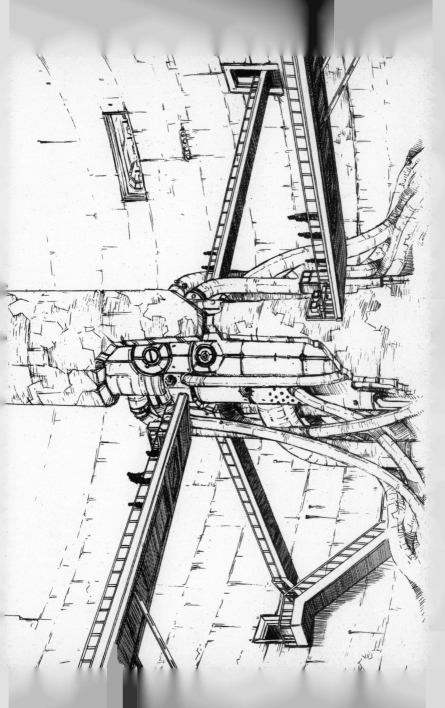

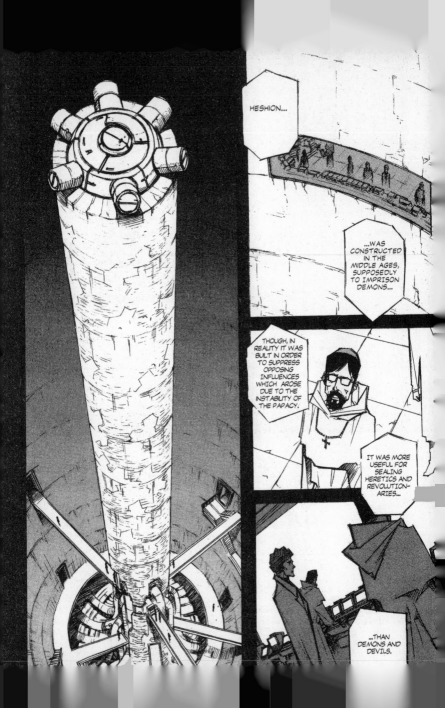

HESHION...

...WAS CONSTRUCTED IN THE MIDDLE AGES, SUPPOSEDLY TO IMPRISON DEMONS...

THOUGH, IN REALITY IT WAS BUILT IN ORDER TO SUPPRESS OPPOSING INFLUENCES WHICH AROSE DUE TO THE INSTABILITY OF THE PAPACY.

IT WAS MORE USEFUL FOR SEALING HERETICS AND REVOLUTION- ARIES...

...THAN DEMONS AND DEVILS.

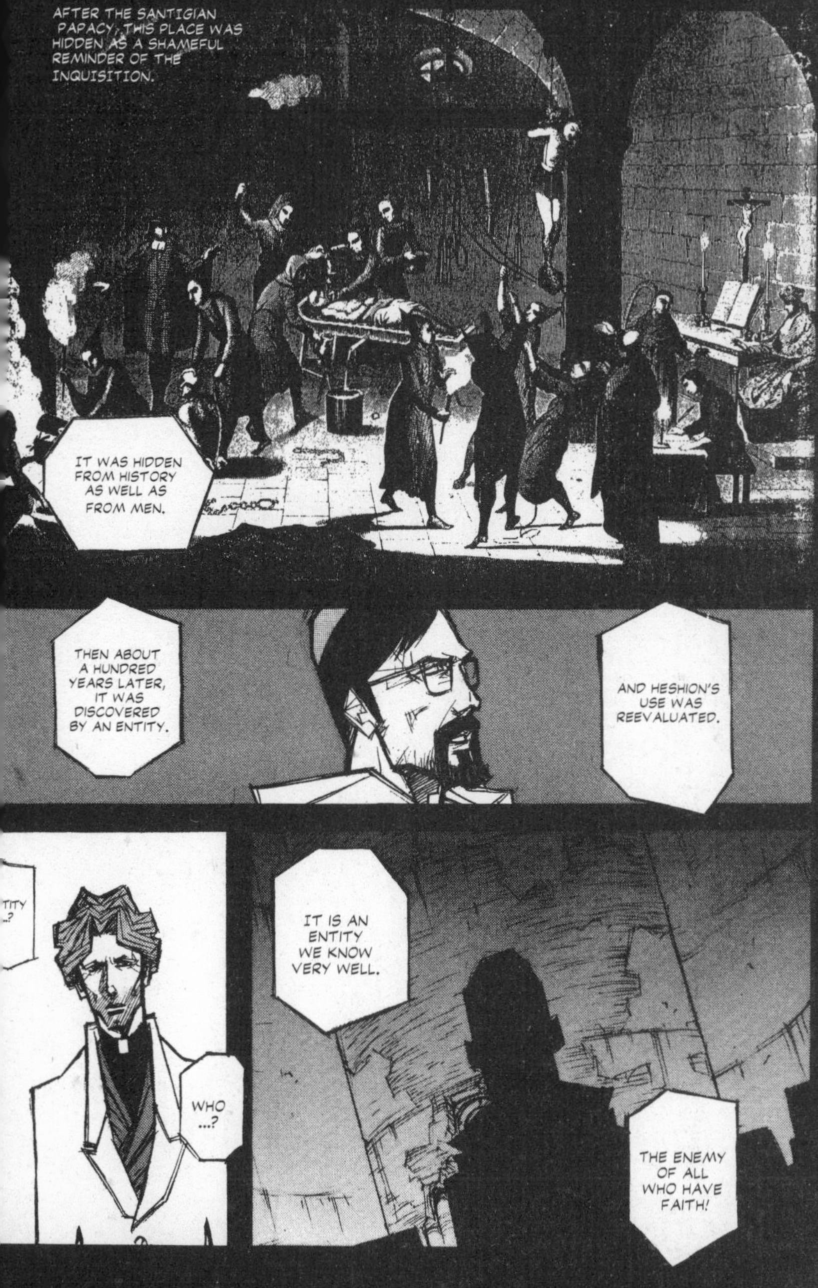
AFTER THE SANTIGIAN PAPACY, THIS PLACE WAS HIDDEN AS A SHAMEFUL REMINDER OF THE INQUISITION.
IT WAS HIDDEN FROM HISTORY AS WELL AS FROM MEN.
THEN ABOUT A HUNDRED YEARS LATER, IT WAS DISCOVERED BY AN ENTITY.
AND HESHION'S USE WAS REEVALUATED.
TITY ...?
WHO ...?
IT IS AN ENTITY WE KNOW VERY WELL.
THE ENEMY OF ALL WHO HAVE FAITH!

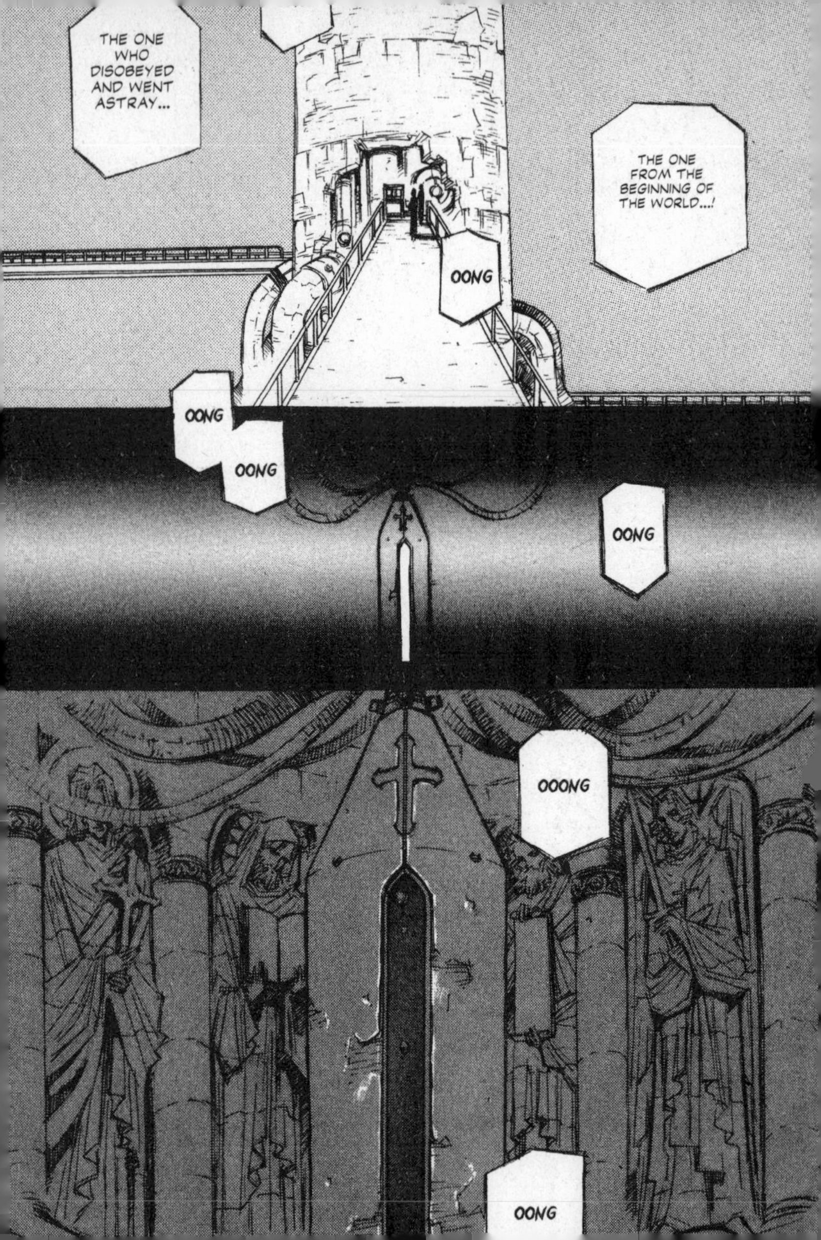
THE ONE WHO DISOBEYED AND WENT ASTRAY...
THE ONE FROM THE BEGINNING OF THE WORLD...!
OONG
OONG
OONG
OONG
OOONG
OONG

THE PILLAR
YOU SEE BEFORE
YOU IS A VACUUM...
A VOID.

SURROUNDED BY
SCIENCE, IT IS
FAITH THAT
KEEPS IT
SEALED.

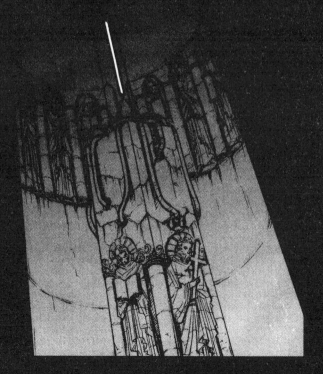

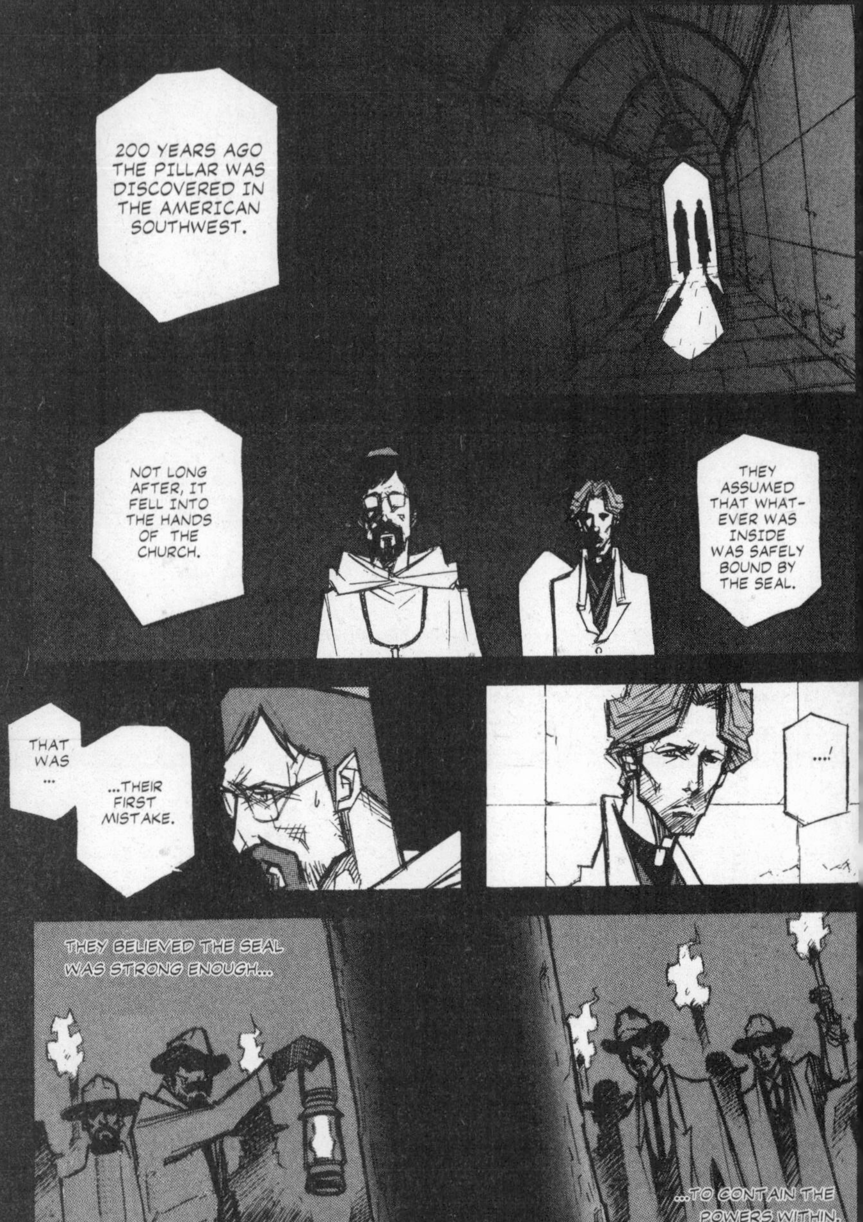
200 YEARS AGO THE PILLAR WAS DISCOVERED IN THE AMERICAN SOUTHWEST.
NOT LONG AFTER, IT FELL INTO THE HANDS OF THE CHURCH.
THEY ASSUMED THAT WHAT-EVER WAS INSIDE WAS SAFELY BOUND BY THE SEAL.
THAT WAS ...
...THEIR FIRST MISTAKE.
...!
THEY BELIEVED THE SEAL WAS STRONG ENOUGH...
...TO CONTAIN THE POWERS WITHIN.

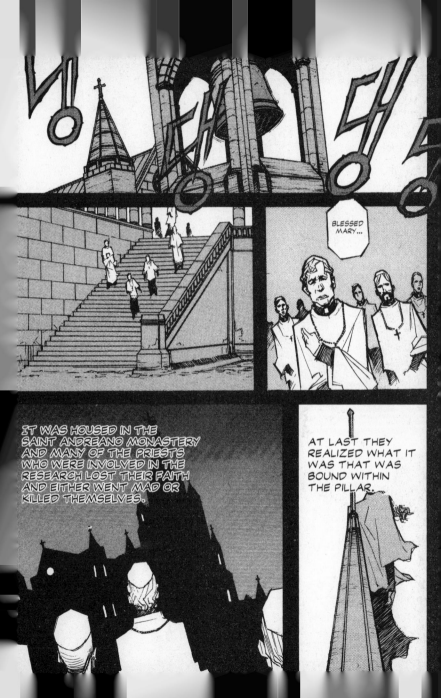

BLESSED MARY...

IT WAS HOUSED IN THE SAINT ANDREANO MONASTERY AND MANY OF THE PRIESTS WHO WERE INVOLVED IN THE RESEARCH LOST THEIR FAITH AND EITHER WENT MAD OR KILLED THEMSELVES.

AT LAST THEY REALIZED WHAT IT WAS THAT WAS BOUND WITHIN THE PILLAR.

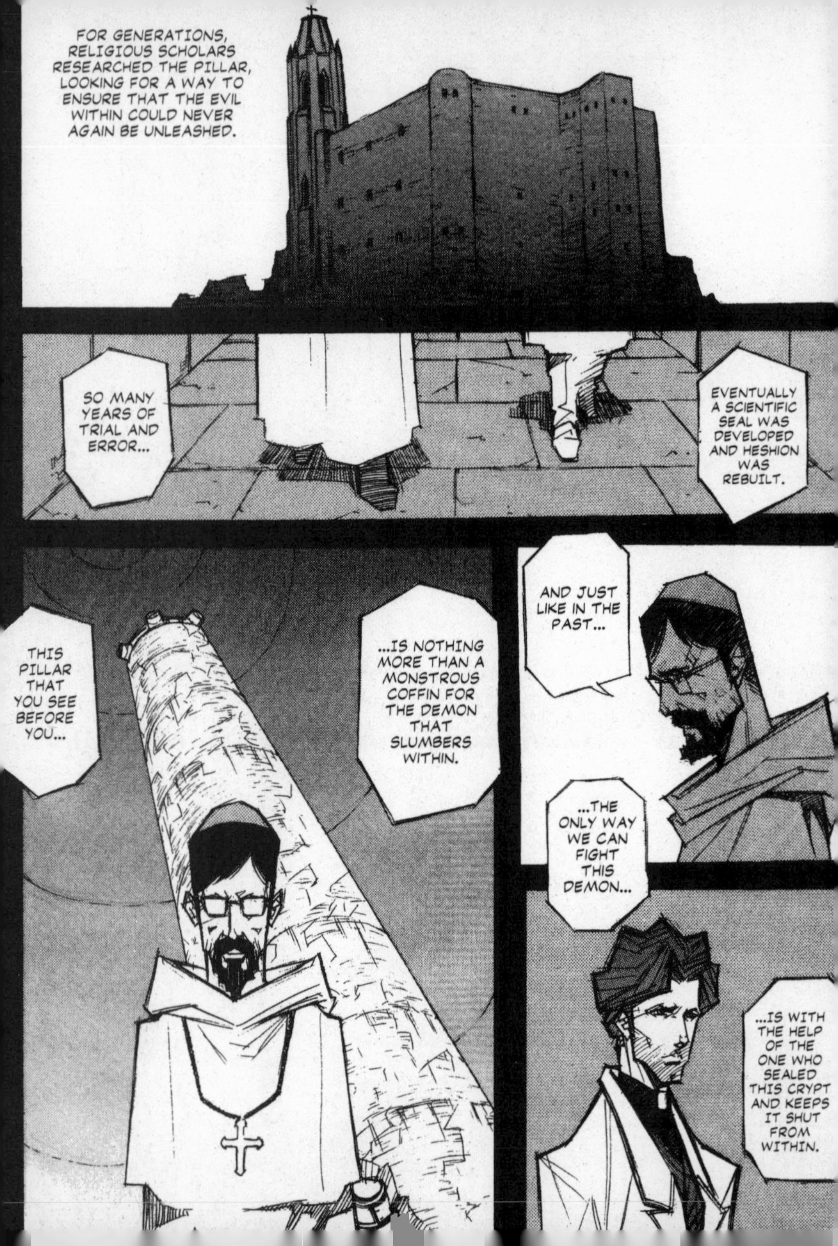
FOR GENERATIONS, RELIGIOUS SCHOLARS RESEARCHED THE PILLAR, LOOKING FOR A WAY TO ENSURE THAT THE EVIL WITHIN COULD NEVER AGAIN BE UNLEASHED.
SO MANY YEARS OF TRIAL AND ERROR...
EVENTUALLY A SCIENTIFIC SEAL WAS DEVELOPED AND HESHION WAS REBUILT.
THIS PILLAR THAT YOU SEE BEFORE YOU...
...IS NOTHING MORE THAN A MONSTROUS COFFIN FOR THE DEMON THAT SLUMBERS WITHIN.
AND JUST LIKE IN THE PAST...
...THE ONLY WAY WE CAN FIGHT THIS DEMON...
...IS WITH THE HELP OF THE ONE WHO SEALED THIS CRYPT AND KEEPS IT SHUT FROM WITHIN.

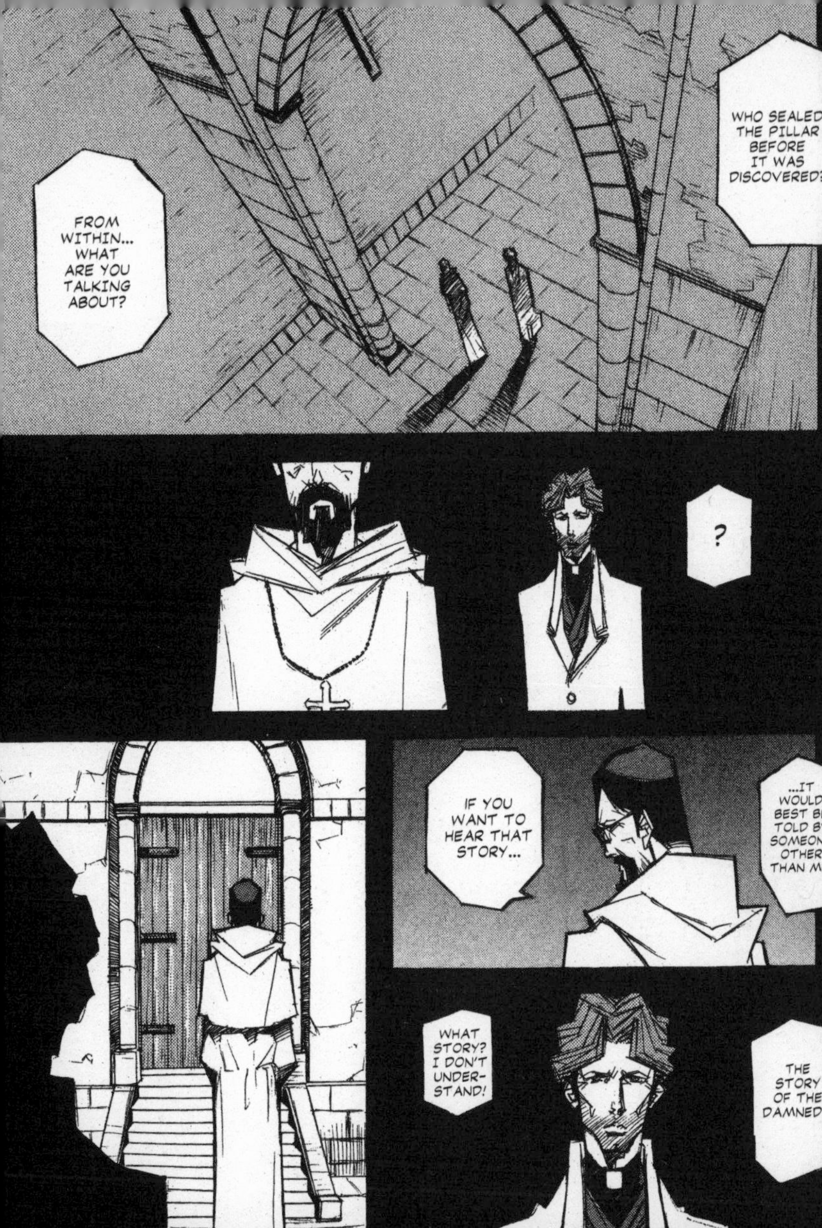
FROM WITHIN... WHAT ARE YOU TALKING ABOUT?
WHO SEALED THE PILLAR BEFORE IT WAS DISCOVERED?
?
IF YOU WANT TO HEAR THAT STORY...
...IT WOULD BEST BE TOLD BY SOMEONE OTHER THAN ME.
WHAT STORY? I DON'T UNDER-STAND!
THE STORY OF THE DAMNED...

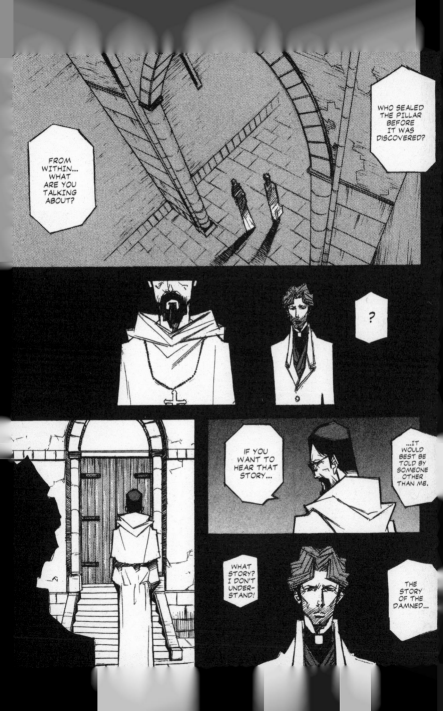

IT'S THE STORY OF
AN ANGEL OF BLOOD...

...WHO CAME TO THIS EARTH
300 YEARS AGO.

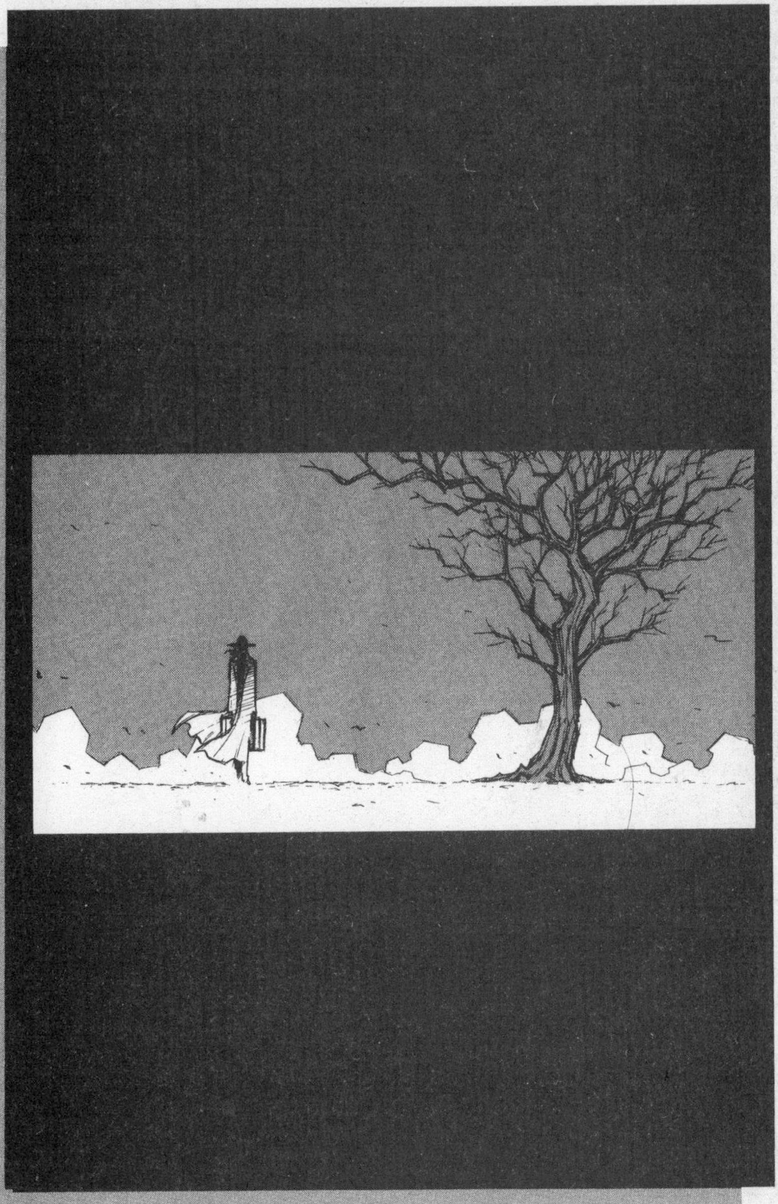

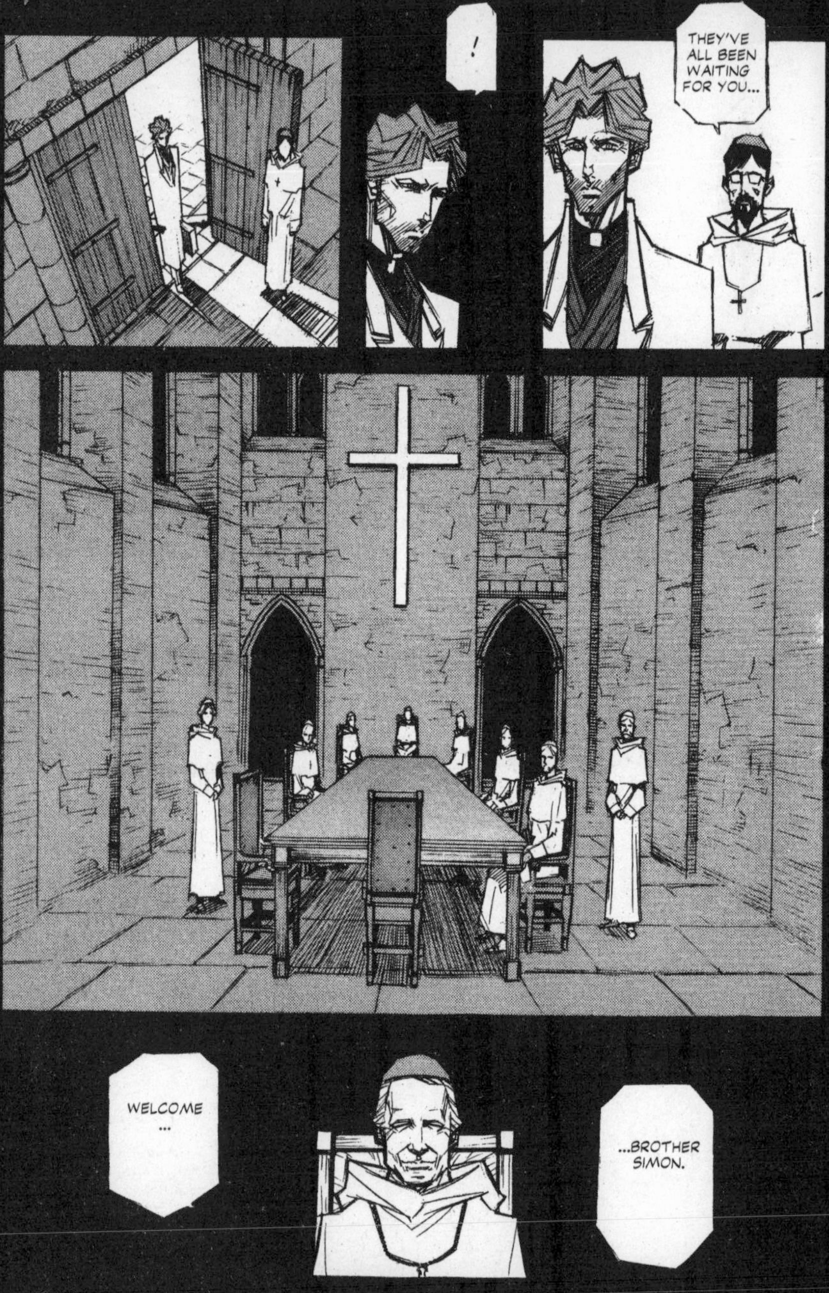
!
THEY'VE ALL BEEN WAITING FOR YOU...
WELCOME ...
...BROTHER SIMON.

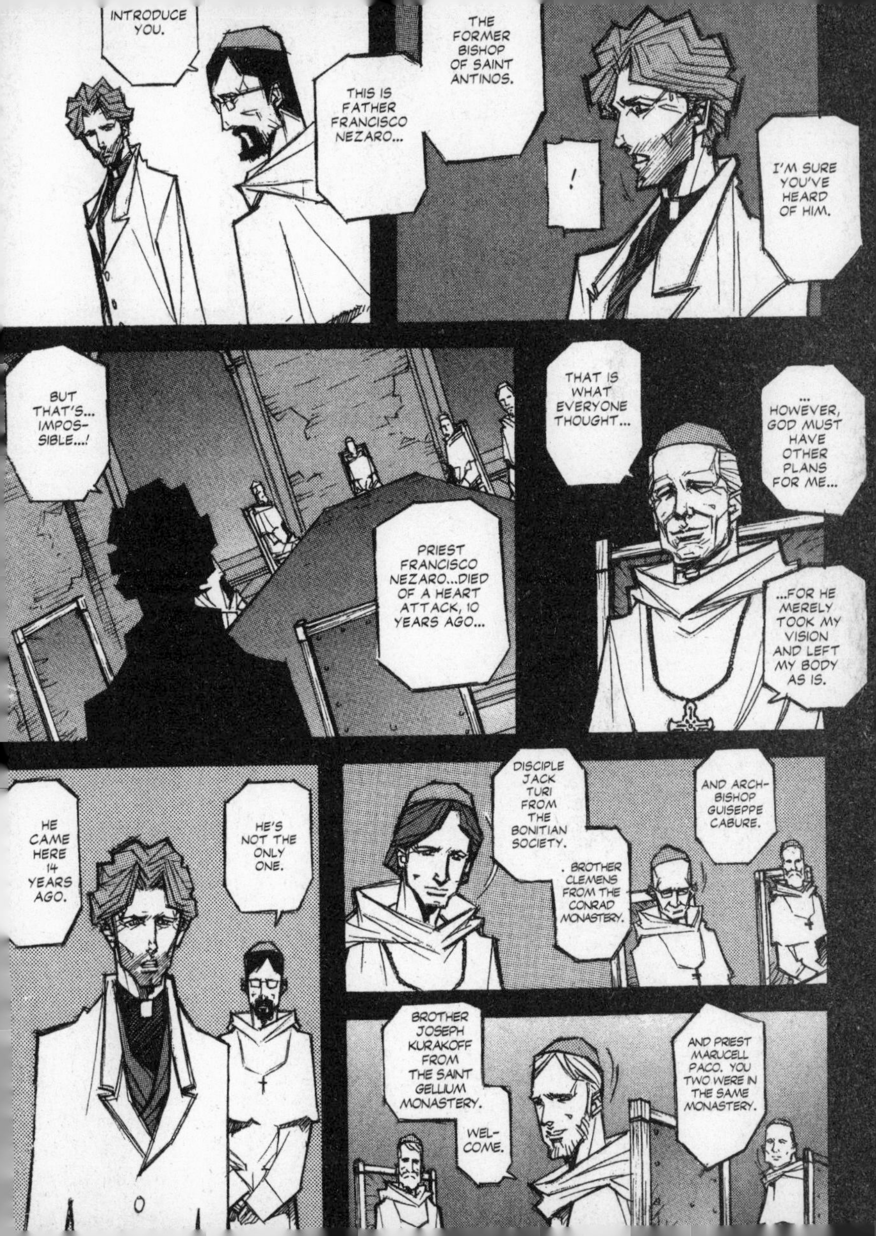
INTRODUCE YOU.
THIS IS FATHER FRANCISCO NEZARO...
THE FORMER BISHOP OF SAINT ANTINOS.
!
I'M SURE YOU'VE HEARD OF HIM.
BUT THAT'S... IMPOSSIBLE...!
PRIEST FRANCISCO NEZARO...DIED OF A HEART ATTACK, 10 YEARS AGO...
THAT IS WHAT EVERYONE THOUGHT...
... HOWEVER, GOD MUST HAVE OTHER PLANS FOR ME...
...FOR HE MERELY TOOK MY VISION AND LEFT MY BODY AS IS.
HE CAME HERE 14 YEARS AGO.
HE'S NOT THE ONLY ONE.
DISCIPLE JACK TURI FROM THE BONITIAN SOCIETY.
. BROTHER CLEMENS FROM THE CONRAD MONASTERY.
AND ARCH-BISHOP GUISEPPE CABURE.
BROTHER JOSEPH KURAKOFF FROM THE SAINT GELLIUM MONASTERY.
WEL-COME.
AND PRIEST MARUCELL PACO. YOU TWO WERE IN THE SAME MONASTERY.

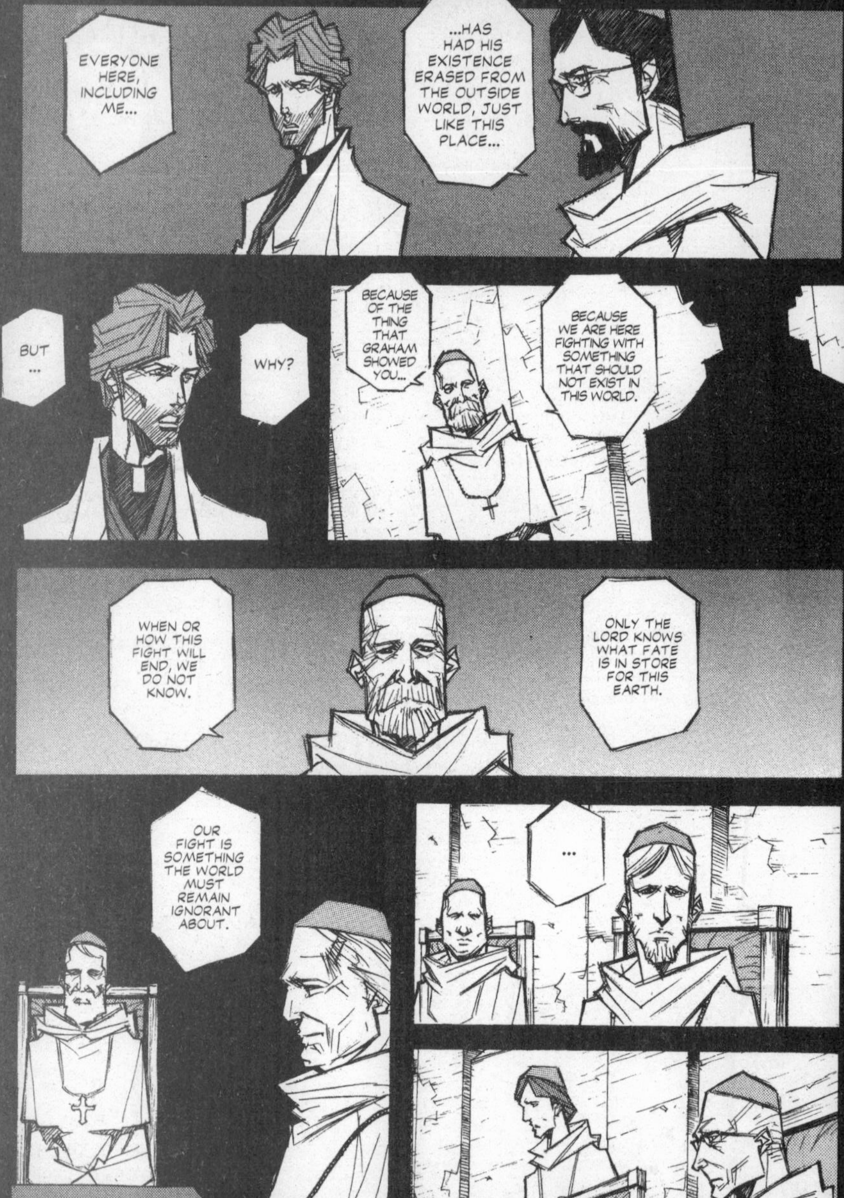
EVERYONE HERE, INCLUDING ME...
...HAS HAD HIS EXISTENCE ERASED FROM THE OUTSIDE WORLD, JUST LIKE THIS PLACE...
BUT ...
WHY?
BECAUSE OF THE THING THAT GRAHAM SHOWED YOU...
BECAUSE WE ARE HERE FIGHTING WITH SOMETHING THAT SHOULD NOT EXIST IN THIS WORLD.
WHEN OR HOW THIS FIGHT WILL END, WE DO NOT KNOW.
ONLY THE LORD KNOWS WHAT FATE IS IN STORE FOR THIS EARTH.
OUR FIGHT IS SOMETHING THE WORLD MUST REMAIN IGNORANT ABOUT.
...

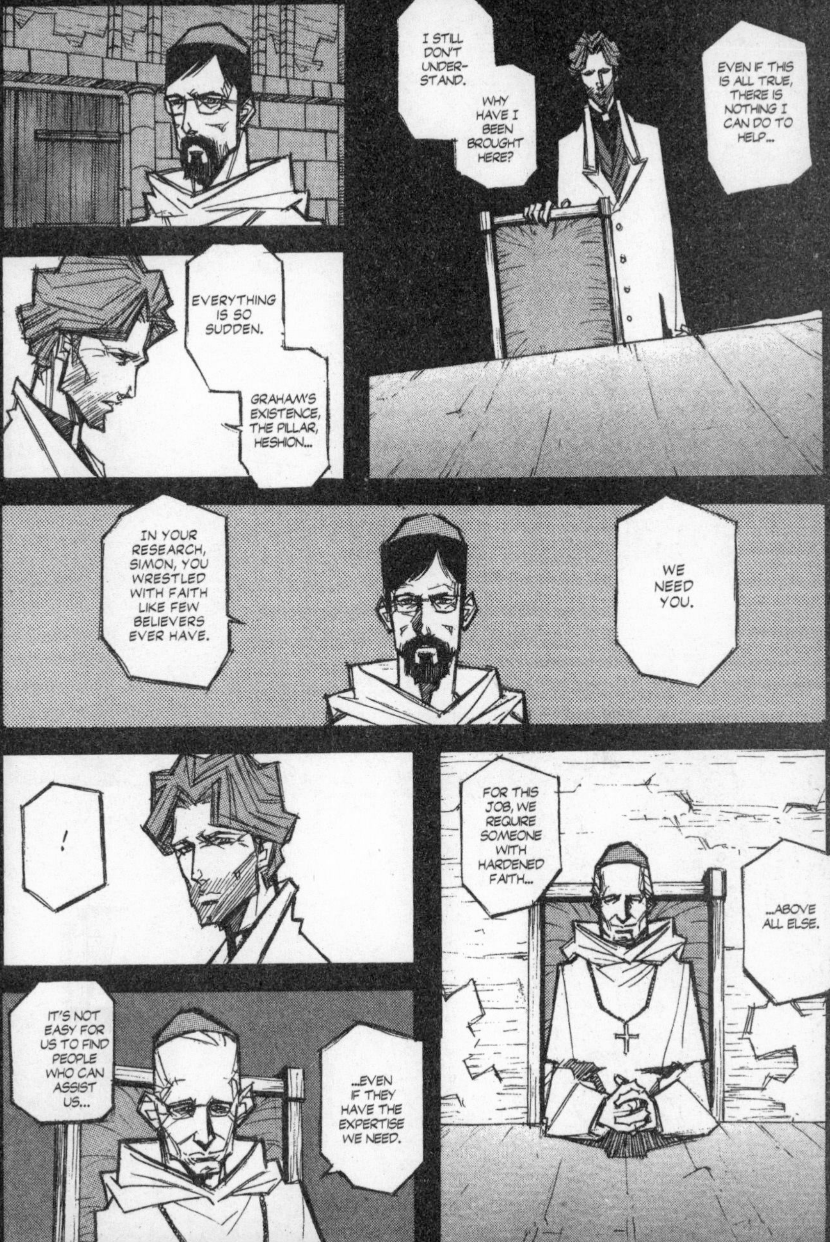
I STILL DON'T UNDER-STAND.
WHY HAVE I BEEN BROUGHT HERE?
EVEN IF THIS IS ALL TRUE, THERE IS NOTHING I CAN DO TO HELP...
EVERYTHING IS SO SUDDEN.
GRAHAM'S EXISTENCE, THE PILLAR, HESHION...
IN YOUR RESEARCH, SIMON, YOU WRESTLED WITH FAITH LIKE FEW BELIEVERS EVER HAVE.
WE NEED YOU.
!
FOR THIS JOB, WE REQUIRE SOMEONE WITH HARDENED FAITH...
...ABOVE ALL ELSE.
IT'S NOT EASY FOR US TO FIND PEOPLE WHO CAN ASSIST US...
...EVEN IF THEY HAVE THE EXPERTISE WE NEED.

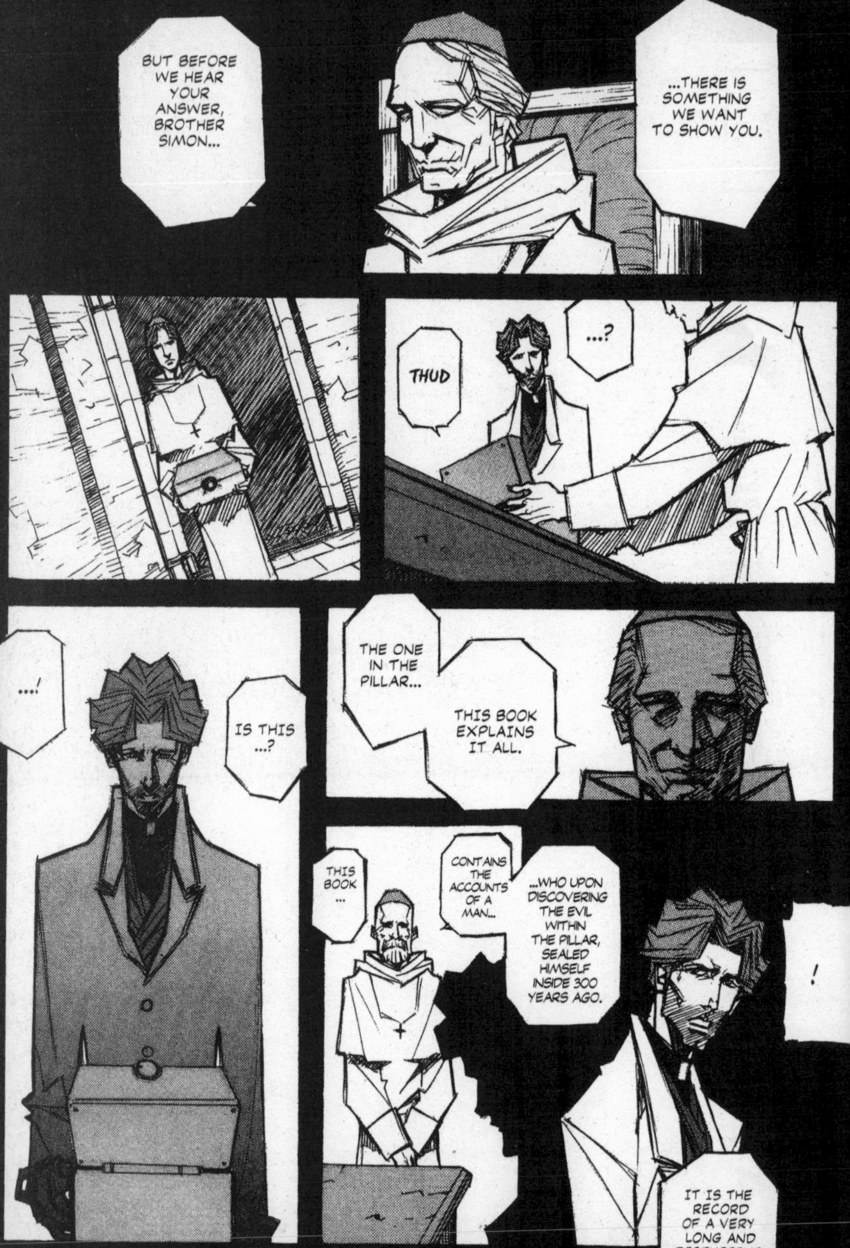
BUT BEFORE WE HEAR YOUR ANSWER, BROTHER SIMON...
...THERE IS SOMETHING WE WANT TO SHOW YOU.
THUD
...?
...!
IS THIS ...?
THE ONE IN THE PILLAR...
THIS BOOK EXPLAINS IT ALL.
THIS BOOK ...
CONTAINS THE ACCOUNTS OF A MAN...
...WHO UPON DISCOVERING THE EVIL WITHIN THE PILLAR, SEALED HIMSELF INSIDE 300 YEARS AGO.
!
IT IS THE RECORD OF A VERY LONG AND DISTURBING BATTLE.

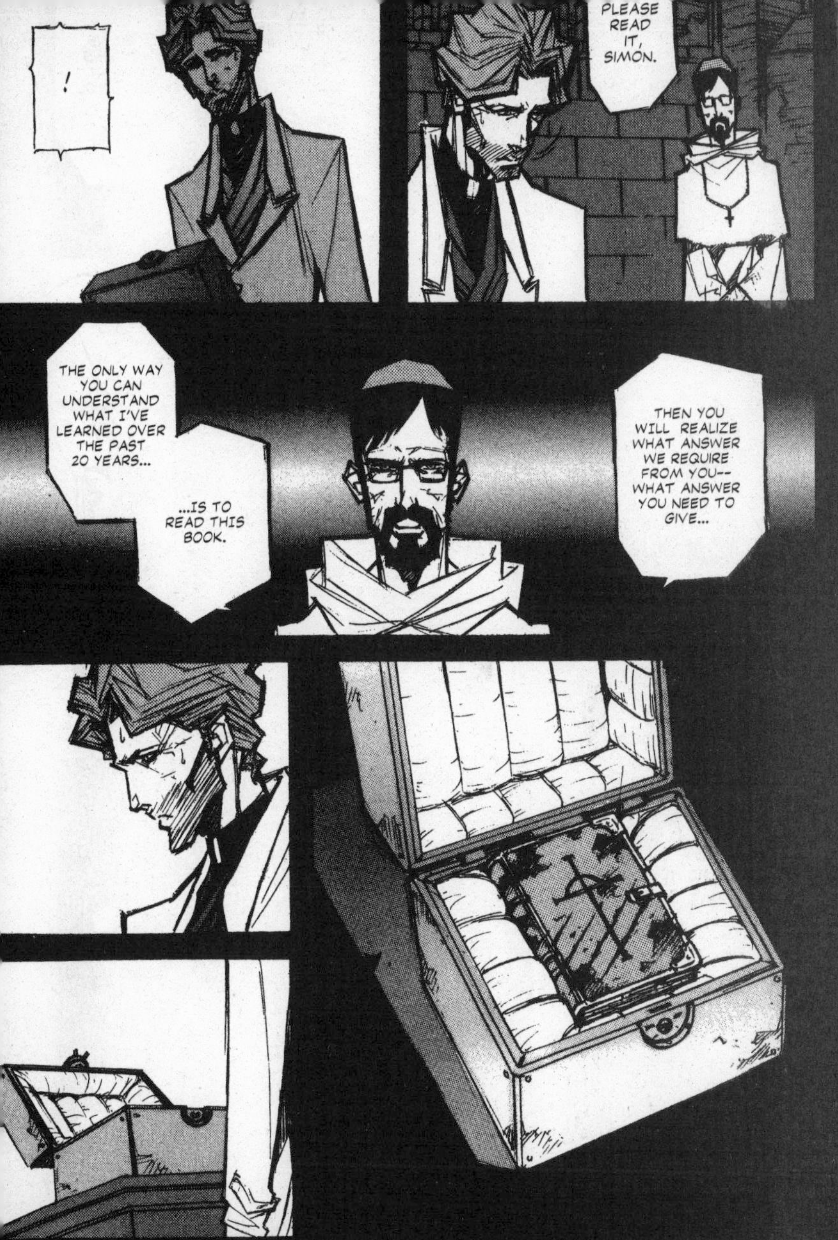
!
PLEASE READ IT, SIMON.
THE ONLY WAY YOU CAN UNDERSTAND WHAT I'VE LEARNED OVER THE PAST 20 YEARS...
...IS TO READ THIS BOOK.
THEN YOU WILL REALIZE WHAT ANSWER WE REQUIRE FROM YOU-- WHAT ANSWER YOU NEED TO GIVE...

IVAN ISAACS WILL RETURN IN PRIEST VOLUME 4: FORBIDDEN DUET

IN WHICH IVAN TAKES US BACK TO HIS YOUTH AND RECOUNTS HIS FORBIDDEN LOVE FOR GENA AND HIS FALL FROM GRACE.

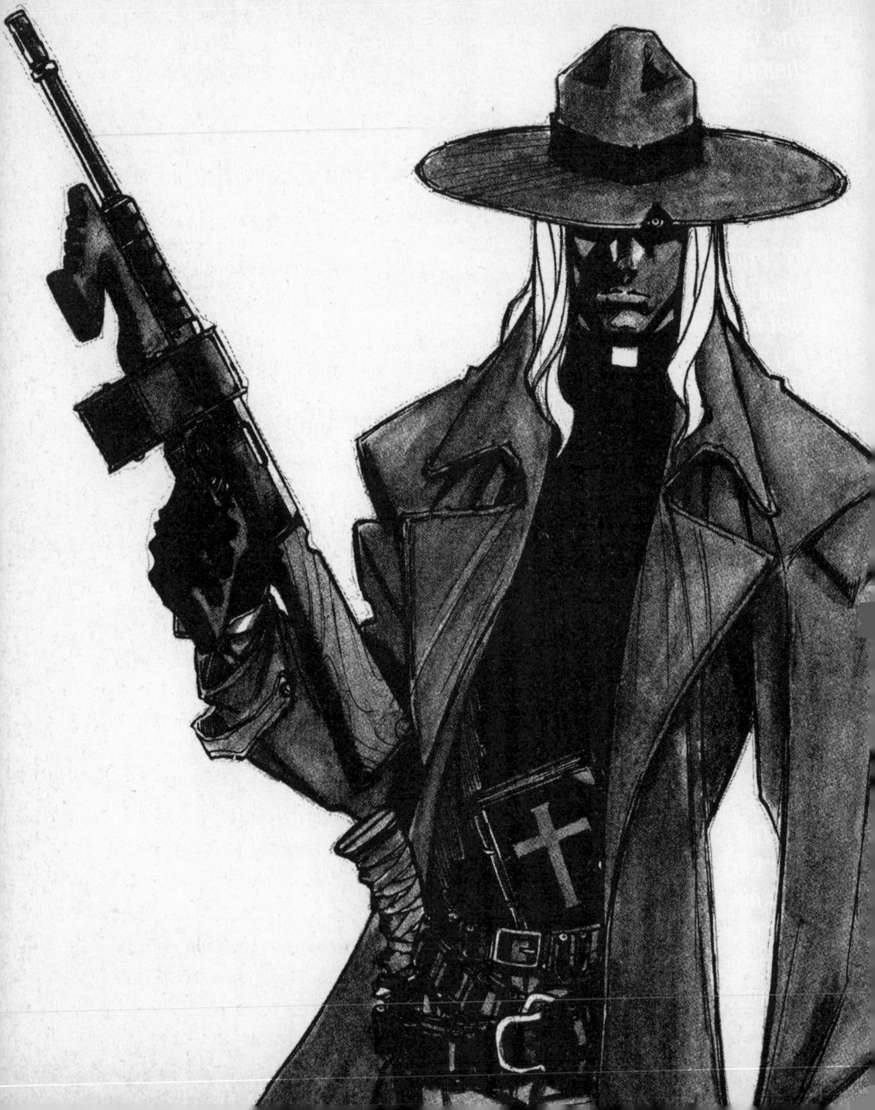

AN INTERVIEW WITH
MIN-WOO HYUNG

Q) What was the first manwha that you worked on and what was it about?

A) Chronicle of a Hot-blooded Judo King *was the title of my first manwha. The concept, in of itself, isn't unique. It's rather a common young adult theme, written purely to entertain.*

Q) When did you first begin work on *Priest*? How did you come up with the concept of combining Spaghetti Westerns with gothic horror?

A) Priest *was conceived from* Blood, *an American PC Game developed by Monolith Productions, Inc. The idea of a resurrected zombie as the protagonist totally fascinated me. Initially, I took the subject matter and began writing a novel, then later decided to draw it instead. In order to preserve the initial charm I experienced from the game's character, I avoided delving further into the character's imaginary world. From an early age, I've always loved Gothic Horrors and Spaghetti Westerns, and* Priest *was very conducive to both genres. It was rather an easy harmonization of both genres, and they naturally and seamlessly seeped into* Priest. *(Of course, the game* Blood *was also created with a horror/western plot. Due to various reasons, both* Blood *and* Priest *are inseparably related.)*

Q) Reading *Priest*, I'm amazed at how "western" it feels. You did a remarkable job capturing the spirit of a Hollywood action movie. Were you influenced by movies in making *Priest*? Can you share any titles that influenced you?

A) *The first Western that I accidentally came in contact with was Walter Hill's* The Long Riders. *I was never really interested in cowboy movies until I saw this movie, though you'd be hard pressed to call it a Spaghetti Western. After this movie, I slowly started getting into Spaghetti Westerns. As a result, I discovered and came to admire Sergio Leone's works and especially* Once Upon a Time in the West. *This movie has so profoundly influenced me that any work I do now or will do in the future will inevitably mirror its stylistic overtures.*

Q) The artwork in *Priest* is very different from other manwha I've seen. What were your influences?

A) Hell Boy. *The first time I saw this comic, I was blown away by its innovative and shocking style. To this day, I cannot forget that series.*

Q) How did you become a manwha artist? Did you have formal training?

A) *No, I did not go through any general training course like other manhwa artists. However, like these fellow manwha lovers, I did undergo a beginning course. And although I had considered manhwa as a mere hobby, now in my late twenties, it has become an occupation.*

Q) In Korea, Japanese manga is quite popular, but I haven't heard about American comic books in Korea. Are American comic books readily available, and are you a fan? Are there any American comics in particular you like?

A) *American comics are very different from the manhwa Koreans have enjoyed and are used to reading. From production, to character development, everything is very different. Therefore, in order for Korean manwha fans to enjoy American comics, American writers need to be mindful of their efforts (assuming that American writers desire to do so). Should we become exposed to American comics, through a long-term exchange, there is no doubt in my mind that American comics will become popular in Korea. I, of course, love American comics. Surprisingly, the comics I read as a child were not Japanese manga but rather American comics. It all started with my Aunt and Uncle. My Uncle, who is American, would visit Korea with my Aunt and bring me American comic books. If I have to choose one, my current favorite would have to be* CREECH *by Greg Capullo.*

Q) *Priest* is currently being adapted into an online game by World Netgames. Are you involved with the development of the game? How closely does the game follow your manwha?

A) *Making two publicity posters for this game was my only involvement. Although the subject matter for the game is from my manwha, the creation of the game was the creative work of others. (I'm sure you can appreciate the irony. As you know my manwha was derived from the game* Blood *and to see my work being made back into a game is very surreal. This type of reciprocal action or interplay is something you would see in Hollywood. Case in point, a Japanese manga-ka, after watching* Mad Max *created* Fist of the North Star, *Hollywood, impressed with the manga, made a movie based on the* manga. Although Priest and Fist of the North Star have been both heavily influenced and derived from their respective reciprocal works, they are undoubtedly new and different creative pieces of work.) The online Priest game has not yet arrived at the conclusion. Therefore, I obviously do not yet know what the differences are between my work and the game. The only thing I do know for sure is that my protagonist will not be in the game.

Q) Do you have an end planned for *Priest*? What will be the final volume?

A) *I've had some ideas for the ending but I'm not sure whether this ending will be feasible. I planned on ending the series at volume 25 but I'm not sure about that either. I'm not the methodical and prudent planner type.*

Q) What do you plan to work on when *Priest* is finished? Do you have any other manwha stories planned?

A) *Warrior, cop, gangster, and skateboard…I'm in the process of choosing from one of these subject matters. (I'm already in the process of developing a Warrior themed manhwa in the US through Image Comics).*

Q) Can you share any details on your project with Image?

A) *As stated in my previous answer, yes, I am. I am currently working on the manwha through a joint publishing venture by a Korean and an American company. It's a work in progress, so I want to avoid mentioning anything about it. One thing I can mention is that the initial concept is completely in the style of American comics, however, beyond that, the style converts completely into my own.*

Q) The black and white artwork in *Priest* is very striking. Do you prefer working in the black and white medium? Would you be interested in working on a color series?

A) *I really love those noisy black and white films with the distorted and elongated screen shots caused by dust and time. That is why I eliminated the margins, in order for* Priest *to give off a similar feel. I don't like tones. I don't like them because they are bothersome, annoying, and all those manwhas that use tones appear to be tied together by one personality. I think colored manwhas are great, although, I have yet to find a coloring method that would convey my individual style. However, I am looking into ways of solving this*

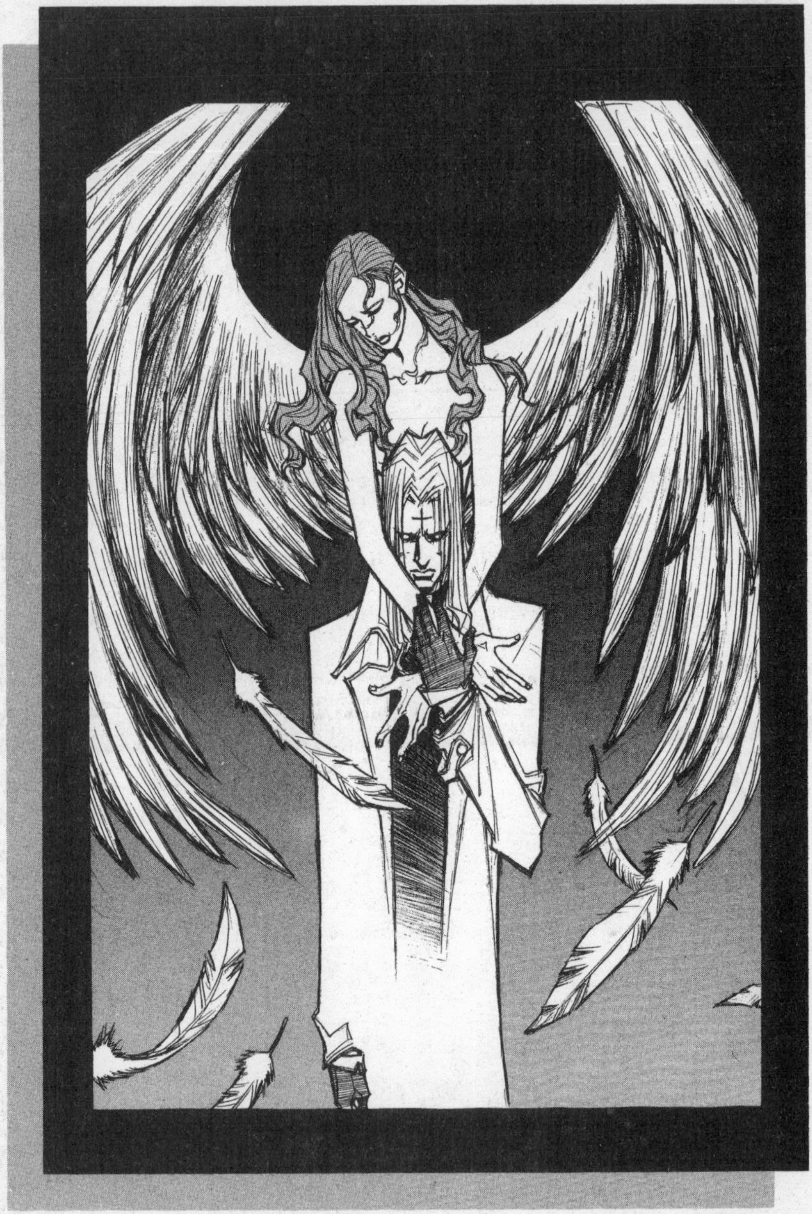

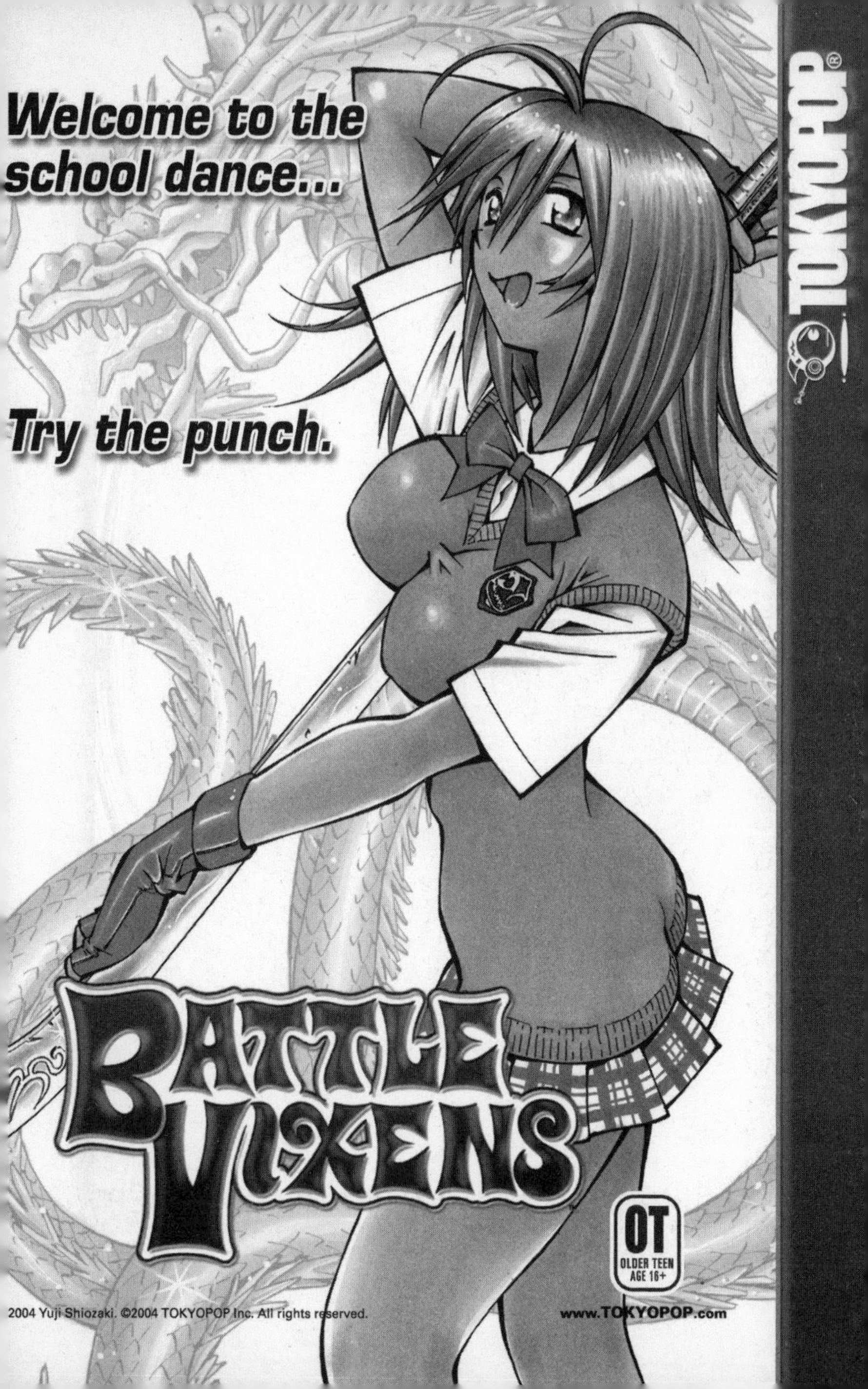
Welcome to the school dance...
Try the punch.
BATTLE VIXENS
OT
OLDER TEEN AGE 16+
2004 Yuji Shiozaki. ©2004 TOKYOPOP Inc. All rights reserved.
www.TOKYOPOP.com
TOKYOPOP

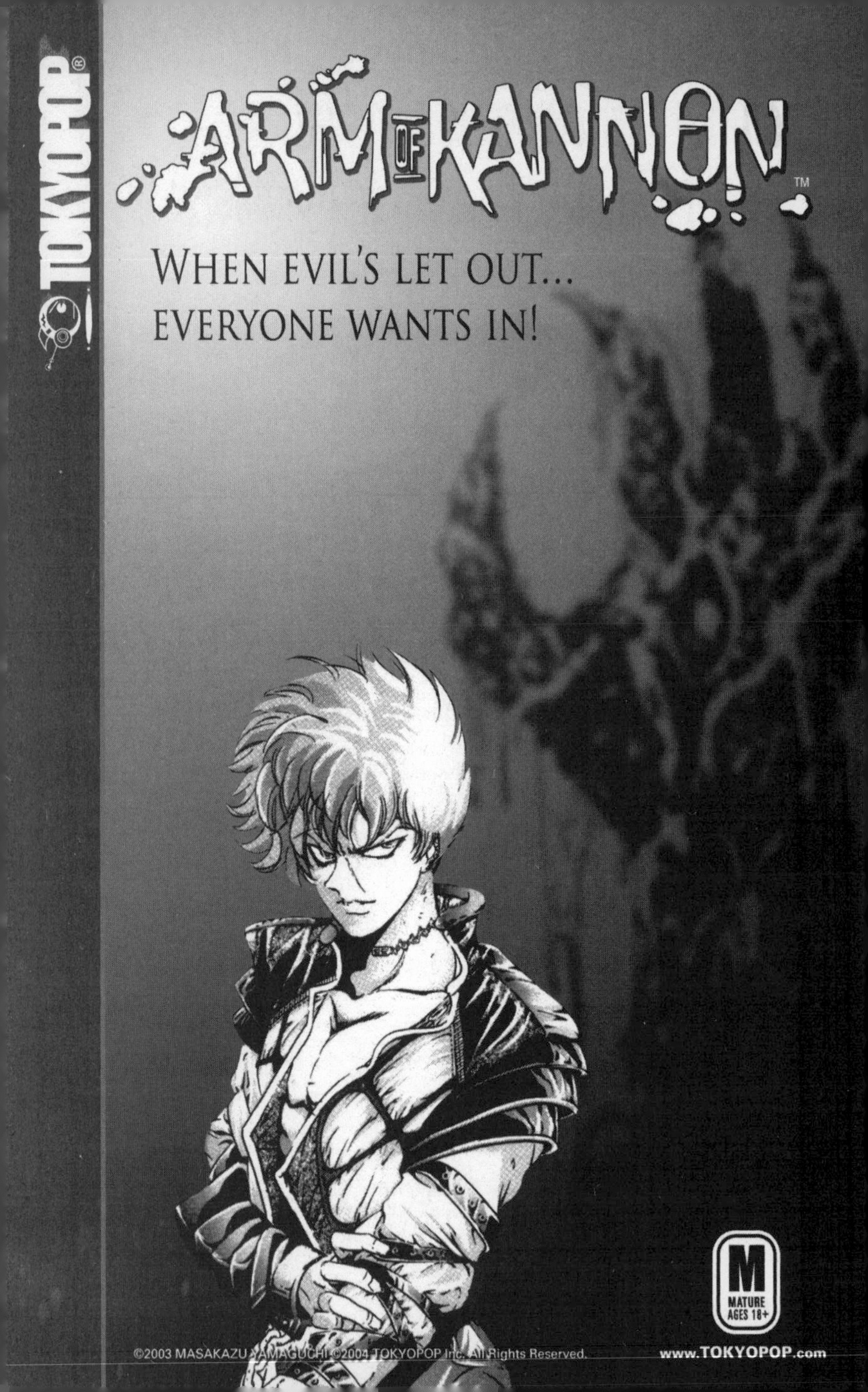
TOKYOPOP®
ARM OF KANNON™
WHEN EVIL'S LET OUT...
EVERYONE WANTS IN!
M
MATURE
AGES 18+
©2003 MASAKAZU YAMAGUCHI ©2004 TOKYOPOP Inc. All Rights Reserved.
www.TOKYOPOP.com

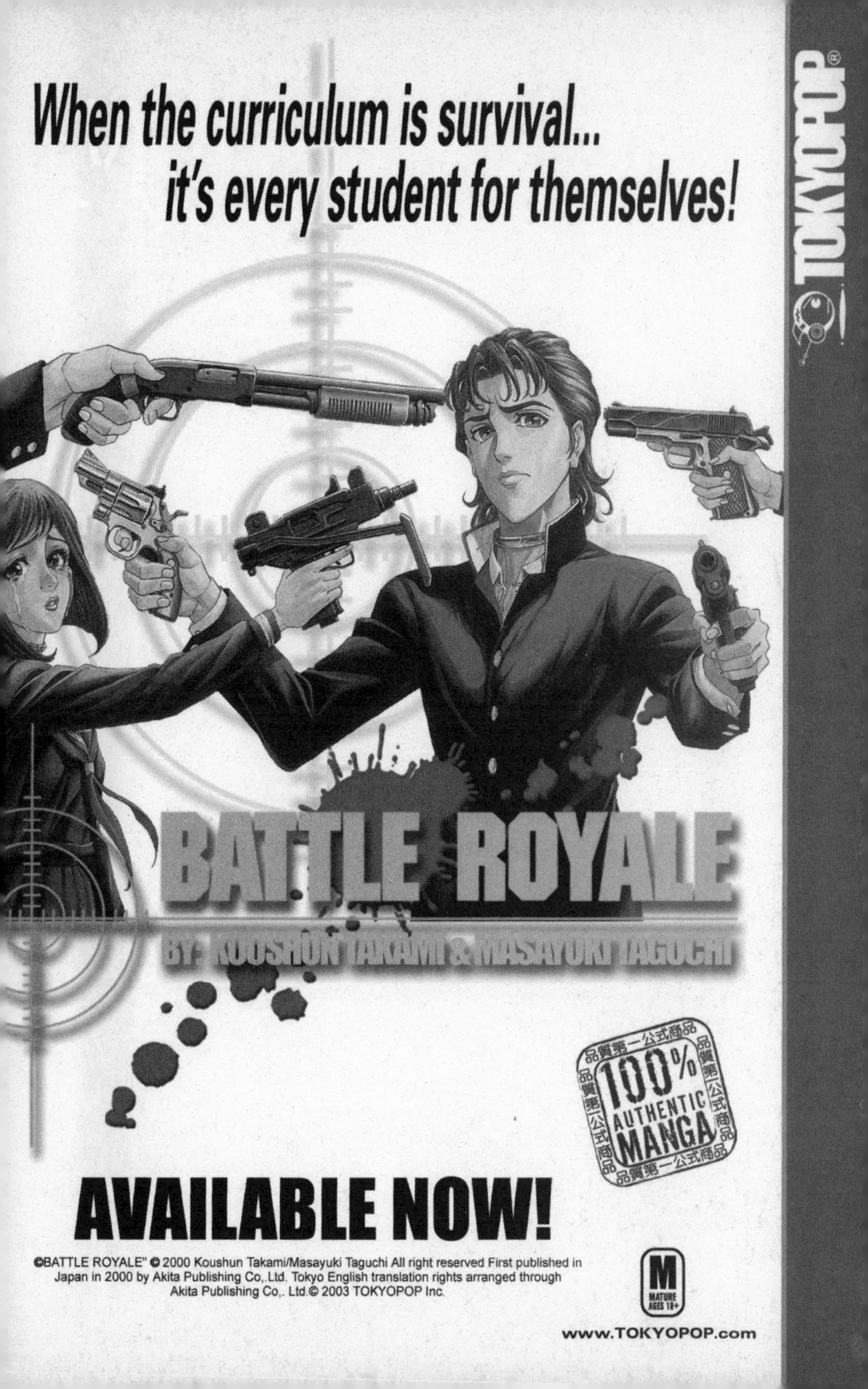
TOKYOPOP®
When the curriculum is survival...
it's every student for themselves!
BATTLE ROYALE
BY: KOUSHUN TAKAMI & MASAYUKI TAGUCHI
品質第一公式商品
100% AUTHENTIC MANGA
AVAILABLE NOW!
©BATTLE ROYALE" © 2000 Koushun Takami/Masayuki Taguchi All right reserved First published in Japan in 2000 by Akita Publishing Co,.Ltd. Tokyo English translation rights arranged through Akita Publishing Co,. Ltd.© 2003 TOKYOPOP Inc.
M
MATURE AGES 18+
www.TOKYOPOP.com

ALSO AVAILABLE FROM 🔲 TOKYOPOP®

MANGA

ALSO AVAILABLE FROM  TOKYOPOP®

For more
information visit
www.TOKYOPOP.com

03.03.04T